1979

l'année
bateaux

the world
of yachting

the world
of sail and power

(U.S. edition)

Editions de Messine
Paris

Publisher
Patrick TEBOUL

Editor in chief
Gerald ASARIA

English Editor
Frank PAGE

Lay out
Jean-Claude MAILLARD

Production
France BOUET
Jean-Jacques DUFAYET
Alexandre BERGEVIN

Translations
Florence HERBULOT
Jennifer GODSCHALK
Daniel NOTTET

Published also in french under the title
« L'ANNÉE BATEAUX »
ISBN 2-86409-001-5

Published in U.S.A. under the title
« THE WORLD OF SAIL AND POWER »
by Sail Books, Inc.
38, Commercial Wharf
Boston MA 02110
ISBN 0-914 814-25-7

Photographic credits. The credits are listed from left to right starting at the top of each page.

6 à 10 : T. Willis ● 11 : J. Knights, F. Allain (3) ● 12 : C. Février ● 13 : C. Février, D. Forster (2) ● 14 : G. Asaria ● 15 : R.R. ● 16 : de Rosnay/Gamma (2), D. Forster, F. Richard ● 17 : A. Corroler (2) D.R, D. Forster ● 18 : D. Forster ● 19 : C. Cunningham ● 20 : Mercury ● 21 Aifo-Fiat, Mercury ● 22-23 : R. Thibedeau ● 24 : R. Thibedeau, R. Bulman ● 25 : R.R ● 26-27 : Design A. Sivirine ● 28 : P. Match ● 29 : F. Allain (4) ● 30-31 : P. Match ● 32 : P. Match ● 34-35 : D. Allisy ● 36 : J. Eastland/Ajax News ● 37 : P. Carpentier, J. Eastland/Ajax News, D. Forster ● 38 et 39 : C. Février, F. Allain (2), C. Février, D. Forster, F. Allain, C. Février (2), R. de Greef, F. Allain, G. Gurney ● 40 : F. Allain (2) ● 41 : J. Eastland/Ajax News, R. de Greef ● 42-43 : G. Gurney ● 44 : A. Black ● 45 : G. Gurney ● 46-47 : D. Forster ● 49 : Stern ● 50-51 : F. Allain ● 53 : D. Allisy ● 54-55 : F. Richard, D. Forster, A. Black ● 56 : J. Eastland/Ajax News ● 57 : Sipa Press, D.R ● 58-59 : A. Black ● 60 : G. Gurney, R.R, G. Gurney ● 62-63 : S. Peacock ● 64 : S. Peacock ● 65 : P. Campbell ● 66 : P. Campbell (3) ● 67 : D. Forster, C. Février ● 68-69 : D. Forster ● 70 : D. Forster (2) ● 71 : Miami-Métro, G. Gurney ● 72-73 : D. Forster (2) ● 74-75 : D. Forster (2) ● 76-77 : G. Gurney ● 78 : D. Forster (3) ● 79 : D. Forster, C. Février ● 80-81 : C. Février (2) ● 82 : D. Forster, C. Février ● 83 : C. Février, D. Forster ● 84 : F. Richard, Bureau/Sygma ● 85 : E. Guillemot ● 86 : Guichard/Sygma ● 87 : Guichard/Sygma (2) ● 88-89 : C. Février ● 90 : B. Deguy/Neptune, E. Guillemot ● 91 : R. de Greef, B. Rubinstein/Neptune ● 92-93 : C. Février ● 94 : Guichard/Sygma, Sipa Press (2) ● 95 : C. Février, Bouhours/Sygma ● 96 à 103 : D. Forster ● 104 à 107 : P. Uhl ● 108 : H. Hansen (2) ● 109 : J. Knights, Baden ● 110 : H. Hansen, Baden ● 112 : P. Carpentier ● 113 : A. Black ● 114-115 : A. Black ● 116 : C. Février, G. Gurney, P. Carpentier ● 117 à 121 : D. Forster ● 122 : F. Richard ● 123 : F. Richard (2) ● 124 : E. Dercksen (2) ● 125 : F. Richard, E. Dercksen ● 126 : Houtvast, F. Richard ● 127 : F. Allain ● 128 : F. Allain ● 129 : F. Allain (3), F. Richard ● 130 à 132 : F. Allain ● 134-135 : P.J. Mello ● 136 : A. Black ● 137 : F. Richard (2) ● 138 : F. Richard ● 140-141 : D. Forster (2) ● 142 : F. Richard ● 143 : P. J. Mello ● 144-145 : F. Richard ● 146 à 149 : D. Nerney ● 150 : D. Forster, D. Nerney ● 152 à 155 : F. Richard ● 156 : D. Forster, F. Richard, D. Forster ● 157 : G. Gurney, F. Richard ● 158-159 : D. Forster ● 160 : F. Richard, D. Forster ● 161 : F. Richard (3) ● 162-163 : D. Forster ● 164 : F. Richard, D. Forster ● 165 : F. Richard, D. Forster ● 166-167 : G. Gurney ● 168 : F. Richard, D. Forster ● 170-171 : D. Forster ● 172 : K.S. Olsen ● 173 : P. Campbell ● 174-175 : S. Peacock ● 177 : A. Black ● 178-179 : Galligani/Mondadori ● 180-181 : Galligani/Mondadori ● 182-183 : P. Uhl ● 184 : D. Cornwell ● 186-187 : Legrand/Vandystadt ● 188 : Legrand/Vandystadt, Alan ● 189 : Aschendorf/Vandystadt, J.-F. de Girard, Ashendorf/Vandystadt ● 190 : S. Powell/All Sport ● 191 : S. Powell/All Sport (2) ● 192 : R. Bulman ● 193 : S. Powell/All Sport, Mercury (3) ● 194-195 : S. Powell/All Sport ● 196 : H. van Maasdijk ● 197 : J.-F. de Girard ● 198-199 : Rusniewski/Vandystadt ● 200 : Rusniewski/Vandystadt, Legrand/Vandystadt ● 201 : Rakic (2) ● 202 : Alan, Rakic, Alan ● 203 : S. Powell/All Sport ● 204-205 : S. Powell/All Sport (3), Mercury (2), S. Powell/All Sport (5) ● 206 : S. Powell/All Sport, Mercury ● 207 à 209 : S. Powell/All Sport ● 210 : Mercury (3), S. Powell/All Sport ● 212-213 : R. Thibedeau ● 214 : J. Crouse ● 215 : R. Thibedeau (2) ● 216 : R. Thibedeau ● 217 : R. Thibedeau, J. Crouse (2) ● 218-219 : S. Powell/All Sport ● 220 : R.R ● 221 : R.R, S. Powell/All Sport ● 222-223 : R. Thibedeau ● 224 : R.R .

Printed in France – Maury S.A. – 45330 Malesherbes

Contents

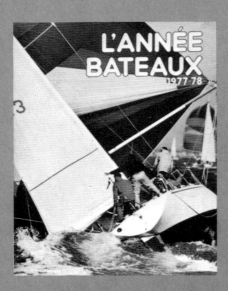
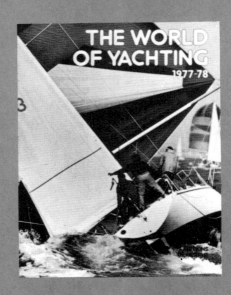
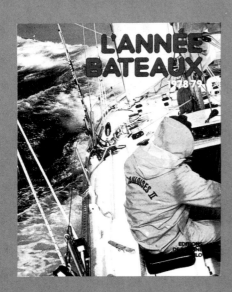
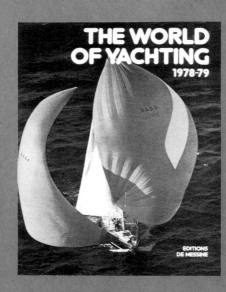
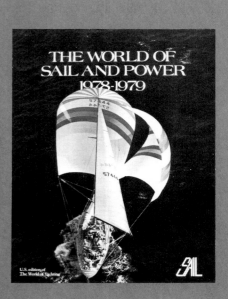

The Boating Year

A year of boating business

New designs but lots of different versions

by Tom Willis

Historically, boating and the industry it supports have been small-scale. Until the 1960's, when the advent of glass fibre reinforced plastics made production line boatbuilding a reality, the sport was limited to dinghy sailors, rich people who could afford the heavy maintenance costs of a wooden boat, or real enthusiasts who were prepared to spend all their leisure time working on their boats.

GRP changed all that. In twenty years pleasure boating has gained adherents by the million throughout the Western world : in the USA, where the sport has become firmly entrenched in the list of the top ten favourite leisure activities, there were over *fifty million* people who took to the water at least twice last year.

But while the cottage industry history of boatbuilding slowly gives way to a big business future, the sector remains remarkably disparate, a hybrid assortment of companies producing a range of goods similar only in that they are designed either to float on water or to go in something that floats.

There is no other industry where the end product varies so widely in sophistication and price. The average working man would except to pay something like two weeks' salary for a small rowing boat. A mid-range family sailing cruiser would cost him two or three years' income. There are even a handful of craft available – standard, off-the-peg production models – which carry a price tag in excess of what he would earn in two working lifetimes.

The builders, too, are as dissimilar as the boats they manufacture. At one end of the scale we can still find the boatyard two miles up the creek which will build from a design in the shipwrights' head, taking a year to complete the job ; at the other end are vast factories like that of Jeanneau, in Les Herbiers, France, which produce some five thousand boats a year and carry a standard range of over forty models ; or companies like J.V. Dunhill, of Basingstoke, England, whose giant Rolinx injection-moulding press can make a topper dinghy hull in seven minutes flat.

People in the industry are fond of drawing analogies between boatbuilding and car manufacture to predict the demise of the small builder. It is not necessarily a valid comparison : the car industry came from nowhere to mass production in a few decades, and when Henry Ford began to take the market by storm with his Model T there was still only a limited number of independent manufacturers in operation. In contrast, the history of boatbuilding is long and innovative ; small yards, producing boats in wood until the arrival of GRP, made the transition to glass fibre building quickly and successfully and most are still trading. The fortunes of the factory boatbuilders are based on a masive growth in demand, as was the case with the car industry ; but the enormous scale of production which allowed the motor manufacturers to reduce their prices until backyard production became uncompetitive is not a real possibility for boat manufacturers. Despite the growth in demand, water sports remain an indulgence ; cars, on the other hand, benefited from the simple fact that some form of transport was necessary for most people. In addition, they were cheaper to maintain than horses.

Many boatbuilders employ less than twenty staff and produce a mere handful of boats annually. However, when prices are compared, these craft are not noticeably more expensive than a Jeanneau or a Glastron, despite economies of scale.

Injection moulding is a development that may change this differential. Introduced in a blaze of glory last year with J.C. Rogers' New Moon, this technique of hull manufacture has substantial advantages for the mass production builder. The saving is largely due to the fact that each boat that comes out of the mould is identical ; thus all bulkheads, joinery and interior fittings can be precut to pattern and positioned without the need for trimming. As a consequence the labour intensive, expensive business of fitting out can be pared to the bone.

There are no signs as yet of this method being adopted on an international scale, but, once initial development problems have been ironed out, widespead acceptance seems inevitable. The equipment is highly expensive to install – far more so than a simple female mould – but will pay for itself in any long production run.

One of the few other companies that have adopted similar resin injection processes is JCL Marine. In this case there is a direct link with the car industry : JCL's chairman, Colin Chapman, also controls the Lotus car company, and the process used for the manufacture of Lotus' lightweight, high-performance body shells was adapted for building JCL hulls.

The last year has not been spectacularly successful for the boat industry worldwide. The threat of another recession hangs over most Western economies, and the first signs of another round of oil-fired inflation are already beginning to appear in the shape of higher prices for oil byproducts – such as the resins used in GRP building. The failure of major boatbuilders, the latest being Reinell (USA), Neptun (Germany) and Macwester (UK), indicates that all is not well ; even the best-known names have not been immune from the effects of a steadily more difficult market – Pelle Petterson, Camper & Nicholson and Chris Craft have all had to close some of their facilities.

One indication of a downturn is the fall in the number of truly new designs to appear at boat shows. « New », of course, is a loose term : the Paris boat show organisers define it as meaning either a completely original model, or an established model which has undergone extensive alterations, or a product appearing for the first time at the Paris show.

Below. This moulding machine can turn out a glassfibre hull in seven minutes.

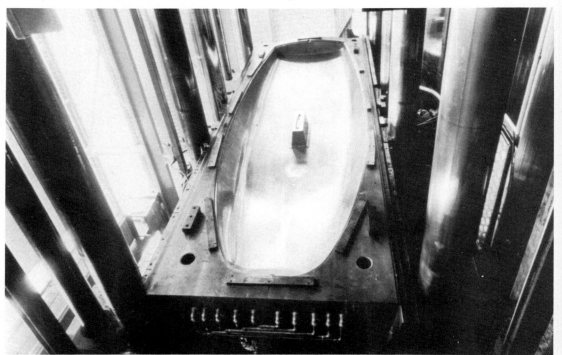

Italian design

Top. The 11.80 m Exocetus Volons, a very special motor-sailer designed by Sonny Levi. Her two 240 hp. Aifo diesels can push her up to more than 33 knots (61 km/h).

Centre. Another Levi design, Commando with her step-drive transmission can get up to 50 knots (92.6 km/h).
Above. Two Rivas the 38 ft Bravo (left) and the 48 ft. Superamerica (right).

which offered two positions for the mast. With the mast in the normal position, the craft is a conventional sailboard; in the secondary slot, and with a sheet fixed to it, the boat becomes a dinghy. Other variations on a theme included inflatable sailboards from Hutchinson, Semperit and several other inflatable manufacturers, whose chief advantage lies in their prices.

Moving up the size scale, the next class of boat worthy of mention is the fun boat. Ranging from the Laser and Topper to the surf catamarans like the phenomenally popular Hobie Cat and Spark, this market has been particularly healthy in Australia, where the mooring problem is so acute that trailerable boats account for all but a small percentage of new boat sales annually.

Given that Hobie and Performance Sailcraft (the builders of the Laser) have appropriated for themselves something like a tenth of the Australian sailboat market, it is not surprising that a sizeable domestic industry has gradually built up which bases its production on similar craft. Lightweight cats and surf dinghies abound in Australia, and the more farsighted builders are starting to establish offshoots in Europe and America. Boats like the Hawke Surfcat – 13ft long and weighing just 132 lbs – can be carried on a car top to the sea, carried to the beach by two people and launched into the surf with a minimum of fuss. They are the ideal craft for a beach-oriented sailing market.

A true trailer-sailer is a light-displacement boat with a limited amount of accommodation, sufficient for a weekend's camping aboard with the family. Once again these are most popular in Australia, but in the last few years trailer-sailers have been developing a market for themselves in Europe. The French magazine Bateaux has been particularly instrumental in spreading the gospel of the trailer-sailer. Two years ago the journal described the rules of a class of small sailing/camping dinghies which became the Micro Cuppers.

Micro Cup regulations stipulate a boat of less than 5.50 m in length with a beam of 2.50 m, a sail area (main and jib) 18.50 m² and adequate buoyancy to keep the craft afloat when swamped. With a maximum displacement of 600 kg, the boats are generally easy to launch and recover, and their similar characteristics ensure that several different makes can race one against the other with no model having an unreasonable advantage. For these reasons the Micro Cupper has to date been a huge success in its country of origin – 1979 has seen the introduction of the Kelt 5,50, the Expression, the Kibell Micro, the Edel II, the First 18, the Neptune 550, the Ultra 55 and several more – and is attracting international attention.

The European boatbuilders who can lay claim to a comprehensive range of small sailing craft have concentrated their efforts over the last few years in developing boats for the bottom end of the market; often these are called trailer sailers for no better reason than that they can be trailed, unescorted, on European roads. A true trailer sailer should be easy to transport behind the average family car, and hardly more trouble to launch and recover than a dinghy.

Nevertheless, there has been a veritable explosion in the number of sailing cruisers of about 20 and 25 ft available. Development capital may be limited, but the volume of production of small boats ensures that preliminary costs are usually absorbed quickly. Unfortunately for the Europeans, few builders have managed to get the recipe as right as the J24

But if we take « new » as meaning a completely original model, we are forced to conclude that development funds have been considerably truncated in the last year or so. A quick look at the European autumn shows turned up few revolutionary concepts, and most of the debuts were for improved or altered versions of existing boats or for boats appearing for the first time in that country.

The major growth area for the industry has been the small boat market. Here we can start with the simplest and most basic of water sports craft, the sailing surfboard. These boards have had a mixed reception in Europe. In countries where the weather is generally reliable, the sport has mushroomed; elsewhere, it has merely

grown. France, Germany, Belgium and Holland are the European centres of board sailing; there are now around sixty different makes of board available in these countries, and well over a quarter of a million enthusiasts.

The fight for a market share has only just begun with sailboards. The winner's laurel leaves, at least this year, go to Baron Marcel Bich, who managed to introduce his ABS thermoformed Dufour Wing at a price well below that of the competition in January, and in the first six months succeeded in producing and selling over 15,000.

A variation of the classic sailboard (is it old enough to have a « classic » form ?) was to be seen this year in the shape of the Whirlwind,

Nautor, the « Rolls Royce of the sea », displays its latest design, the Swan 76 (right), modelled on Kialoa (left) largely.

built by J Boats of Rhode Island, USA, and Westerly Marine of England.

Further up the market we are beginning to see the Far Eastern countries of Taiwan and Korea gaining ground steadily. In the USA, Taiwanese boats are imported in quantities which dwarf the American sales of other countries. Although these have in the past been mostly motor yachts of the trawler type and their standard of decor and interior finish unreliable, the yards have now come of age and are producing high-quality blue-water ketches like the new Transpac 49 or Scylla 36, as well as the extensive selection of luxury displacement motor cruisers. The conditions are ideal for a Taiwanese or Korean boatbuilder: wood is relatively cheap and plentiful, labour even more so. Put the two together and there is no reason why these countries should not be able to build any number of handcrafted but competitively-priced yachts.

The same situation obtains for what must be one of the world's most improbably-sited boatbuilders. Specialised Mouldings, a Kenyan company building workboats and a new sailing cruiser called the Samantha 39, operates in what it insists is the best climate in the world for fibreglass manufacture – 5,000 ft above sea level and 200 miles from the Indian Ocean. Be that as it may, SM is able to mould its hulls, fit them with hand-carved oak furniture, transport them to the coast and ship them to Europe while still managing to sell at a price lower than an equivalent Europe-built boat.

Back in the West, the sailing boat manufacturers are as yet not under real attack from the Far East. But they are, nevertheless, having a lean time. The bigger yachts are an exception, and for these there seems to be a never-ending stream of customers with cheque books at the ready. One of the largest production boats to date is the maxi-rater due to appear in the next few months from the Finnish company Nautor, which does not seem ever to put a foot wrong when it comes to planning for a new market. As with all the longer Swans, the Swan 76 was designed by Sparkman & Stephens and based on the record-beating Kialoa.

Turning to the powerboat scene, the name of one designer has held a well-deserved pre-eminence. The Italian Sonny Levi, as well as being one of the most prolific designers of powerboats, is also one of the most innovative. The most radical product of Levi's fertile imagination must be the V-5, his 30 knot planing motor sailer. First conceived in 1972, the idea remained unfulfilled until IAG Nautica agreed to fund the development in 1976. Towards the end of last year, the prototype trials showed both designer and builder that they had not been over optimistic in their hopes for the craft. V-5 proved capable of achieving a top speed in excess of 30 knots with her twin 200 hp Fiat Aifo diesels and cruised effortlessly at 25 knots. The 39ft (11,9m) boat also showed up well under sail, although an improved rig is under consideration.

Levi's other major contribution to powerboat design is seen in such boats as the Laver Manta and Mikado and the Triana fast freighter, with its revolutionary stepped stern. His obsession with getting the most out of an engine has led him to produce diesel-powered boats with the performance of petrol-driven craft. His designs are stark but functional, and appeal to the fuel-conscious enthusiast – although, as Levi points out, it takes seven to ten years at 100 hours' use a season before the saving in fuel compensates for the higher cost of the boat.

Levi is by no means typical of the Italian design school. His versatility and his ability to work on power, sail and even aircraft set him apart from many. But his name crops up

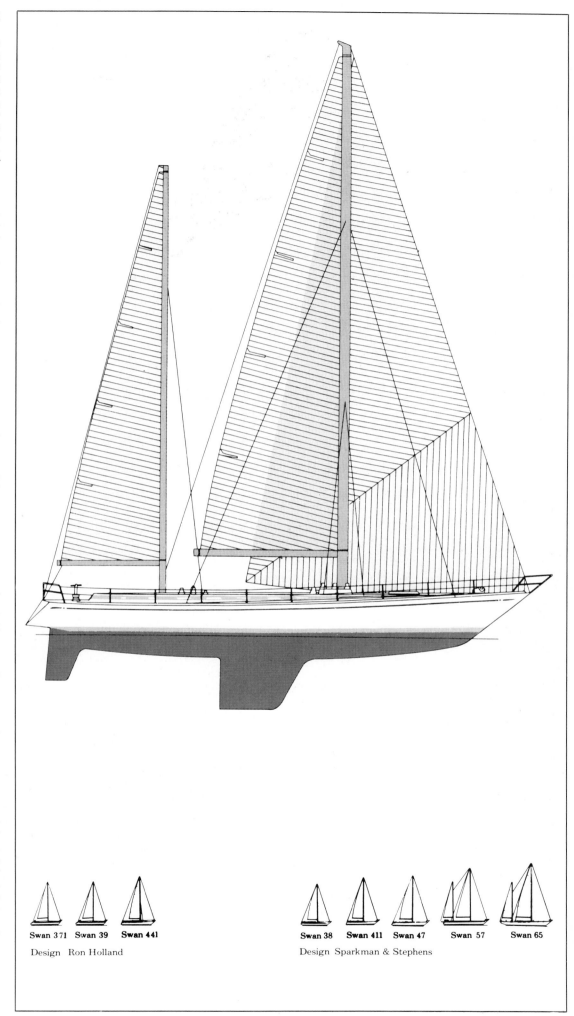

Swan 371   Swan 39   **Swan 441**

Design Ron Holland

Swan 38   **Swan 411**   Swan 47   Swan 57   Swan 65

Design Sparkman & Stephens

Above. *Aluminium and even steel are being used more and more in the construction of small boats, like the Mare-29.*

everywhere : in Italy, England, even among the products of the mighty AMF conglomerate in the USA. It is refreshing to note that the desire for innovation is not quite moribund.

Because that is how it would appear to anyone who has spent time visiting the shows of Europe and the USA this year. The 1979 crop of new craft was distressingly lacking in radical changes. On the one hand were builders bringing out new boats to fill their ranges ; on the other were builders who had merely restyled existing models.

There have been signs of trends away from conventional materials, such as the increasing use of Kevlar and aluminium in production hulls. One recent example of the use of Kevlar is the Italcraft M-74, which has a top speed of 47 knots and is claimed to be the world's fastest motor yacht. In this case, the wonder material is estimated to have reduced the hull weight by 40 per cent.

One way of supporting a poor market in pleasure boats is to sell for military purposes. Many of Europe's major power boat builders are doing just this, with coastguard, customs, naval and rescue versions of their most powerful models. An amusing spin off to this appears to be that a number of Third World rulers have ordered military vessels with surprisingly unmilitary specifications. More than one naval patrol boat has been sold to a Persian Gulf state without a single piece of ordnance on board – unless you count the clay pigeon shoot on the flying bridge.

Picchiotti is one builder which has established a firm market in this type of dual-purpose craft, but several others – Baglietto, Aresa, Gallart, Moonraker – have succeeded in selling

far more production than would have been possible had they kept to the pleasure boat specifications.

Whatever the state of the pleasure boat industry, there is one sector which enjoys a healthy growth rate through boom and slump. Here the best known names are Dutch – De Vries, van Lent – and at least part of the reason for their relative prosperity is the fact that they experience little competition and rarely have to chase orders.

These builders produce luxury motor yachts in steel, a material which is very popular among Netherlands boat owners. What sets the De Vries or van Lent boat apart from the rest, however, is the size and expense of the undertaking. An enormous amount of publicity surrounded last year's completion and delivery of the 65m Al Riyadh, built by van Lent for King Khaled of Saudi Arabia ; so strong is the Middle Eastern desire for one-upmanship, the story goes, that Al Riyadh was not even off the stocks before a certain potentate began hawking plans round the yards for a yacht just a metre longer.

The largest yacht built in 1979/80 is likely to be an Italian production from the Benetti boatyard. At 83m this leviathan certainly has the edge over Al Riyadh in terms of length, but it is hard to see how the purse of an Italian businessman can run to the lavish appointments of the Saudi king's vessel.

This year saw the first Monte Carlo boat show. Unfortunately there was little or no advance publicity for this event, an omission which caused the public to stay away. Nevertheless, there were 25 yachts on display with a combined estimated value of £ 4 1/2 million. Prominent among them were, inevitably, the

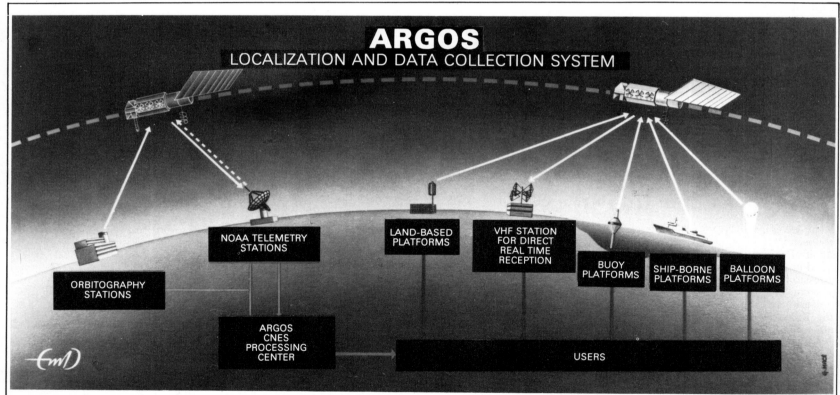

For the first time in any trans-oceanic yacht race, all the competing boats in the Transat en Double were equipped with a system of identification through the satellite Argos, which could give their precise locations. Of French design, Argos was built by Electronique Marcel Dassault in collaboration with NASA. Each of the boats was equipped

with a small transmitter which sent a coded signal into the sky every minute. The Satellite TIROS N received and recoded these transmissions, and then retransmitted them by radio to three receiving stations – in Virginia, Alaska and France. Less than six hours later, the information could be disseminated to the race organisers.

In the Transat race, this system was used to pinpoint the wrecked yacht Charles Heidsick and to get help to the boat rapidly. This convincing demonstration opens the way to a general adoption of the Argos system in ocean races of the future and it is probable that similar application could be found in other areas.

Italian contingent, including Technomarine, Benetti, Posillipo and others, but almost all the boats showed the influence of Italian styling in their design.

The trawler yacht is one of the few classes of cruiser to owe none of its characteristics to the Italians. In this case the origin seems to have been the drawing board of Floyd P. Ayres, of American Marine, whose Marine Trader was one of the first of the modern breed. According to his employers, most Taiwanese yachts are fundamentally copies of Ayres designs – a statement with which, no doubt, the Taiwanese builders would disagree, but one with more than a grain of truth in it if one goes by the extraordinary similarity between different makes of trawler yacht.

Hong Kong, Taiwan and Korea are the major Third World producers of pleasure boats, but the list is growing. The Peoples' Democratic Republic of Libya has recently built a factory where the Storebro Royal 40 cruiser, priced at over £100,000 each, is being produced under licence from its Swedish originators; but from South America to the Philippines there are newly-opened manufacturers building established European and American designs for the export market. One feature of these builders is that the senior staff rarely indulge in boating themselves – as is almost invariably the case in the West. Indeed, in Taiwan the employees of boat factories are prevented by government decree from owning pleasure craft.

The effect of these non-consuming producers on established boatbuilders has yet to take full effect on European and American pleasure boat markets. Equally we cannot yet gauge whether the gradual encroachment by Japanese boats is the start of an invasion of Western preserves; whenever a country increases its export share, the industry in the importing country is the loser.

But many of the problems being experienced by the boat industry stem from the fact that boat owners are still a very small group in most areas. While water sports are by no means as elitist as they once were, they attract little government support either financially or legislatively. Indeed, it often seems as though sailors are singled out for punitive tax measures; it was only with great difficulty that the Swedes this year managed to head off legislation which would have added another 20 per cent luxury tax to the 20.62 per cent VAT which boat owners already pay. More disquieting is that this occurred in a country where the incidence of boat ownership is one of the highest in the world, and where some form of waterborne transportation is for many people a real necessity.

The US boat industry bears investigation, if only because it has developed further and faster than its European counterparts. This has been helped in no small measure by a cohesion and a professionalism which is all too often lacking in other countries' industries. The two main trade associations, the National Association of Engine and Boat Manufacturers and the Boating Industries Association, amalgamated this year after an extended courtship; with the additional lobbying power that speaking with one voice gives the US boatbuilders, and the sheer number of jobs that the new organisation represents, the industry can confidently expect to receive a fair measure of government support.

Another reason for the relative stability of the American boat industry lies in the boat factories' production of runabouts, sports fishermen and power cruisers. Here the model year has established itself as a concept vitally relevant to continuing sales by encouraging owners to trade in their perfectly serviceable craft for the next year's model.

The disadvantage of this system is that it can result in built-in obsolescence and an over-cautious attitude towards radical change in design. The 1980 version of a production line boat from some manufacturers will bear a remarkable similarity to the 1975 version, despite much-vaunted "model improvements" annually for the last six years. But whatever reservations design purists may have about this point, it does make for an exceptionally healthy market in the USA. To sum up, the last year has been notable for consolidation rather than development. Boatbuilders throughout the world have been chiefly concerned not to introduce new craft but to find new markets for their existing ranges. 1979 will be looked upon as a period spent marking time, trying to maintain growth in a static sector of the economy.

When the 1980 models appear, several changes in design trends will owe their genesis to one single event. The Fastnet tragedy, in which 19 people lost their lives and 24 boats were sunk or abandoned, will have far-reaching effects on the design of racing yachts. Time will tell how many craft sank because a race-tuned prototype fitting proved insufficiently strong to weather the storm; or because the yacht itself had been slimmed down and lightened in order to gain the maximum advantage from the racing rules. Are many yachts now inadequate for the task of coping with really heavy weather? Experimental materials can win races, and only by trying them out under race conditions can the sailor see whether they are worthwhile improvements; but surely this should not be allowed to jeopardise the seaworthiness that is a prerequisite of all yacht design, whether the boat is destined for a life of cruising or one of offshore racing. □

Above. *A truly popular catamaran is being turned out by the Cougar factory. The Cat-900, with its twin coupled engines, provides a huge sun-deck, a luxurious bedroom and an astonishing bathroom.*

Latest of the offshore monsters. The Maltese 53 footer is built in Kevlar-49 by Magnum Marine. Measuring 16.13 metres long and 4.80 metres in the beam, she weighs about 20 tons. Either of the twin GM diesel 1,200 horse power engines will drive the boat at nearly 40 knots. Her flush deck encloses a luxurious saloon, a galley and two cabins with bathrooms.

Men and boats of the year

Sailing

by Jack Knights

In such a crowded year of yacht racing, who are the true heroes ? Is it Ted Turner of Atlanta, and his crew of eighteen, for winning the stormy Fastnet Race (besides many others) or is it Alain Catherineau of La Rochelle and his crew of five for rescuing the crew of the British yacht Griffin which had to be abandoned in that race ?

Who deserves more acclaim for the remarkable Transat en Double... Eugene Riguidel and Gilles Gahinet for winning, or Derek Kelsall and the Chantiers Barberet for designing and building their trimaran « VSD » or, those whose generosity provided such a large and costly craft ?

Do Eric Tabarly and Marc Pajot deserve the congratulations of all for sailing « Paul Ricard », untried and experimental, from Lorient to Bermuda and back, being fastest out and third fastest back for a razor-close second overall or, considering the money and human ingenuity and skill expended, was second place failure ?

And how does one equate the Olympic class sailors ? A whole new generation of American youngsters, raised on Lasers and inter-collegiate racing, stormed the Finn Gold Cup. They left the other 125 competitors from 26 nations almost out of sight astern. Headed by twenty two year old Cam Lewis they brought new skills to a branch of the sport that had seemed to be reaching maturity. John Bertrand, one of these young tigers had already won most of the big Finn events but he had seemed unique, a phenomenon. The Gold Cup showed there are many more where he comes from.

Then there were the world championships at Kiel of the Tornadoes and Flying Dutchmen. Blending the vitality of youth with the wisdom of his forty three years, Britain's Reg White whose son Rob was steering a rival catamaran, came through to add the '79 World title to his 1976 Gold Medal and afterwards he said that he owed his success to the improving tactical judgment of his new crew, eighteen year old Steve Olle. Meanwhile, on an adjoining course. Marc Bouet and Thierry Poirret were winning the FD Worlds for France. As so often, consistency paid... the American headed by Augie Diaz and Mark Reynolds may have been fastest in the light, the Spaniards Alejandra Abascal and his new crew Miguel Noguer may have been fastest in the fresh but as the French pair proved with results of 6,1,9,13,2,2,5 in a fleet of fifty, only they were consistently good, whatever the weather.

How can you measure the singlehanded dinghy racer against the ocean crosser ? Much depends upon your point of view. The dinghy racer will tend to think that his skills are more highly developed, supreme physical conditioning more necessary. The ocean voyager can point out that his speciality is far more comprehensive in its demands. Racing an ocean calls for stamina and daring. navigation and weather lore, seamanship and strategy.

One thing is certain, to win at the top level in any branch of yachting today, calls for very highly developed skills, painstaking preparation and that special ingredient which may be called « The will to win ». Who is the greatest hero of them all is a question that is as unresolvable as asking whether Beethoven is greater than Rodin. But it is possible to say that some events stand out as being extra difficult to win, while some winners win with a special style.

Take the 1979 Three Quarter Ton Cup sailed from Denmark's Hundestedt on the open Kattegat...the long distance race coincided with the same weather disturbances that had so tragically disrupted the Fastnet Race hardly more than a week earlier. Of the thirty-nine competitors at Hundestedt only two survived that final long race and of these two one, the aptly named « Love and Fight » continued to race throughout the storm. The other, which was the overall winner of the event was the Peter Norlin designed « Regnbagen » from Sweden. She anchored in the lee of Anholt Knob, the island which formed the race's weather mark and for eight hours she sat out the worst of the weather before cautiously pushing on under storm jib. For the entire 300 mile race the wind stayed above Force 6. At its height the gale blew at sixty knots. Lars Nylinder and his « Regnbagen » crew as well as her builders, deserve a special round of applause.

The One Ton Cup, on the other hand, sailed from Newport, Rhode Island, deserves hardly more than a footnote. Only twelve yachts competed, the medium distance race had to be voided after one of the turning marks was discovered to be miles out of position and in the end the winner turned out to be not a One Tonner at all but last year's winning Three Quarter Tonner, Pendragon, with a larger rig.

1979 was the year for old boats to win the level rating events. Apart from Pendragon there was that other Laurie Davidson design, Waverider. Sailed once again by Tony Bouzaid, Helmer Pederson and Tony Bassadone, this three year old yacht took the Half Ton Cup for the second year running. (Had she not made a couple of mistakes towards the end of the 1977 Half Ton Cup she would have won three times running). The event was this time held on the bleak and turbulent North Sea from the Dutch port of Scheveningen. There were thirty eight yachts and conditions were variable. The yacht that pushed Waverider hardest was yet another three year old New Zealander - Swuzzlebubble but she fell foul of the, protest jury.

Who will ever forget the incredible finish of the Route du Rhum, when the 11.5 metre trimaran of Michael Birch sprinted to the line ahead of the big monohull Kriter V, sailed by Michel Malinovsky ? Just 98 seconds between them helped to consolidate the genuine friendship of the two skippers, seen here sailing together on Mike's boat Olympus Photo.

Above. *Ted Turner, the happy owner of Tenacious, the winner of the Fastnet amongst others...*

Below. *John MacLaurin carries off the One Ton Cup this year, in his modified Pendragon, last year's Three Quater Ton Cup winner.*

Waverider and Swuzzlebubble had both been modified to meet the major changes in the IOR rules which were passed last autumm. Their centreboards were fixed down as keels and their hulls were slightly deepened. Swuzzlebubble was eventually beaten out of second place by the new British yacht Roller Coaster from the drawing board of the young journalist and designer Rob Humphreys.

Another level event which was won by the same boat for the second year running was the Mini Ton at Estartit in Spain which attracted an entry of forty-three from eight nations. The successful boat was Wahoo of Italy, designed by the Maletto, Navone, Fontana partnership and sailed by them. This time she won three races including both offshore events. The wind was light, most of the time but Wahoo was just as fast when in the long race, the wind briefly freshened to Force 5.

The Two Ton Cup, held from Poole in England just before the Admirals Cup to guarantee a reasonable entry was won by an old boat too. Strictly speaking « Gitana VII », owned by Baron Edmond de Rothschild was brand new - so new in fact that measurement problems and then a breaking rudder kept her out of the French Admirals Cup team, but her design was drawn by German Frers Jr some two years back and her completed hull had been waiting on the shelf at a British yard for some months, looking for an owner.

« Gitana VII » with an all French crew and her Frers designed sisters, Madrugada and Sur II showed beyond doubt that in the prevailing light conditions they were best of the ninetten from ten nations. They had about the biggest sail area, the longest waterlines and they seemed to sail just that little bit closer to the wind. In more wind, with better handling, the considerably lighter Police Car from Perth, designed by the young Englishman Ed Dubois, might have won.

The French captured another level rating event in 1979 and this one, the Quarter Ton Cup, attracted the largest entry of all, 57 boats from 15 nations. The Yacht Club Italiono staged the series from the new marina of Portosole and the racing was made extra special by the presence of Paul Elvstrom at the tiller of the Italian Son of a Gun. For once Elvstrom had to be content with second, for the one time Moth champion and experienced Mini Ton campaigner Jacques Fauroux had the legs of him in a vessel of his own design named Bullit. Elvstrom led on points coming into the final race and led this too till the closing stages but when the wind became tricky he dropped to 8th while Bullit came up to win.

The most unusual world championship of 1979 was without doubt the Twelve Metres regatta at Brighton's huge new sixty million pound marina. This was sponsored at a cost of at least £ 100,000 by a commercial television company, Southern Television. They were hoping to help Britain's 1980 America's Cup challenge and at the same time give themselves an exclusive. Unfortunatexly one of those long-running trade union disputes for which Britain is well known, darkened the television screens both before and during the racing so the commercial side came to nought. Six Twelve Metres - Lionheart, Constellation and Columbia with Britsh crews, Gretel II from Australia, Sverige from Sweden and Windrose, ex Chancegger from Holland - did race when the weather permitted. Lionheart won and Sverige broke the same new mast twice. Gretel II was easily beaten by these two. She then returned to Australia where she was to race the Twelve « Australia ». This would provide the first good guide to European form, since the Americans at the last moment, boycotted Brighton.

When all is said and done the event that attracted the greatest assemblage of talent and state of the art technology in 1979, and which took place in the most memorable weather, was the twelfth Admirals Cup from Cowes. Since its humble start in 1957 with two teams, this event has became the « ipso facto » world championship of fully crewed offshore racing yachts. In 1975 and again in 1977 the weather did not match up to the competition and feeble airs predominated but not this time. The event began

Alain Colas

Alain Colas has gone. Where or when, we shall never know exactly. Quietly, without flowers or wreaths, without even the press eulogies which would normally mark the death of a great sailor. Perhaps this was because Alain Colas was not the most popular of the great French navigators, undoubtedly because he was one of the originals – and originals are always rather disruptive.

Colas was a man from the land who came from the countryside to beat the sailing men at their own sport. He was also a man who surrounded himself with sponsors, financial backing, press publicity, the media, public relations, and electronics at a time when that wasn't quite the done thing.

It threw him into sharp contrast with the image of the taciturn yachtsmen who braved the elements with their strong arms, tough muscles and physical fitness, rather than with the aid of the sophisticated techniques of modern technology. And some people seemed to forget that to be original and innovative doesn't necessarily cancel out the struggle and risk ; that to make progress is sadly, very hard, without money to support those innovations.

I saw Alain Colas at work where few others did : on a hospital bed, with his two legs clamped together, linked by grafts of flesh and connections of bone and artery.

That was where he achieved his greatest victory, one that will never appear on any roll of honour but which should never be forgotten. Remember.

Trinity in Brittany, April 1975, on board Manureva, the trimaran he knew by heart, and on which he had learned to sail with Eric Tabarly, then used to win the 1972 Observer Singlehanded and later to sail round the world singlehanded.

A stupid manoeuvre ? Bad luck ? It doesn't really matter. I was there ; I saw the leg crushed by the anchor chain, a horrific mass of mangled flesh and the almost severed foot which seemed to exist bloodily separate from the body of the man who continued, despite everything, to command and direct the boat without even crying out at his grievous wound. And then, as we carried the body, the face which fought against foundering, the hospital. So it came about that I was close to Colas when few others were : at the hospital bed, where the medical experts gave him very little hope of ever going to

sea again and begged him to take tranquillisers to ease the pain which threatened to overcome him. But the proud Colas refused, so that he could maintain all his faculties, so that he could carry on organising his dream project : to build his cathedral of the sea for a singlehanded sailor', as he called it. It was a wild project which came into existence, despite everything, one year later under the name Club Méditérranée. Then, I saw him again less than 16 months later, at Newport, Rhode Island, at the finish of the 1976 Observer Singlehanded, where he did succeed in crossing the ocean in his giant four-masted schooner, despite his fearful wound. And where he was received with no fanfares because he had not succeeded in the great challenge : to win the race on a 236 foot boat which had cost three million dollars. He had sullied the seas with his famous boat, his constant radio broadcasts to the French stations, his syndicated writings for the provincial press. And others, just as courageous, had crossed the Atlantic in almost the same time without the help of all these commercial overtones.

And still today these others are understandably reluctant to use Colas's methods – and that is even sadder. Colas understood that sailing would become the most fantastic sport of this century of energy problems, and that the old order would have to change. He saw that, as in so many other sports, the era of the gentleman amateur was drawing to a close and that romantic idealists would have to concede the top places to athletes of the first order, sustained by all the technology of the age.

Worse still, although this man from the countryside in the heart of France had proved that he could do just as well as the men born beside the ocean, he, like Gerbault and others had been unable to spread the word that the great growth of yachting would draw more and more men from the villages and towns towards the sea, a fact that hasn't been fully comprehended even now.

Colas the originator is no more. He was killed by his total commitment, by his defiance. Some people said by his despair. Colas the landsman has gone, vanished into the sea like the great sailor that he was. For his epitaph, I believe he would have liked the world to remember him as a man of intellect and a man of courage in a class apart from the crowd. I will stand witness to that for as long as I am able.   *Gerald Asaria*

in a moderate wind, continued in Force 7 and climaxed at the Fastnet Rock with Force II and waves of a severity which an oceanographic institute judged were unlikely to recur at this time of year for the next fifty years.

The Hong Kong team which had done so well in 1977, led after the first two races. Another small country, Ireland, took over after that but the Fastnet storm decided the trophy's destiny. It shattered two Irish rudders, slowed the British and Americans scattered the Hong Kong sailors and provided the tough and seasoned Australians with the opportunity that the tight manœuvering of the inshore races had not provided.

Only the French and the Italians of the other eighteen nations, came close to matching the skill, seamanship and stamina of the crews of Ragamuffin, Impetuous and Police Car in this epic struggle.

Individually, the outstanding yacht of the fifty seven that started in the Admirals Cup was unmistakeably Eclipse owned by the British yacht builder Jeremy Rogers. Before the Fastnet she lay a close secod on overall points to Regardless, a Ron Holland designed, Florida built, Irish owned and American crewed yacht. The gale took away Regardless' too-light rudder (rudders designed by Holland were being shed like autumn leaves in 1979) and it flattened Eclipse time and again but even so she came through unscathed to be the first Admirals Cup yacht in the race and was only beaten by one other - Ted Turner's sixty one foot Tenacious which being seven years old was helped by her MkIIIa rating.

Eclipse is one of five hand-built prototypes of the new Contessa 39 class which the Rogers yard at Lymington are now building. The design, by Douglas Peterson of San Diego, was intended to rate close to the 30 ft lower limit of the Admirals Cup range. In production form the Contessa 39 is a very middle of the road design with a displacment of 14,250 Ibs of which 6,000 Ibs is ballast with a beam of 12ft3 in and berths for as many as eight without overcrowding in her roomy interior which also has a large galley, chart table and enclosed head.

About the only features Eclipse and the other prototypes share with the production version, apart from the hull shape and dimensions are the double mould, injection system of lamination which is exclusive to Rogers. The flat-out racing prototypes were extremely lightly built and as bare inside as an empty saucepan. Eclipse had more Kevlar than glass in her hull, together with

a great deal of Plasticell foam. Her all up displacement could not have been a great deal less than that of the production boat since for rating purposes her DLF needed to be as close as possible to unity but the proportion of the all up weight which went into the hull and deck was extremely small. Yet she came through the Fastnet storm without damage, in spite of being knocked flat and swept by waves on several occasions.

Her crew took with them an absolute minimum of supplies for the Fastnet. Much of their food was dehydrated and the cooking stove was of the simplest possible type. One reason the boat was as empty as it was, was that in the rush to prepare customers' boats Jeremy Rogers had little time to build his own boat. In the end the crew rallied around and did much of the work - roughly - themselves. She didn't even carry the normal electronic instruments. Yet unmistakeably, Eclipse and her crew were the Boat and Crew of the Admirals Cup and since it was such a memorable Admirals Cup this must surely qualify Eclipse to be Boat of 1979.

In shape, she follows on from Doug Peterson's Jena of 1978 which was the most successful IOR yacht in the Mediterranean that year. (Jena, ranamed Jubilé, had a very good Fastnet too coming third overall). Eclipse has a full powerful hull with a high prismatic coefficient, big keel and rudder and lofty masthead rig featuring a very small section spar. Her cockpit extends considerably further forward than in the production version and she is as simple on deck as below. In fact you could say that Eclipse and her one-off sisters, Assiduous and Inishanier which were both in the Admirals Cup, looked downright plain.

The winningest yacht of 1979, under IOR rules, must be Ted Turner's Tenacious. Tenacious has in addition to the Fastnet Cup, won the Miami Nassau, the Miami Montego Bay, the Annapolis Newport and the Britannia Cup, the main event of Cowes Week. Built by Palmer Johnson for Lyn Williams as Dora IV in 1972 she can be said to mark, along with the similar

Running Tide, the high water mark of the offshore design development of Olin Stephens which began with Dorade in 1930. Part but by no means all her success stems from a low rating under the MkIIIa provisions for older yachts which is usually augmented further by a direct old age allowance. Yet she is fast by any standards, particularly in a blow. And with her very substantial spar and deck gear and her ample alloy scantlings she never breaks down. Moreover, she is fitted down below with proper cabins for owner and navigator and bunks and lockers for her crew. She is in fact the very epitome of the large cruiser racer and it is hardly surprising that Ted Turner has fallen in love with her and refuses to be seduced by something younger and flightier.

Ternacious was regarded as distinctly beamy when launched but now her shape seems very moderate. Certainly her long and easy ends help her to stand out when moored among more modern rivals.

So far we have considered individual yachts but in many ways 1979 belongs to yachts in groups. In the U.S.A, Britain, Denmark and elsewhere it was the year in which various new classes of habitable one design lay the foundations of future success. In the U.S.A the Tartan Tens and the New York 40s began racing in earnest. In Denmark forty Aphrodite 101s attended their second world championship (won

like the first by Poul Richard - Hoj Jensen). In Britain, Cowes Week, most conservative of regattas, included special races for the Impalas, the 00D34s, 101s and J24s for the first time.

By the simple test of popularity it is the sporty little J24 which must be crowned « generic boat of the year ». Today there are over one thousand six hundred J24s in the world. Three hundred of these are in Europe with the biggest fleets in Britain and Sweden whilst nearly all the others are in their native U.S.A. where the 1979 world championship took place. The first European championship was held at Poole in England and was won, to his considerable surprise, by the Swedish sailmaker Rolf Haeggbom - sailmakers figure prominently in this class, they also came second and third.

Compared with a typical Quarter Tonner, the J24 is, because of its low freeboard and flush deck, considerably less roomy below, but because it is much stiffer it is easier to drive hard and it is simply more fun both for skipper and crew. The lack of standing or even, for tall people, sitting headroom hardly seems to matter. Like the Laser, the J24 has already spawned many imitations but, again like the Laser we trust that having been launched first it will be able to retain its leadership. We also trust that the class rules will be kept strict so that crews can fly around the world to race borrowed boats without disadvantage. Because it has accommo-

"A ping-pong ball in a washing machine". The ball was Gerry Spiers, the 39-year-old sailor who, singlehanded, was the first to cross the Atlantic solo in a boat of just 3 metres length - 10 ft 6 in.

His tiny yacht Yankee-Girl was the washing machine in a storm. But together they crossed the Atlantic from the United States to England in 54 days. Both ball and washing machine arrived in good order.

A very unusual crossing – across the Bering Strait on a sailing surfboard was made for the first time in 1979. Close to the Arctic circle, this 60-miles stretch of water also forms the frontier between the United States of America and the Soviet Union. The man who established this new record is a 32 year old French baron, Arnaud de Rosnay. He sailed from Wales in Alaska to Ouelen in Siberia in 12 hours on the May 31, profiting from 15 knots winds all the way across. The seas he crossed never become warmer than 4 degrees C, so if he had fallen in, his life expectancy would have been no more than ten minutes.

The Aurore singlehanded race, staged at the same time as the disastrous Fastnet, created a little of its own drama with the miraculous rescue of Pierre Follenfant by Olivier

Moussy. But further problems were avoided by the wise decision to cancel the last leg of the race. It turned out to be a benefit for 27-year-old Breton Patrick Elies, who won all

four legs of the race on his half-tonner Chaussettes Olympia, a new design by Jean-Marie Finot.

Left-hand page, lower left. Williwaw, version 79, has a good free-board and simple flush deck bridge, typical of Doug Peterson's designs. The boat's stern is large and powerful.
Right. Lionheart, the new British 12 m. J.I wins the World Championship of this famous series.
Above. Jeremy Roger's Contessa 39 prototype Eclipse (right and p. 19) was the star of the Admiral's Cup. Still not quite finished it took second place.
The J 24 continues her career. There are now 1800 in the world, and this popular success earns it the title of « boat of the year ».

dation however rudimentary and has to have an engine, however like an eggbeater that little unit may be, the J24 offers a scope, a width and depth of enjoyment that such craft as the Soling cannot. In consequence it is rapidly overhauling the small open racing keelboats in total numbers.

We cannot quit 1979 without thinking for a moment of the nineteen who were drowned during the Fastnet Race. Yachts are not yet so good that extremes of weather may be faced in them in complete safety. Racing yachts are not built to be lifeboats. They are as light as human skill can make them... as light as racing rules permit them to be. Those rules carry a very heavy

burden ; by permitting huge spinnakers as well as bloopers, there is little doubt that the IOR rule has led to a generation of yachts which can easily get out of control, even in sheltered water. While remaining highly resistant to sinking, these lively craft have shown they can throw their crews overboard or stun them or frighten them silly. 1979 should have reminded us all that the sea must still be treated with the greatest respect. □

Men and boats of the year

Power-boating

by Ray Bulman

1979 was a notable year for powerboating. It not only saw quite outstanding performances from drivers, both offshore and circuit (inland), it was also a period when new engines and craft made an impact on the sport. Most important of all, it was a period when basic costs soared to a new peak.

The increase in fuel prices in 1979 had a greater effect on powerboating than on any other sport. With top offshore racers using approximately 80 gallons (363 litres) per competition hour, it became one of the world's most expensive water sports. But it was still a year where some battles for champion-ship titles were won early in the season and where other leaders fought up to the last heat in a series.

Offshore racing and its inland brother (circuit) appear to have individual allegiances on either side of the Atlantic. Offshore is the premier sport in America, whereas the majority of supporters for circuit, together with the best events, centre on Europe. This was certainly the case in 1979.

European offshore racing was dominated by one man; Italian Guido Nicolai. Driving his Don Shead designed 38ft (11,5 m). Picchiotti monohull, he won all but one event for which he entered, and finished the season with a huge championship points margin over second man Derek Pobjoy of Gt. Britain. Unlike Nicolai however, Pobjoy used a boat which would be considered long past its prime in the United States. She was the eight-year-old Don Shead designed Enfield built in aluminium – the same material used in Dry Martini 2 – for Tommy Sopwith in 1971. This craft has been extensively modified over the years and is still competitive in European races.

Cougar Marine, the world home of the offshore catamaran, located near Southampton in England, had many successes with their craft; most being achieved in the United States. They produced a new Class 1 catamaran for Ted Toleman at the beginning of the season, later driven in Europe by circuit veteran Nick Cripps. This was a new innovation inasmuch as the crew sit in the wing rather than stand in the sponsons, with the engines also centrally installed instead of the more usual mountings in each hull.

This boat, although potentially very fast, was plagued with mechanical problems and by the time these were cured, the season was over.

Although this British-designed Cougar catamaran was unsuccessful, those sold in the previous 12 months to American drivers had several victories. At the end of 1978, Japanese entrepeneur Rocky Aoki – a resident of the United States – purchased the original Class 1 Cougar catamaran which had been built for Britain's Ken Cassir the previous year. This boat had not only won the 1977 Cowes/Torquay/ Cowes classic, it also set up a new Class 1 speed record of 92.12 mph nine months later.

Aoki saw little success on his American debut but later, as he improved with experience he began to realise he owned a world beater. His early outings were dogged with mechanical problems and hull failure mainly due to driving the fragile craft in rough weather, but these tactics changed for the Benihana Grand Prix off the New Jersey coast in July. Instead of racing ahead of the fleet, he was content to sit back behind the leading boat, letting the conventional monohulls set the pace. It was an approach which paid off. With the finishing line in sight he moved ahead to take the chequered flag – his first win for 12 races and the overall prize in America's major offshore classic.

Not content with this, Aoki then went on to win the Long Beach race held in aid of the John Wayne Cancer Charity four weeks later and suddenly found himself with 800 points in the American Championship series. His efforts on the final American heat were to determine whether or not he would finish third in the championship and hence qualify for a place in the World final at Venice in October. Unfortunately he was seriously injured when the monohull he borrowed for this rougher event broke in half and hence he failed to gain the vital points needed for Venice.

Another driver who has faith in the multihull configuration is 1977 World Champion Betty Cook. She was the second American to purchase a catamaran after Joel Halpern ordered a Cougar following the success of Yellowdrama in the 1977 Cowes/Torquay/Cowes. Her early outings were dogged with mechanical problems which seem to prevail in these high-speed aerodynamic craft. Unlike their monohull counterparts they need setting up for ultimate speed but once this obstacle is surmounted, their performance is far superior in moderate weather conditions. Betty Cook scored her first success in Detroit at the end of June and set a new average speed race record of over 84 mph.

From these performances it now seems that 1980 will see more catamarans exported by Cougar Marine but it is only a matter of time before the demand will force their builders, James Beard and Clive Curtis, to look for new light-weight materials to permit mass production. They are currently built in wood and with high intensified labour costs are not only slow to produce, they are also expensive relative to the racing monohulls built in the United States.

The home of offshore racing is undoubtedly in America, but in 1979 the demand by the American Powerboat Association (APBA) to increase the prize money for championship heats suddenly had a reverse effect. It had steadily risen over the past few seasons from a minimum of $10 000 to $30 000 (US dollars) per heat. With such a high level of sponsorship it was obvious that organizers would find the money difficult to obtain and this indeed happened. The American offshore calendar had planned 10 championship heats, but because high financial support was not forthcoming in all cases, it was reduced to seven. It now looks as if the APBA will have to re-examine this rule for 1980 otherwise growth could either be reversed or swing to the less costly Production craft which compete for separate prizes.

Opposite. *The brilliant Mercury team.*
Left to right, below. *Mike Seebold, Curt Todd, Reggie Fountain, Bill Seebold, Earl Bentz, Lee Sutter and Tom Percival.*

Fiat,
Diesel record

The new outright world speed record for a diesel-powered craft was put up at Tremezo on Lake Como in Italy on 23 May, 1979.
The record speed was 182.80 kilometres per hour, the mean of two runs, with a maximum achieved speed of 183.6 mph.
The engine used, a 5.5 litre supercharged six cylinder Fiat, develops 180 hp at 3.200 r.p.m. and a torque of 530 kg, and was specially prepared for this test.
Tullio Abbate, builder and driver, broke the previous record with his first run at 172.9 mph. which was held by a VM 250 hp. turbo and a Kevlar hull. 200 km/h is not too far in the future.

Between offshore and circuit racing lies an area where enthusiasts with a special lust for speed seek fame on the record breaking circuit. They are a lonely group, for their only competitor is the electronic stop watch. Since the tragic death of Donald Campbell in 1966, there have been few attempts on the world water speed record. The exception is Australian Ken Warby.

Ken Warby's turbo-jet engine Spirit of Australia was initially a low budget attempt to capture the title for his country. Much of the boat he built at his own cost, but the craft proved successful and in October 1978, he established a new record two way average of 317 mph.

Warby's record was incredible and it illustrates the heroism and determination of a private individual in an area where others have relied on enormous financial assistance. He regularly undertakes demonstrations in the region of 200 mph as easily as others travel at 30 mph, but it is unlikely that Warby's record will be broken before he increases it still further.

American Lee Taylor Jr, the former record holder, has a new 40 ft (12,1 m) hull called US Discovery II built in aluminium and titanium. She is a reverse three – pointer and will be powered by hydrogen-peroxide rocket motor giving a thrust of 8 500 pounds. Should Lee Taylor be successful, and 1980 could be his year, his boat, designed to reach 500 mph, may encourage Warby to make another attempt. Those who set such records are brave men indeed with national prestige at heart, but it is doubtful what benefit such speeds bring to the average boating enthusiast or commercial vessel designer in an area of outmoded transport.

1979 saw the introduction of a new Mercury racing out-board which had a marked effect on the international circuit calendar. This engine first appeared at the British Embassy Grand Prix at Bristol in June. Two boats entered, one driven by American Bill Seebold, the other by his fellow countryman Earl Bentz.

The motors were cloaked in secrecy and no one except Mercury engineers were allowed a glimpse under the hood, but they could alter the sport over night.

The lap record at the Embassy Grand Prix, over the 3 kilometre winding course in the Bristol Dock, was set at 85 mph (136 kpl) in 1975 by English driver Peter Thorneywork. This was held for 3 years until Bill Seebold bettered it by 2 mph (3,2 k) in 1978. Such a lap average is quite outstanding on these narrow waters and it was thought that no driver would ever achieve 90 mph (144 kph) in safety. This theory was to be shattered in 1979 when Earl Bentz reached an incredible 98.24 mph (158 kph) in practice. With the only straight section being less than 300 yards (274 m) in length, it meant that Earl Bentz was touching 150 mph. (241.3 kph).

These engines were immediately whisked away by Mercury Marine and not seen again until the third heat in the Canon Series at Drammen, Norway, in September. Their appearance on this circuit also annihilated the competition and the four 20 minute heats were won on aggregate by Bill Seebold at a race average speed of 112 mph (179.2 kph).

Such performances are now pushing Formula 1 circuit racing into the realms of motor sport, but unlike the grand prix motor race driver who earns vast sums, his powerboating counterpart receives a pittance in return for risks which are probably far higher.

One of the world's leading circuit drivers is Italian Renato Molinari. He has more powerboating titles to his credit than any other driver. Unfortunately he made few appearances outside his own country during the '79 season. After finishing well down the prize list at Bristol, he decided to withdraw to home ground where he won the second event easily in the Canon Series at Casale Monferrato in July. Luckily on this occasion the prototype Mercury engines were not racing and it was a standard OMC Evinrude which gave Molinari his success.

The 1979 powerboat season was a period where enthusiasts waited for the introduction of new rules. The Offshore World Championship has proved highly unsatisfactory with a one race final and plans are in hand for this to be modified in 1981, when it will revert to a series of

Opposite. The latest stage in the technical evolution in power boat racing. These hydraulic brakes make a definite improvement in boat performance. Frist trials in the previous season were not very convincing, but it seems that they have' come right' this year.

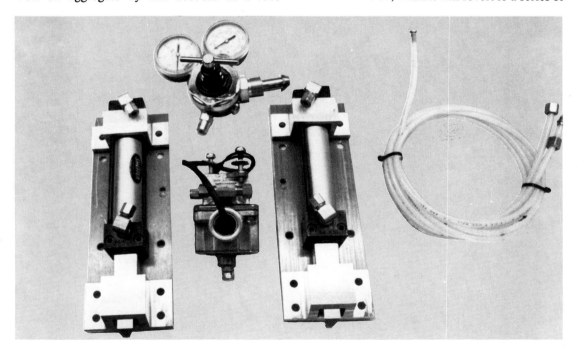

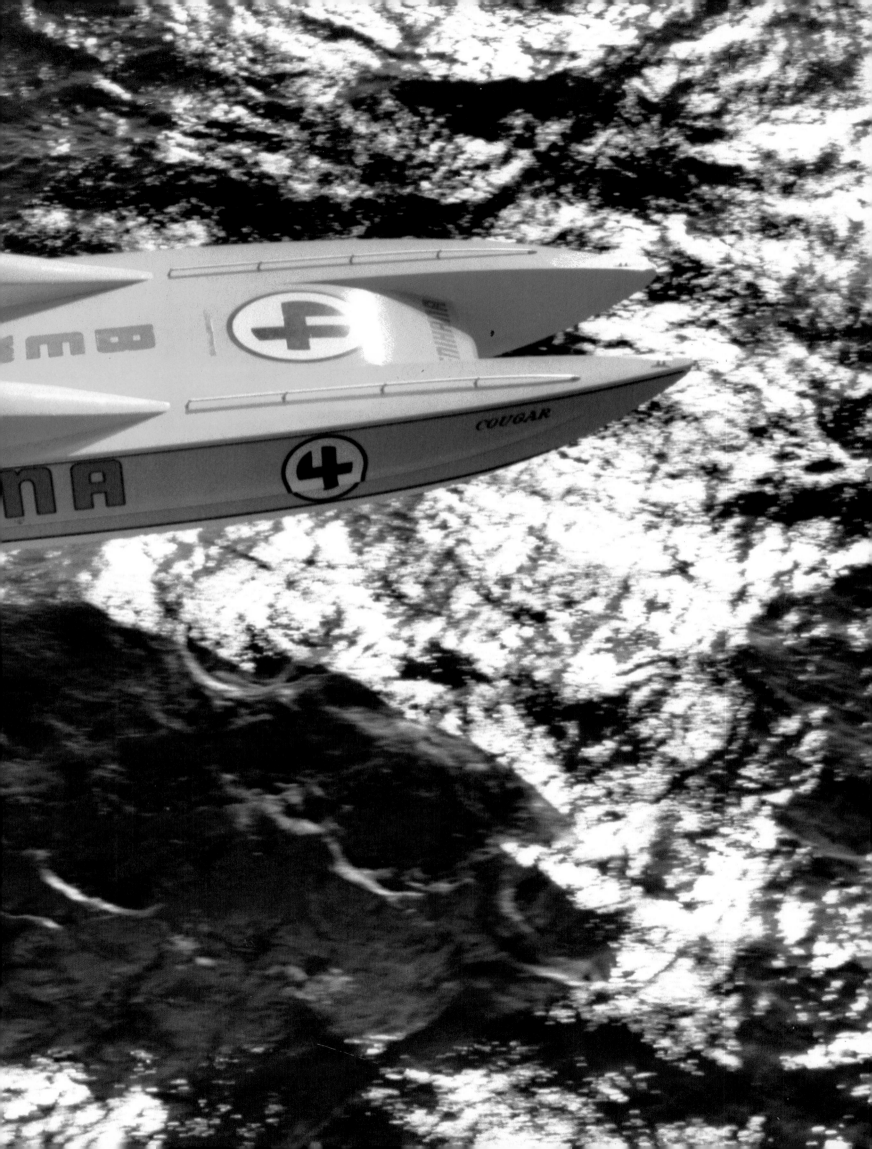

Rocki Aoki beats
the Key West - Cuba record

Although the heavy seas almost incapacitated his 100 miles per hour English built 38' Cougar Cat tunnel hull « Benihana », (P. 22-23) tearing off both its engine hatches, splitting its deck and sides, and rupturing a fuel tank, Japanese-American ocean racer-restauranteur Rocky Aoki was able to establish a new speed record by boat from Key West, Florida to Varadero Beach, Cuba on May 3 rd of '79.

Expecting seas of 3-5 feet an publicly predicting an ambitious 90 miles per hour pace for the 65.6 statute mile run from the U.S.'s southernmost city to the once gay Cuban resort. Aoki of New York City, and his throttleman Errol Lanier ran head on into water almost twice that size but still managed to complete the trip at an average speed of 55.15 mph.

Taking 1 : 44.25 to reach their destination, the pair were forced to abandon their plans to make a return dash to the United States after surveying the damage done to their twin podded wooden boat during the initial run.

Although both of the two big 482 cubic inch Mercuiser engines remained in excellent condition at the end of the hectic journey, the same could not be said for the other parts of the famed boat which holds the world straightaway record for offshore hulls at 92.2 mph.

Within a half hour out of Key West and a few minutes past the official starting point three miles out, both of the engine hatch covers had ripped off and a bilge pump stopped. One vicious sea caved in Aoki's clear plastic face mask.

Lanier then discovered that raw fuel was coursing through his pod forcing him to pop his head high above the protection of the port cockpit to escape the fumes. When he did, the seas whipped his goggles loose.

By then it was obvious to both the men in « Benihana » and to the observers and officials following overhead in four Bell Jet Ranger helicopters that the delicate cat was the wrong boat for the day.

Once tied up at the docks in Varadero, cracks across the aft section of the deck and vertically down the port side next to Lanier's station, were discovered as was a loose engine mount that allowed the port engine to flop dangerously.

Despite the political differences, the venture came off without a hitch as the Cuban officials cleared the red tape.

It was the first time that any speedboats have publicly made the trip between the two countries in speed runs since 1958 when the late Forest Johnson of Miami, Fla. won a race from Miami to Havana in his 28' Prowler « Tooky » beating the legendary Sam Griffith in the only other boat to finish the 259 mile event. « Tooky » was powered by two 275 hp Cadillac Crusader engines, taking 5 :53 to complete the course with a stop at Key West. In 1932 the celebrated American sportsman-inventor Gar Wood, Jr. won the inaugural Miami-Havana race in 9 :23 in one of his own 50' Gar Wood hulls powered by a pair of 450 hp World War II Smith-Liberty airplane engines.

grand prix in the United States and Europe. Until this happens, few people are willing to invest large sums of money in Class I for a single championship race where the slightest malfunction can rob a competitor of the title.

Circuit racing has also proved unsatisfactory. There is a lack of young blood progressing up the formula ladder to take over from the veterans who currently drive on the world circuit. The average age of top formula 1 stars is now mid to late thirties and this is far too old for the quick reactions needed with these ultra fast boats.

The sport generally shows a bad lack of investment and unless it can be made more attractive to the commercial sponsor along the lines of a motor racing world championship circuit, it will stagnate with only the works drivers left to compete.

This opinion is held by many, but the future rests in the hands of the Union Internationale Motonautique (UIM). Their rules must be overhauled in the next 12 months period for, although powerboat racing in all its forms is well supported in the low horsepower categories, it is the large Class I offshore craft and the highly sophisticated Formula I circuit boats which are slowly slipping away. □

Previous pages and above. *Rocky Aoki on his catamaran Benihana. He was to have an accident several days later and for several hours his life hung on a thread.*
Above. *James Beard, designer of the Cougar catamarans which have had a remarkable season with Rocky Aoki's achievement and particularly Betty Cook's world title.*

Calypso

*Alexis Sivirine, close friend of Commandant Jacques Cousteau,
has just published a remarkable book on the most famous boat in the world.
He gives us here a history of the Calypso,
with his own superb illustrations.*

The word Calypso evokes, in some people's minds, the beautiful fair-haired woman who loved Ulysses ; in others the illuminated sign over a restaurant or some other outpost of our consumer society. But for those concerned with the world of the sea, it conjures up a little black and white ship which ceaselessly travels the oceans of the world to bring us marvellous pictures of life above and below the sea.

Built at Seattle in the United States in 1942, and originally a mine-sweeper, the ship was given to Britain under the lend-lease act and became part of the Royal Navy. She finished her naval career in Malta in 1947 and was returned to the United States on August 1st. She was then put up for sale, and it wasn't until May 1949 that she was bought by Mr Gazan, a shipping agent, to be made into a ferry, shipping passengers and vehicles between Malta and Gozo, the island off to the north. Numerous commentators on the Odyssey said that it was on Gozo that the nymph Calypso lived, so Mr Gazan called his boat by that name. He used her for some time, although he was still trying to sell her, a minesweeper not being too suitable for ferry work.

Then along came someone to lift this humble boat out of her mundane surroundings and give her a real history. He was an officer of the French Navy, well-versed in underwater exploration and already known for his exploits in the National Marine and his underwater films which had aroused the imagination of the general public. At this point he was trying to set up a private organisation which would enable him to do oceanographic research of all kinds without administrative pressures ; and which would make the best possible use of the newly developed equipment which had opened up the oceans to man – the self-contained underwater, diving suit which he had designed with the collaboration of the engineer Gagnan in 1942.

This officer was, of course, Jacques-Yves Cousteau, a corvette captain, commander of the Elie Monnier, a naval research vessel. He was put in touch with Mr Gazan in July 1950, through the good offices of Messrs Auniac and Rambaud from Antibes, who also found him an English patron in Loel Guinness, who wanted to buy two minesweepers – one to make into a private yacht for himself, and the other, the Calypso, to hand over to commander Cousteau.

To modify and equip the Calypso for his own purposes, Cousteau asked for, and received, a temporary leave of absence from the Navy and set up a non profit-making organization called the Friends of French Oceanography. In July 1950, Calypso was in Antibes for the wholesale modification which was to prepare her for her third career on the seas. The work to be carried out was formidable. They had to add a false bow so that the crew could film under water ; create an after deck as a working area ; add various winches and hoists ; devise a working platform

that could be lowered and raised from sea level ; install a lookout platform in the prow to allow for safe navigation in coral reefs ; equip the boat with compressors, pumps and so on ; install a depth-sounder, gyroscopic compass, automatic pilot, and radio transmitters ; enlarge the fuel and water tanks so that the ship could go longer without replenishing stocks and completely alter the ship's arrangements to provide for life on board for scientists, and all their gear.

Remember that, at this time, there was no oceanographic research vessel in France, unless you count the Theodore Tissier, a fishery research ship. So Cousteau set himself a very broad programme : observation of the under-sea world, its flora and fauna ; morphological study of corals and development of specialised measuring equipment for use on the ship and by the underwater divers.

He was not only concerned with providing written reports of his work, but wanted to film, to hear and see how the world beneath the waves behaves by taking samples and using all the equipment. He wanted to increase man's knowledge concerning the topography as well as the geology, physics and chemistry of the globe.

This programme suited Cousteau perfectly. Thanks to his personal initiative and the extraordinary logistical support provided by the Calypso, France has become one of the world's leading nations in oceanographic studies. She will hold that position while Cousteau has the means to explore more widely and exhaustively.

It would take a whole library of books to record all the research carried out by Cousteau, the boat's crew and its scientists. There are already more than 20 books recording the research completed, which are linked by the common title « Scientific results of the Friends of Calypso » and published by the French

Oceanographic Institute.

So in an article like this we can only summarise this rich work and list the various voyages of the vessel, their main achievements and the discoveries made in under-sea exploration – for Calypso has scored many world firsts.

1951 – Preparation of the ship and first sea trials. Missions for the Museum of Natural History in Paris ; study of the coral and life in the Red Sea close to Djeddah. Great success ; return in February 1952.

1952 – Beginning of the large underwater workshop on the archeological site of the Grand Congloue close to Marseilles. World-wide acclaim for this work, which has resulted in thousands of amphoras and ancient pots being recovered and the examination of a Roman vessel by television cameras – the first time they had been used under the sea.

1953 – More work on the Grand Congloue workshop for the Department of Archeology for Provence and Corsica : 3,500 dives to a depth of 40 metres. Then a mission to Greece and Sicily and trials of the first electronic flash under water – developed by the pioneer of such equipment, H.G. Edgerton, who was on board Calypso at the time.

1954 – Calypso undertook a programme of oil exploration research for BP. It was the first exploration of the sea in the Gulf of Bahrein and the opening of these riches to the Emirates of Abu-Dahabi and others. For the first time ever, the Calypso crew used Gravimeter research

Jacques-Yves Cousteau with his son Philippe. When he had become the skipper's right hand man, Philippe Cousteau was to disappear tragically during the summer of 1979 while he was piloting his amphibious airplane.

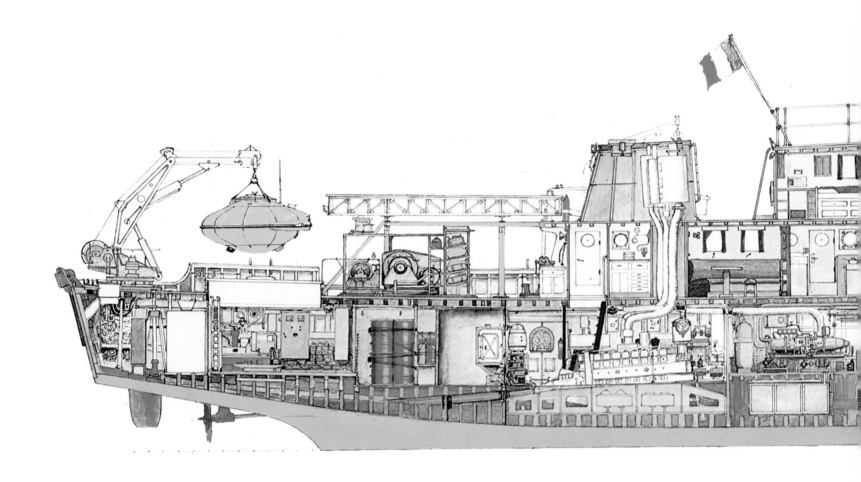

1942

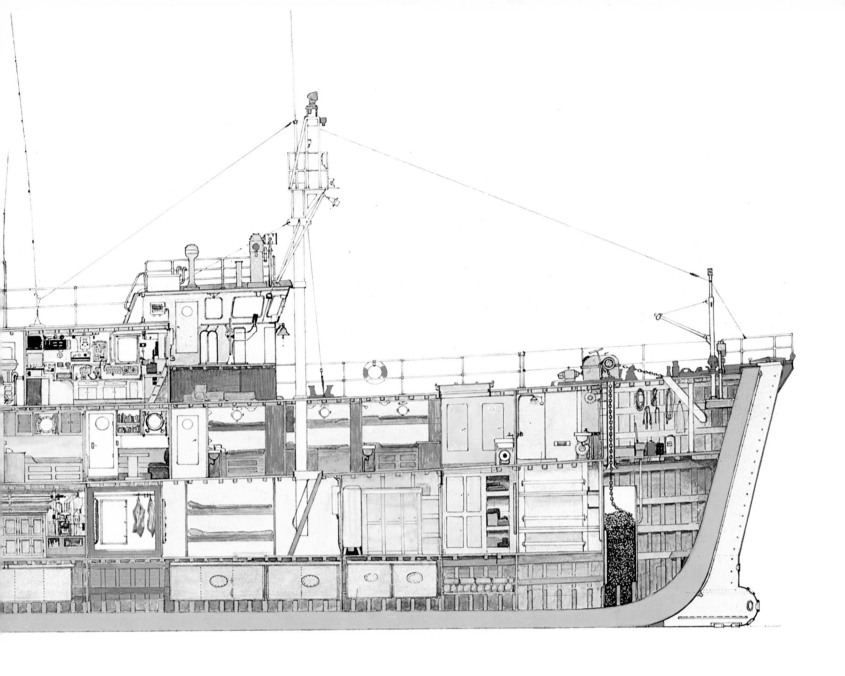

1968

equipment under the water – and got excellent results. They also carried out four special missions with French scientists : the Seychelles with Professor Charbonnier ; the Sicily-Tunisia shelf with Professor Peres ; Port Vendres with the Arago de Banyuls Laboratory, and research between Nice and Corsica for Professor Bourcart's geological studies. Calypso became the official oceanographic research vessel for France.

1955 – A cruise in the Indian Ocean to the Seychelles, the Isle of Aladabra and the making of the first full length underwater film « The World of Silence ». Then a scientific assignment in Sicily and in Greece (the Matapan Trench), Crete and Turkey.

1956 – Mission with Professor Forest along the coasts of Guinea, Cameroon, Senegal and the Ivory Coast. On the way back a unique exploit : mooring the ship in the middle of the Atlantic 7,600 metres above the Romanche trench on a nylon cable 10,000 metres long. Also taking pictures with the Edgerton electronic flash showing the busy life which exists at these enormous depths.

1957 – Calypso's silhouette was modified – she got a new false bow and various other improvements. Creation with ORTF of the first Eurovision programme for television featuring direct pictures from under the sea – coming from the Grand Congloue to Marseilles and featuring shots of the workshop on the sea bottom. Also important work in Gibraltar, the Azores and the Atlantic for the International Geophysical Year.

1958 – Installation of a new hydraulic crane on board. New assignments in the Atlantic near Gibraltar and Madeira. First trials of an underwater sledge « The Troika » which is still a world first, and which allows the taking of stereo pictures and film at great depths. More work in Alboran, Genoa and Cannes.

1959 – The company Gaz de France asked Calypso to undertake an unusual topographical survey as a preliminary to the possible laying of a pipe line between Mostaganem in Algeria and Carthaginia in Spain – which required an accuracy 10 times greater than normal sea bed surveys. A precise survey was carried out by means of a special Decca system installed on board. Launching of the diving saucer SP 350 which was to become the number one auxiliary vessel of the Calypso (an underwater craft for two people, capable of going down to a depth of 350 metres). Voyage to the United States with an Atlantic assignment which resulted in stereo colour pictures of the huge trench in mid-Atlantic, revealing to the world the presence of under-water fissures with lava emissions – this 15 years before the Franco-American expedition

on the Famous. Other pictures show animal life 8,400 metres down.

1960 – New assignments using the SP 350, because the machine had fascinated all who saw it, both in France and abroad – in Corsica, Spain and Algeria.

1961 – Work in the Mediterranean, Brazil, Argentina and Uraguay.

1962 – Return from Argentina. Many local assignments concerned with geological work – using the new very powerful acoustic depth sounder. Then the setting up of the first ever underwater house, for a study of « saturation diving » – men living under the sea for long periods. This « Diogenes operation » saw two oceanauts living under the surface for eight days at a depth of 45 feet. The year finished with more hydrological and geophysical missions plus radioactivity measurements for the Atomic Energy Commission.

1963 – Work in the Red Sea, and a second experiment in saturation diving. This time a whole village was set up at Shab Rumi – some houses at 30 feet, some at 75 feet. This was followed by four months of work in Corsica and around Nice with the RANA navigation system which enabled the team to produce a very precise chart of that area.

1964 – Another world first : the setting-up of a floating laboratory on the Froude strip between Nice and Corsica, then voyages in Greece and Crete and trials of dives using powered projectors.

1965 – Various missions in the western Mediterranean between March and November.

1966 – This was a crucial year for Calypso which, as we have seen, had been cherished and encouraged by the directors of oceanographic research in France. But then a big sister to Cousteau's boat arrived – new, and totally equipped for any kind of oceanographic work. After one short mission, Calypso was given no more official work. CNEXO, derived from the COMMEXO which Cousteau helped to set up, had elected a different board of control which gradually gave less and less work to the old servant who had helped to show the way. Nevertheless Cousteau – undeterred, adapted his trusty boat so that it would do the job which

nobody could take from him – the production of beautiful films of undersea life even better –.

1967-70 – After the re-fit, the first jobs were in the Red Sea, where conditions are ideal for filming. But international events now began to intrude. The Six Day War, the closing of the Suez Canal, the general tension : all this made it necessary for Calypso to return to the Atlantic by way of the Cape of Good Hope, having replaced her old diving saucer with two one-man machines capable of going down more than 1,500 feet. So instead of going back to France, Calypso headed for the Caribbean, Panama, Chile and the Galapagos Islands, where she very nearly came to a tragic end when she struck an uncharted rock at full speed. Then on to Mexico, the West Coast of the U.S.A. and eventually to her birthplace, Seattle. Further still, to the Aleutian Islands, where Calypso reached the furthest point west of her whole life. She returned by way of Los Angeles and Belize, where the team visited the marvellous under-water grottos. And so to France. This whole voyage produced colour films for television

Left. *Calypso looks for an anchorage between cliffs of ice.*
Opposite, right. *Calypso moored at Marseilles.*
Top to bottom. *The instrument room : navigation gear is complemented by very accurate electronic measuring apparatus.*
This torpedo-launcher is used for filling diving bottles. The saucer allows Cousteau's men to explore the greatest depths of the ocean, diving to more than 25,000 feet beneath the Atlantic.

stations in both Europe and America and also books for the Requin series.

1970-71 – Based at Marseilles, Calypso undertook a number of missions for private companies and produced various films - on the Sicily-Tunis bank, about dolphins and coral-fishermen of Corsica.

1972-73 – With two ambitions – to find the best places for filming and also to make a comparison of our polluted waters and those barely touched by man – Cousteau turned his ship towards the Antarctic. This was to prove the sternest test for the now 30-year-old Calypso. A helicopter ; an indispensable aid for anyone exploring the ice pack because it provides a vital link between the ship and shore-based outposts, was used. But sadly it brought about the death of a well-loved lieutenant, Michel Laval. There were other adventures : a blizzard, ice which shut in the ship and a furious sea during a storm. All provided vivid memories of this trip which finished at Punta Arena for repairs of the worst damage. Then a return to the sheltered port chosen in the U.S.A., Galveston. This return trip

and the stop-over for repairs lasted a year – it seemed like the end of Calypso's travels to the crew, tired and disorientated as they were by the tough experiences of the Antarctic.

Calypso had a very hard time in Galveston, for finances were low, and the team was waiting for some of their films to be syndicated. I saw the boat myself with Jean-Marie France in May 1974 and was able to judge the damage and what it would take to put her back in order – damage caused in the Antarctic, and also by a collison with a tug almost as big as Calypso herself, which happened in the port, and from a fire which – luckily - had gone out before it got a real hold –.

1973-74 – Despite problems in the land-based company which helped Calypso with its research, the OFRS then the CEMA, Cousteau carried out the re-fit and again began to make films for television. In the Caribbean, he shot films of lobsters, coral reefs and shipwrecks. On this cruise he also used a flying auxiliary – a seaplane of the Catalina type which was piloted by his son Philippe Cousteau who thus added

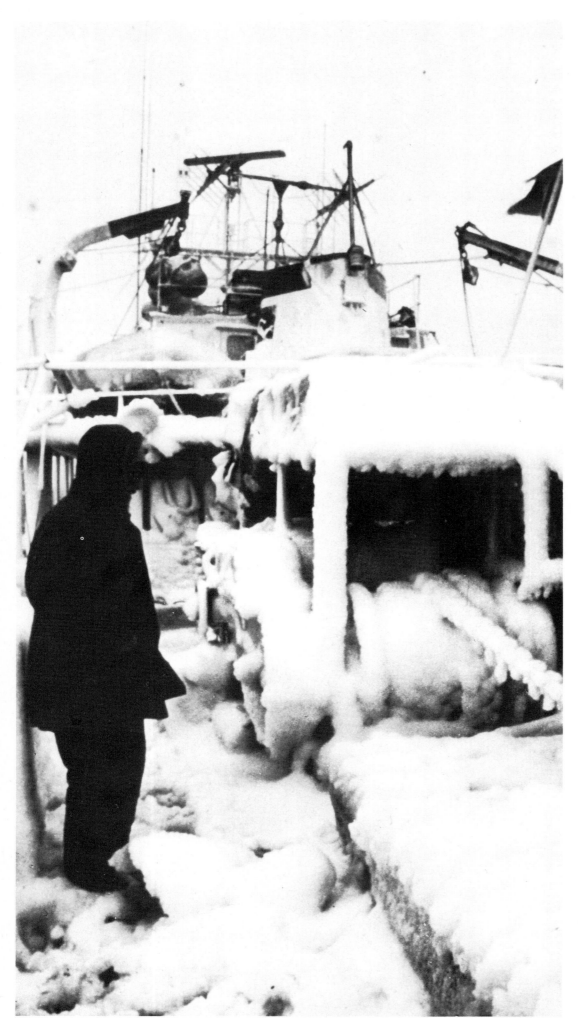

another dimension to Calypso by opening the way to airborne oceanography.

1975-76 – An assignment for the Greek government which kept Calypso in Greek waters for some months and saw the collection of a huge number of ancient actifacts – all now in Greek museums.

1977 – While always looking out for suitable areas for films on and below the water, Cousteau used some of the money collected by the Cousteau Society in the U.S.A. (a non profit-making company, set up to carry out research into marine pollution) to make a trip around the Mediterranean and produce an analysis of the levels of pollution in various areas. The resulting report gave him valuable ammunition for his continuing campaign against the pollution of the sea.

1978 – Calypso while making different films, investigated wrecks of old vessels and carried out a systematic exploration of the zone around Marseilles.

1979 - After another re-fit at Barcelona, the boat was standing by for a contract which was to see it exploring the coasts of Venezuela for a report on pollution there. Finally leaving Marseilles in May, she headed for Newport, Rhode Island, U.S.A. to film a wreck – the famous Monitor, from the War of Independence, then she got ready to travel to Guadeloupe and on to the Venezuelan coast. It was then that Cousteau heard the news about the loss of the Catalina and the death of his son Philippe.

Whatever Commander Cousteau plans for the future, it is a fact that for more than 30 years Calypso, always flying the French flag, has been a remarkable tool of oceanographic research. She has provided a work-base for numerous scientists, technicians, film-makers and sailors – a means to their various ends which may not always have been as comfortable as they might have liked, but usually with a working team atmosphere it would be hard to find anywhere else. The Calypso crew, which seems to come back time after time with the same stalwarts, has always known how to generate a spirit of unity, friendship and an understanding of the value of life which many of them say you cannot match elsewhere.

The total of all the crew members, and all those experts who have worked on the ship, adds up to hundreds, so it is impossible to name them all. Still, it would be unthinkable not to mention Madame Simone Cousteau, certainly the one person who has spent the longest time on the ship and who gives such essential aid to the skipper in his work. Then there is Commander Alinat, who runs the museum at Monaco and has often been on the Calypso, ever since she first began her work, running her operations and arranging for the installation of new equipment. And Albert Falco, the chief diver, who joined the team in 1952, and who Cousteau is happy to trust with the ship on the most difficult assignments.

So despite the difficulties she has come through and the terrible Cousteau family tragedy, The Calypso is destined to carry on the good work planned for her by Commandant Cousteau. □

Preceding pages. *Philippe Cousteau's hot air observation balloon prepares to take off.*
Opposite. *Calypso in shrouded with a mantle of ice after a snow-storm near the Argentine coast.*

The Major Event

Cowes' Story

150 years of sailing history

by Frank Page

Cowes has been at the centre of yachting in Britain for more than 150 years, but in all that time there has never been an event at Cowes of more historic interest than the race which started from there Saturday 11th August 1979. It was the '79 Fastnet Race, crowning event of a fiercely-disputed Admiral's Cup and peak ambition of more than 2,000 yachtsmen on over 300 boats. It was to become the greatest disaster in sailing history.

The evening before the start of this Fastnet Race, the town staged its traditional Friday-of-Cowes-week firework display, Thousands thronged into the town and packed the promenade. Many more stood on the decks of hundreds of boats moored in Cowes Roads. As the rockets flew higher and soft billows of smoke drifted gently across the water, the yachtsmen were - as always - tempted to join in the show. First one red flare shot into the night sky. Then another, and another. Soon those innocent smoke clouds had a lurid tinge of red which seemed to hint at some malevolent influence, some foreboding of peril in store. On board one big motor yacht, the professional skipper shook his head and looked away. ' I can never see a red flare go up without my heart sinking. It's something that means a lot to me as an experienced seaman. I don't think they should be allowed to do that. ' He finished his drink and went below. On a yacht moored nearby, which was destined to be one of the smallest boats in that huge fleet of 300 that sailed west the next day, one sensible yachtsman also had his doubts. 'I remember thinking to myself - " I just hope they are not going to need those red flares in the next few days ".

But at that time there was little cause for concern about the Fastnet Fleet. Yes, the weather men had been saying that one or two of those depressions scuttling in from the Atlantic might turn nasty. The weather adviser to the British team put it bluntly to Edward Heath and the crews of the three British boats on Saturday morning before they set off. ' I told them we could have one or two depressions which could blow up explosively' he said. " It could be like July 1956, when there was a force 10 in the Channel, so be prepared. My forecast was for a force 8 blow. You couldn't possibly have predicted a force 10 at that stage, because it didn't come until Monday afternoon. "

And by that Monday afternoon the huge fleet was strung out across the Western Approaches, most of them just about half way between Land's End and the Fastnet Rock off the southern coast of Ireland. The maxi-raters and top class I yachts had turned the rock and were heading south again, but the rump of the fleet - the class III, IV and V yachts - were in the region of the Labadie Bank.

This is an area of comparatively shallow water, and when the barometer suddenly plummeted and the wind just as suddenly whipped up to force 10 or 11, it was the insubstantial waters of the Labadie bank which were churned into a howling, boiling maelstrom. The waves were gigantic, and short, and confused. Many yachtsmen spoke of monster rollers which came together from different directions, piled up into huge pyramids of water and crashed down on to the tiny, helpless boats in their path.

This was a total contrast to the Fastnet Races of the rest of the seventies. Then, the secret of success had been finding a way out of the belts of calms. In 1977 some of the smaller yachts had even run short of food and water, the race went on so long. There hadn't been a really tough Fastnet since 1963 : it was hardly surprising that, when the storm came, it found some yachts and their crews unprepared for the ordeal.

Of the record fleet of 302 yachts which set out from Cowes that bright and blustery Saturday, only 85 completed the course back to Plymouth. No less than 217 boats were forced to retire - scuttling away to safety in sheltered ports in Ireland, Wales and England - and 23 boats were sunk or abandoned.

The British armed forces and life-boat service combined with the coastguards to mount one of the biggest rescue operations in history. A final total of 136 yachtsmen were snatched from peril by helicopters and rescue boats. But the ferocity of this storm would brook no denial : 15 yachtsmen were lost from boats competing in the Fastnet and another four perished from a trimaran which had been following the race. It was the worst calamity in the history of sailing for sport. Inevitably, the great storm provided a searching test of both men and boats. At least 14 rudders broke under the strain and designers are clearly having to re-think some of the previously accepted standards of strength for lightness. On the other hand, few boats were dismasted and

the spar and rigging makers may well feel that they have come out of the disaster with some honour. A few boats were severely damaged by the huge waves, but only five were actually sunk. The other 18 abandoned craft were later recovered and most will be fit to race again.

Design faults emerged, too, Some hatches proved too weak, some washboards came out of the boats far too readily, so that water could pour in as each succeeding wave crashed over the yacht concerned. Cookers became lethal flying objects - one even went clean through a yacht's window - when the big seas threw a small boat about.

But perhaps the worst anxieties arose from the fallibility of safety gear on the Fastnet boats. Some life-rafts proved disturbingly fragile, with canopies ripping off, sea anchors snappping, the rafts themselves capsizing far too easily and one actually ripping into two pieces under the force of the waves. There were also reports of rafts which failed to inflate when needed. Safety harnesses did not always stand up to the strain, either. It should be said that many Fastnet survivors owe their lives to their harnesses, because there are countless stories of boats knocked down and men in the cockpit being hurled into the sea but able to get back aboard because they were clipped on. Against that, there are also instances of harness lines snapping, buckles giving way, and hooks which simply pulled straight under the force of a sudden jerk.

All of these matters are being considered by a special Inquiry set up by the Royal Yachting Association and the Royal Ocean Racing Club, under Commander Bill Anderson. At the time of writing it had issued 900 detailed questionnaires to Fastnet Race competitors at the beginning of September and received nearly half that number back by the end of the month. The answers to the questionnaires will be fed into a computer in the hope that this will show whether it was the design and construction of each yacht, the skill of her skipper and crew or her position relative to the worst of the wind and sea which were the most important factors in her survival of the storm.

At the same time, the Inquiry is talking to the main authorities concerned with the search and rescue operation to see whether more detailed contingency planning might have helped the competitors to get more help more quickly. And the Inquiry members are also investigating structural features and equipment - particularly rudders, harnesses and life-rafts. It is anticipated that the Inquiry report will be published towards the end of 1979. One other question which is bound to feature strongly in the Inquiry report concerns radios. Until the 1979 Fastnet Race competing yachts were required to carry radios capable of receiving weather forecasts, but it was not mandatory to have transmitting sets. Critics of the Fastnet rescue operation - particularly yachtsmen from Australia, where two-way radios are required - said after the race that some of the inexperienced crews on small boats might have been advised how to cope if they had been equipped with transceivers. Against that, some

experienced radio operators complained that at the height of the storm thers was much confusion caused by improper use of VHF sets, and it was dificult to establish clearly who was in danger and where they were. If all the boats in the fleet had been equipped with Transceivers, the argument went, then nobody would have been able to make out anything, that storm-tossed Monday night and Tuesday morning.

Whatever the outcome of the Inquiry, it is certain that the Fastnet Race will never be the same again. It seems certain now that too many people had begun to take this race for granted ; it had become a kind of biennial " jolly " which put little strain on either boats or men. It was a race which owners and their friends thought they would like to do even if they had little experience of sailing outside the comparatively sheltered waters of the Solent. Even if the authorities do not restrict the fleet for 1981 there seems little doubt that far fewer boat owners will want to go next time. The Fastnet is now seen in its true perspective : a race which can be the sternest challenge of all a boat's strengths and of all the crew's seamanship and skill. Robert James, who has twice sailed round the world in Whitbread

races, was aboard the record-breaking maxi-boat Condor of Bermuda for the 1979 Fastnet Race. He said afterwards that the seas and winds he experienced were the equal of anything he had seen in the Southern Ocean.

And, in one sense, that is the sort of reputation the Fastnet ought to have. Certainly it is in line with the original conception of the race when it was first dreamed up by Lieutenant Commander George Martin and a few friends, 54 years ago. Back in 1925 they came to the conclusion that what yachting really needed then was a true ocean race. The yachting around Cowes was all very well, but most yachtsmen seldom went out of sight of land. Their navigation was seldom seriously tested, their race courses never took them out of easy distance of a sheltering port.

A real challenge would be a 600-mile and more race from Cowes - where else ? - down the south coast and round Land's End, across the Atlantic to the Fastnet Rock, then back south-eastwards to round the Scilly islands and finish at Plymouth.

To them, at that time, it seemed like the ultimate challenge. They were amazed when seven yachts actually entered that first year. And they could have had no real idea of what they were starting, because that first Fastnet was not only the beginning of a new classic event in the sailing calendar ; it also led to the foundation of the Ocean Racing Club, later to be given Royal patronage, and much later again to the Admiral's Cup series which has really become the World Cup of off-shore yacht racing. Indeed, if you stand back a pace and look at the history of Cowes and yacht racing in Britain, that vital date of 1925 is one of the landmarks. The Fastnet gave a greater purpose and importance to Cowes

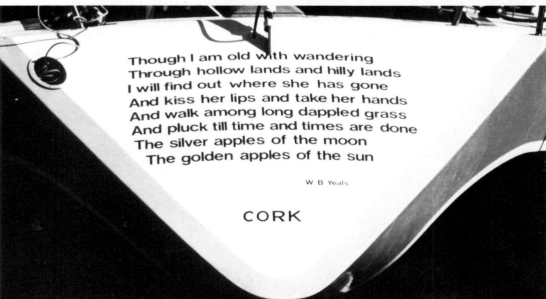

Though I am old with wandering
Through hollow lands and hilly lands
I will find out where she has gone
And kiss her lips and take her hands
And walk among long dappled grass
And pluck till time and times are done
The silver apples of the moon
The golden apples of the sun

W B Yeats

CORK

Pages 34-35. *Close racing in good winds during the Fastnet Race between the American entry Boomerang and Britain's Yeoman XXI.*
Left-hand Page. *A close start reminiscent of a dinghy race.*
Centre. *The top sailor and sail-maker Lowell North was aboard Williwaw.*
Right. *Britain's ex-premier Edward Heath has been campaigning for the Admiral's Cup since 1971.*
Opposite. *Ron Holland's Golden Apple, lower stern.*

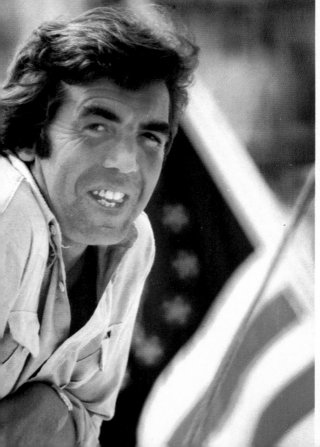

Week ; its incorporation into the Admiral's Cup in 1957 consolidated that position and made Cowes the centre of the most intensely-fought big boat racing championship in the world.

The distinction was a long time coming to the little port on the Isle of Wight, for it had existed for many centuries before it was thrust into the limelight as the sailing centre of Britain - and a fashionable one at that.

Historians believe that there has been some sort of settlement on the Medina River, where Cowes now stands, since at least the 16th century. Originally called shamblers, it seems to have gained the name Cowes in the 16th century, possibly deriving from the twin castles or " cows " guarding each side of the river, which were erected in the reign of Henry VIII. But there must be some doubt about this, as the town is called The Cowe as early as 1512, yet the castles were not built until 1539.

The place soon became a small commercial and fishing port, typical of so many along the south coast of England, with boat yards and sheltered moorings. But it probably grew faster than most because of the rapid expansion of Britain's Navy, whose home was Portsmouth, just across the Solent. Certainly in 1633 Cowes played an important part in the colonisation of America, because Leonard Calvert and his party set out from there to cross the Atlantic and set up the Palatinate of Maryland under a charter granted by the King of England. This conferred on the people of Maryland all the rights of Englishmen, to be theirs in perpetuity : rights which today's citizens of Maryland still cherish. The Calvert party sailed in two small ships called the Ark and the Dove, and they were the first of many ships to propagate a flourishing trade with the settlers in the American colonies. In 1677 4,000 hogsheads of tobacco were exported to Cowes from Virginia. The new Customs House in East Cowes was undoubtedly a very busy place.

By the end of the 18th century, yachting was beginning to emerge as a sport. The Royal Cork Yacht Club had been founded as early as 1720 and there is some evidence that sailing races were beginning to be organised in the Solent, probably from Cowes, at about this time or soon after. The earliest " races " were probably between the fast luggers which were used for smuggling and the equally swift revenue cutters of the excise men. Both kinds of boat were specialities of the Cowes yards. There are indications that sometimes the boats sailed against each other for wagers, but the first official record of a race is in 1788, when there was a race round the island by a fleet of cutters - earliest forerunner of so many round-the-island races.

By the beginning of the 19th century Cowes had grown to a thriving comunity of about 2,000 people, with the villas of retired naval men overlooking the harbour and the small houses of the tough seamen and boatbuilders clustered round the docks. A number of important naval craft were built in the town : ships like the Repulse, a 64-gun ship of 1,387 tons which was present at Rodney's victory at The Saints, off Guadeloupe, in 1782. The same year saw the Cowes-built H.M.S. Astrea, 32 guns, capturing the American 40-gun frigate South Carolina.

But though commerce and inustry were the main sources of income for the people of Cowes, their town was still attractive enough to attract rich and titled people to use it as a holiday town. In 1811 the Duke of Gloucester began to place bets on local boats in unofficial races, and two years later a formal regatta was organised for boats which had been chartered to race but were sailed by professional seamen. Soon the gentlemen began to join in the races and in 1815 Britain's first yacht club was formed. A bunch of 'enthusiastic gentlemen' met at the Thatched House Tavern in London under the guidance of the Honourable Charles Pelham, later Lord Yarborough. They formed The Yacht Club, with 42 members. Entry qualifications were simple : the member should be of good social standing, own a yacht of a certain tonnage and be able to pay the entrance fee. The Prince Regent soon asked to join and when he became King George IV in 1820 the club was renamed the Royal Yacht Club. Its uniform was a common blue jacket with white trousers – this was considered to be 'far from unbecoming to such as are not too square in the stern'.

Until 1825, summer meetings of the club were held in the Medina Hotel in East Cowes, and then the club acquired the Gloucester Hotel, now called the Gloster.

The Royal Yacht Club had a serious purpose apart from sailing races. Its members owned several craft fitted out as men-of-war, including Lord Yarborough's Falcon, which was built on the lines of a 20-ton corvette. By the 1840s, the

total armament of the club was 400 guns, and when William IV succeeded to the British throne in 1833 it changed its name to the more appropriate Royal Yacht Squadron. In 1857 it moved into its present home, West Cowes Castle. The sister fort at East Cowes was a ruin by the end of the 17th century.

In the first half of the 19th century, Cowes gradually became the mecca of the world's sailors. Queen Victoria's mother presented a challenge cup in 1833 and the young queen and her husband Prince Albert became members of the Squadron in 1838, a year after her accession. Tsar Nicholas of Russia also joined that year, his qualification being a Cowes-Built yacht called, appropriately Queen Victoria.

There were, of course, many rituals in a club of such prestige and royal patronage. None but members and Royal Navy officers could land at the Squadron landing stage; to make a mistake in the complicated flag-etiquette was social death and the clubhouse was, naturally, a male domain. Ladies were restricted to the Castle lawn and there was no ladies room provided until the 1920s.

But then, yachting was a man's sport, and it was flourishing. Cowes Week became an essentiel part of the English social scene, with the wealthy aristocracy descending upon the town for the first week of August after coming across the water from Sussex where the preceding event in the calendar was the horse racing at glorious Goodwood. In 1851 the schooner America came to show the British that they knew a thing or two about yacht racing on the other side of the water, too. It won a famous victory in a round-the-island race – a victory which was to be the starting point of one of the world's great yachting competitions, the America's Cup.

In 1863 the Prince of Wales, later Edward VII, became a patron of the Royal Yacht Squadron, and he was its commodore for 19 years from 1882 onwards. This was the peak period of rich men's yachting in Cowes, when owners bought huge sailing craft and employed big crews of professional seamen to man them. Uffa Fox, one of the most colourful characters in the history of the town, gave three main reasons for its popularity as a sailing centre of international repute. First, the Solent provides one of the most challenging yacht racing courses in the world. On this stretch of water there is every danger and every difficulty, including strong tides, strong winds, rocks, shingle banks, mud banks and sand pits. In addition to these natural hazards there is the presence of the largest liners in the world, plying their trade between Southampton and overseas. The second reason is that Cowes provides a range of skilled craftsmen to build and maintain the yachts, and the third that Cowes has always enjoyed royal patronage – and still does. No Cowes week goes by without a visit by some members of the Royal Family.

It was apparent early in the 19th century that not all those who wished to race at Cowes would be accomodated by the one yacht club. The Royal London Yacht Club, which had been formed in 1838, moved to Cowes in 1854. The Island Sailing Club, now one of the biggest and most popular in the town, was formed in 1889. The Royal Corinthian Yacht Club took over the

house close by the Squadron's Castle which had once belonged to the redoubtable Rosa Lewis, owner of the famous Connaught Hotel in London. Finally, in 1952, the Cowes Corinthian Yacht Club was formed.

Together, all these clubs have fostered the proliferation of regattas based on Cowes, and together they have seen the great days of the various famous classes come and go. Perhaps the most romantic period in the history of Cowes was when the monster J-boats were in their prime. And perhaps the most romantic element of Cowes today is the continued health and

intensive competition of the old-established day boat classes which link modern Cowes week with those glorious leisurely events of Victorian and Edwardian times. The Redwing class is as healthy as ever, yet it was first founded in 1896. The X One Design class provides 50 or more boats for the Cowes Week races, although the class was formed as long ago as 1908. And there are many more: Solent Sunbeams, Sea View Mermaids, the West Wight Scows – all types of yachts which have woven strong threads into the very fabric of the Cowes tradition.

But tradition alone will never keep racing

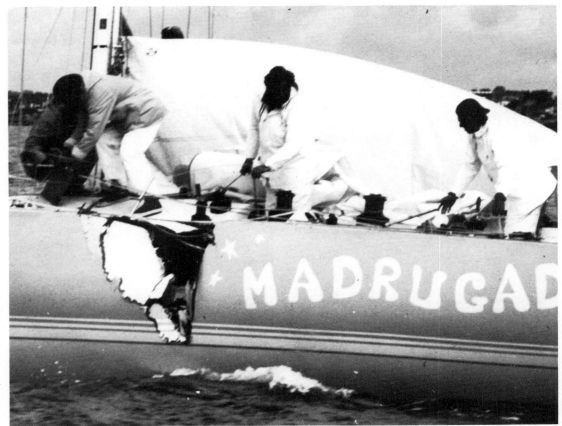

Left-hand page, top. *Police Car, an Ed Dubois design, helped to take the Admiral's Cup back to Australia.* Below. *Vanguard, another Dubois design, shared third place in the Admiral's Cup with the Hong Kong team.*

Right, top. *Jeremy Roger's Contessa 39 Eclipse finished second overall in the Fastnet Race.* Opposite. *Madrugada (Brazil), a Frers design, was in collision at one start with the Argentine boat Sur.*

healthy and competitive. The sport needs the impetus of demanding new targets to stay lively. That's why the start of the Fastnet Race was so important in 1925. And that's why the beginning of the Admiral's Cup series was so crucial in 1957.

The Admiral's Cup is a beautiful gold plated cup which was presented in 1957 by Sir Myles Wyatt, C.B.E., Captain John Illingworth, R.N., Peter Green, Geoffrey Pattinson and Selwyn Slater. They were all members of the Royal Ocean Racing Club and Sir Miles Wyatt was the Admiral : hence the name. The original intention was 'to encourage overseas yachtsmen to race in English waters'. It has certainly done that ; from two competing nations in 1957 (Britain and the United States), the list has grown to encompass all the major sailing nations of the world, and during the seventies the competition has been fought out between 16 to 19 different countries every two years. Britain won the Cup the first year it was constituted, and three of the five presenters of the trophy – Geoff Pattinson, John Illingworth and Selwyn Slater – used their own yachts to pull off a narrow victory over the Americans, led by Dick Nye in an early Carina.

The Americans did not come back in 1959, but the French and the Dutch swelled the numbers to three countries. Britain again held the Cup, with the Dutch second. The French killed their chances by retiring from the Fastnet – it was a tough one. In 1961 the Americans returned and the Swedes joined in, too, so there were five countries in the list. The American team of Windrose, Figaro and Cyane took the Cup back across the Atlantic, and the British organisers began to think about organising proper selection trials to choose the team.

It seems to have worked, because Britain won again in 1963 and 1965, and each time a Ron Amey yacht (Noreyma III and Noreyma IV) played a key part in the success. By the mid-sixties the prestige of the Admiral's Cup competition was growing. Germany was in the list for the first time in 1963. Two years later Australia and Ireland joined in.

Australia came back in 1967 and, like the Americans, took the Cup at the second attempt. The team consisted of Mercedes III, Balandra and Caprice of Huron. Caprice. Gordon Ingate's boat, which was already 13 years old when she came over in 1955, was the star of the side, performing incredibly well despite her age. In 1969 the number of countries stepped up yet again – Sweden had dropped out for a while, but Finland was in, so was Bermuda. Italy and Argentina both began their regular entries.

This time the American method of selecting a team – see who is going to Europe anyway and stick them together – really paid off. Mainly because the designer Dick Carter, already winner of the 1967 Fastnet Race with his Rabbit, was hoping to repeat this success with his latest design, Red Rooster. It was a very competitive series. The Australian ace Syd Fischer sailed his then brand new Ragamuffin into first place in the Channel, race and then Carter won the New York Yacht Club Cup – one of the two inshore races. But the clincher came in the Fastnet, which lost its wind when most of the fleet were still struggling back to the Scillies. The American team got all three boats in before the wind died and emerged triumphant, thanks mainly to a superb set of results put up by Red Rooster.

In 1971 the Admiral's Cup was notable for the presence of one man more than anything else. Edward Heath, Prime Minister of Britain, had taken time off not only to sail his own Morning Cloud for this country but also to captain the British team. And he led that team to victory in a series which had suddenly leaped from 11 to 17 competing nations. Austria. Belgium, Brazil, New Zealand, Poland and South Africa were all in for the first time. But Britain's win was convincing, even if Syd Fischer's Ragamuffin did score a resounding success in the Fastnet Race.

1973 was the year of the upsets. It was the ninth staging of the Admiral's Cup and until then the spoils had always been shared by Britain, the United States and Australia.

Obviously they were the favourites this time, though one or two of the better-informed commentators reckoned that Germany had a chance. But those yachting correspondents were also closely watching Robin Aisher. son of the RORC Admiral, Owen Aisher, and a comparative youngster who had made his name by winning an Olympic medal in the 5.5 metre class.

His boat, which he bought with Tony Boyden, was Frigate, a Dick Carter design. She was the best boat in the British trials, third highest scorer in the Admiral's Cup series and easy winner of Class II. But she couldn't match Saudade, the outstanding yacht of the German team, brilliantly sailed by Hans Beilken. With good support from the other two German boats, Rubin and Carina, Saudade led the way to a famous victory. It was a definite shake-up for the yachting establishment, which began to realise that meticulous preparation and dedicated crew training had a lot to do with both the German success and the high placings of Frigate. Clearly the battle for the Admiral's Cup was going to get tougher every time.

The lesson was well learned. The next two stagings of the Admiral's Cup were both won by Britain and Robin Aisher was a key figure in that success each time. In 1975 his Yeoman XX was in the team with the latest Ron Amey Noreyma and John Prentice's Battlecry. Noreyma turned out to be the outstanding yacht of the series, which saw Canada, Hong Kong, Norway and Switzerland all competing for the first time, although the total number of countries was only 19 because some had dropped out.

Yeoman XX was back for the 1977 series, but this time her fine performance was overshadowed by Moonshine, a Peterson 43 footer built and sailed by Jeremy Rogers. She was second highest points scorer in the whole series, beaten only by the outstanding American yacht Imp, a Ron Holland design and undoubtedly boat of the year. But although Imp won the Fastnet race and was top Admiral's Cup boat, the British kept the Cup, because Moonshine's second place in the triple points-scoring Fastnet Race was backed by Yeoman's excellent third. The American team had to be content with second place yet again, and the surprise performance came from Hong Kong which took third place at her second attempt – even if she did recruit some very good English yachtsmen, such as John Oakeley, to do so.

So the wheel turns full circle to 1979 and the Admiral's Cup series which everyone will remember for its horrific Fastnet rather than the international struggle for the Cup. Nevertheless, the record books will show that Australia took the Cup back 'down under' for the second time, mainly because her tough crews and sturdy boats all scored very well in the Fastnet, taking third, fourth and 13th places. Police Car was the second highest points scorer of the series behind Britain's Eclipse, Impetuous was fifth and Ragamuffin 11th. It was enough to push the Americans into second place one more time, with Hong Kong and Italy equal third.

It shows the ability and the tenacity of the Australians that they should come through that holocaust of a Fastnet Race to clinch their second Admiral's Cup victory and their first success in 12 years.

It is a fair bet that none of the Australian yachts let off red flares the night of the fireworks party in Cowes. They are too dedicated for that. □

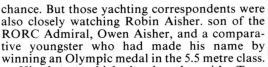

Preceding pages. *Vanina and Formidable, key boats in the Italian and Dutch teams.*
Opposite. *The Argentinian yacht Acadia, chartered by her designer German Frers, was the first of the Admiral's Cuppers to finish the Fastnet.*
Right. *Ron Holland's design Regardless won both the second and the third race of the series.*

Cowes Week

The unforgettable Admiral's Cup

by Jack Knights

August 4th-12th, 1979, England.

Even without the infamous Fastnet storm which claimed the lives of nineteen, this past year's gathering at Cowes for the twelfth Admirals Cup and the umpteenth Cowes Week would have been memorable.

Nothing about it was ordinary. There was more wind, more protests, more to ponder afterwards. Ultimately, Australia took the Admirals Cup whilst the Fastnet Cup went to America's Ted Turner and his low-rated, eight year old Tenacious. Eclipse, one of the first of Jeremy Rogers' Peterson designed Contessa 39, emerged as the top-scoring Admirals Cup boat. Bones were broken and hulls were holed in collisions. Arsonists set fire to refreshment tents. The helicopters of the Royal Navy were called to the rescue of yachtsmen... and all this before the Fastnet even started.

Yet, in the second half of July, everthing had seemed so serene. There had been three weeks of, for England, unusually warm, sunny and settled summer weather. Reefing gear and small jibs had quietly fallen in to disuse ; oilskins were beginning to mildew on their hooks. Yachts such as Chris Dunning's new Marionette, which had been designed to be powerful in a breeze, were finding themselves left out of teams because their particular virtues had hardly been tested.

The change began with the first Admirals Cup race on Wednesday 1st August, held over an inshore Solent course of thirty miles. After a slow start, this turned out to be a boisterous and breezy day, yet the sun and the warmth remained. Thursday 2nd August brought, for the second Cup race, squalls of up to Force 7 and now there was black menace in the sky.

From then till the ragged conclusion of the Fastnet in late August the weather heaped surprise upon surprise. Thursday 9th August, towards the end of Cowes Week, produced a full bore Force 8 gale. As the world now knows, the third day of the Fastnet Race, Monday 14th August brought one of the most savage depressions to disturb an English summer in several years. Winds gusted to seventy knots and turned the sea face into charging walls of water up to thirty feet high. Meanwhile, the rain came in every style from light and showery to heavy and continuous.

There were also some intermittent days of light and shifty winds. The third Admirals Cup race started in a light nor'easter. The Fastnet itself began, misleadingly, in a mild westerly. Yet somehow, even when the weather was mild it wore an air of uneasy uncertainty. The first Fastnet dusk came wrapped in a chill dank fog.

The weather was only one of the components making for so much action and reaction. The Admirals Cup had attracted teams of three from nineteen nations and though this was no more than in 1977, the quality was better than ever.

The first race showed how evenly matched at least half the boats and crews were. In consequence racing was extremely close and close racing always leads to incident.

Many fine yachts, including a score which were too big for the Admirals Cup, had come to Cowes simply to join in the week and then test themselves against the Fastnet course. There were the full bore maxi raters Kialoa, Condor, Siska and Mistress Quickly. These were supported by the only slightly smaller Gitana VI Gauloises 3 from France (which anti-advertising rules caused to be renamed 'G3') Il Moro di Venezia from Italy, Boomerang, Tenacious and others from the USA, and the ex Twelve Metre War Bay from Bermuda. The special Fastnet Class zero for those rating over 42 ft produced no fewer than fifteen entries. English coastal waters had not seen so many large racing yachts since the Thirties.

The Fastnet storm overshadows all else. The odds against the roughest (though not the longest) summer storm in recent years coinciding exactly with the three days period, occurring once in two years, when up to three hundred yachts will be exposed and vulnerable to the west of Land's End in the turbulent Western Approaches, must be a great deal more than a thousand to one. Yet it happened. To make things worse, the severity of the storm, which reached Force 11, was not anticipated by the weather forecasters, not by the British weathermen at least. Had it been predicted the loss of life would have been reduced.

This storm, lasting hardly more than twelve hours, caused more trouble than in any previous ocean race, anywhere, ever. The rescue services, headed by the Royal Navy helicopters from their base at Culdrose near Land's End, claim to have rescued one hundred and thirty six yachtsmen. Twenty three yachts were abandoned and at least five of these were said by the Royal Ocean Racing Club to have sunk. Among the official race entries, fifteen lives were lost in seven different incidents. A further four were lost with the capsize of the trimaran Buck's Fizz which had been pacing the race unofficially.

After first saying that 333 and then 306 had started, the RORC eventually cut this further to a final figure of 302. Of these they eventually announced that 75 had completed the course. Of the 79 named starters in Class V only one, the Contessa 32 Assent, a veteran of the Two Handed Round Britain Race, made it to the finish. Scores of yachts were knocked flat by the galloping waves. A dozen and more were rolled

all the way through 360 degrees. Almost as many broke rudders. Some attempted to keep on sailing and steering. Others removed all sail, made their upper deck as watertight as possible and then retired below to let the craft fend for itself. Some turned tail and ran before the storm, often trailing warps and other gear. Others tried to get the bow to look towards the weather. The result was much the same whatever the technique... sooner or later an extra steep and angry 'rogue' wave would loom into view, a wave so fast moving with its upper part so steep that it would carry everthing including a small boat with it as it went. After this brute had passed on its way the boat might be left upright, with its rig still intact. Or it might not.

For cold-blooded, sustained horror no story could quite match the experience of the crew of Ariadne, a Carter designed, wood-built three-quarter-tonner which was American-owned and based on the East Coast yachting port of West Mersea. The first time Ariadne was rolled she lost her rig. The second time, lacking the pendulum effect of the mast she went so quickly her crew hardly knew what had hit them. But for those of her crew still surviving the worst was yet to come : their worst agony proved to be having in their exhausted condition to scale the tall heaving sides of the coaster Nana which eventually came to rescue them. Four of Ariadne's crew perished.

The larger, faster yachts at the head of the great fleet were around the Fastnet Rock before the storm peaked. This helps to explain how the first home, Bob Bell's Condor, came to create a new course record of 71 hours 25 minutes and 23 seconds. The mid-sized Admirals Cup boats were confronted with the Rock as the storm neared its peak but before the wind had veered dead ahead. The cut-off point came around the Two Ton size. The Canadian Two Tonner Magistri weathered the Rock but only after four and a half hours of unremitting struggle. The Two Tonner Caiman tried for almost as long before finally admitting defeat. From then on, the only boats to get round were those who waited till after the storm had done its worst. The lone Class V survivor Assent turned some twenty hours after Condor had finished at Plymouth.

The enquiries and post mortems are going to be long and comprehensive. In certain technical details such as the design of liferafts and personal harnesses, and hatchways and the stowage of batteries for instance, lessons will be learned. But the greatest lesson of all, which should never have been forgotten in the first place, in spite of three very easy Fastnet Races in '73, '75 and again in '77, is that when the sea grows really angry, a yacht and its crew, even the best of modern yachts and the most seasoned crews, are at its mercy.

Some lives would have been saved if yachts had not been abandoned so precipitately. Here the wide use of radio transmitters and the very speed of the Navy helicopters presented many with the option of rescue who would otherwise have fought through and won, unaided. One or two would not have sunk if hatches had been better designed or more carefully secured. Outside assistance would not have been required in many instances if rudders had not broken. For two years and more, spade rudders have been breaking with a frequency which reflects little credit on certain of our more fashionable designers and builders. In sheltered waters it is usually possible to rescue oneself with jury steering gear but not in a storm in the Western Approaches.

Yet when a wave can pick up and toss, in a complete revolution, a yacht as large as the fourteen metre long Jan Pott from Germany one

can only wonder at the awesome power of the sea.

The Fastnet decided the outcome of the Admirals Cup and nobody would quarrel with the justice of that. After the first four races and before the Fastnet, Ireland stood as the comfortable points leader. Her glass fibre Regardless, designed by Ron Holland, built by Kiwi Boats of Florida, with Californian hotshot Ron Love aboard and a very low figure on her rating certificate, had won races two and three outright. Her Golden Apple, Cowes-built in wood by Souters with Holland, Harold Cudmore and double Olympic gold medallist Rodney Pattisson aboard, had been well placed in every race. In the Fastnet itself she had turned the

Rock probably leading on handicap. Yet neither of these fine boats finished the race because both broke their rudders. For Regardless this was the second rudder failure within three weeks. Later, Golden Apple's crew of ten were winched to safety by a Navy helicopter, the yacht eventually being towed into Newlyn, Cornwall.

For a boat so lightly built, in conditions so heavy, Britain's Eclipse achieved miracles. She beat all her Admiral's rivals on handicap in the Fastnet and was beaten by only one boat – Ted Turner's very different 61ft Tenacious for the Fastnet Cup itself. But Britain didn't win again because of upsets in earlier races and because Eclipse's team mates, Blizzard and Morning Cloud were no better than 31st and 29th among

the Admirals fleet in this final, treble point event.

The USA after a fine showing in the fourth race and with a tradition of success in the Fastnet, looked poised to seize the lead if anything happened to the Irish boats. But the storm took their crews by surprise. For too long, their first priority was survival.

The nation that deservedly won the Admirals Cup on the strength of the way in which it came through the storm was Australia. Till the Fastnet this team had laboured long and diligently but without distinction. Peter Cantwell's Police Car, the lightweight, three-quarter rigged design by Ed Dubois had shown winning potential but had failed to steer clear of trouble. Once she had been involved in a bad starting line collision. She finished this race with three protests out against her. Those who steered her, seemed unable to shake the boat free of the larger boats she was always running up with, under spinnaker. Of the other two, Syd Fischer's Ragamuffin was never ahead of and hardly ever abreast of her American sister Williwaw. Williwaw, skippered by Dennis Conner and with Lowell North aboard till the Fastnet, was always given the better start and after that looked the better handled. The Ron Holland designed Impetuous, though well steered by Jim Hardy was slightly over-shadowed by Regardless, Imp (back hoping for her second Fastnet win), Eclipse and others of much her size. She looked at one time to be winning the second race but that was before she grounded on the Bramble bank.

After the first race, Australia lay fifth (behind Hong Kong, Britain, USA and Italy in that order). After the second race she had improved to third, clearly enjoying the hard wind. Now, only Hong Kong and the USA were ahead. Then came the double point scoring, Channel Race, which clearly favoured smaller yachts. In spite of finishing no better than 8th (Police Car), 19th

Pages 46-47. *Aries (right) a Holland design, and Williwaw, drawn by Peterson.*
Above. *Even on Tenacious, the crew look as though they are having a hard time.*

(Impetuous) and 31st (Ragamuffin), Australia actually pulled up to second overall. Now Ireland with its two small and one medium boat was the leader. Hong Kong and USA both bit the dust in this tricky race.

The fourth race emphasised running speed (since the run was against the tide and the beats with it). This should have favoured Police Car but at the first start she collided with and holed Brazil's Indigo. John Mooney, one of Police Car's crewmen, was thrown overboard and his arm broken. During the race Police Car attracted protests from Morning Cloud and Japan's Koteru Teru and acknowledged one of them by accepting a 20 % place penalty which took her from 5th to 17th. Ragamuffin came 22nd (her sister ship Williwaw won with team mate Aries second), Impetuous was 23rd.

At this stage, with only the fifth and final act remaining, Ireland had 649 points, USA 635, Australia 626, Hong Kong 575, Italy 539, France 516 and Britain 515. If the Fastnet was to be an easy affair, like those of '73, '75 and '77 Ireland looked set to confirm her lead. If the breeze was to come up then the USA with her two largish yachts and the 1977 Fastnet Cup winner, Imp, looked the better bet. Australia didn't appear to figure in any condition.

But that was to reckon without the storm. Till Land's End, reached after nearly two days of light weather sailing, the Americans and the Irish were both well on top of the Aussies. From Land's End towards the Rock, the Aussies were improving even before the storm. Half way along this 150 mile leg, Impetuous had come up with Imp, Ragamuffin for once was ahead of Williwaw whilst Police Car, right on the rhumb line was up with the larger Uin-Na-Mara and Vanguard of Hong Kong. When the full force of the storm caught the leading Admirals yachts as they were turning the Rock, the Australians kept on racing. They all made good use of trysails, a sail which many of their rivals had not given space to. They were fully prepared to see their decks disappear beneath welters of spray and even tons of solid water. One Impetuous crewman said that at one time the whole boat was three feet beneath the water's surface.

Then, just as soon as the storm first showed signs of abating, those tough Aussies were cracking on more sail. While many others remained under bare poles or storm jibs, they were adding boomed out staysails to storm jibs or number fours and close reefed mains or trysails. They were racing all through. They never stopped racing and this made the vital difference.

Argentina's Acadia, navigated by Britain's Sammy Sampson and with her designer German Frers Jr as charterer, was easily first of the Admirals boats to finish, crossing at 0719 on Wednesday. Then, hardly more than four hours later, third of the fleet (Red Rock IV was the only other boat to beat her in) came Ragamuffin. This time she had beaten Williwaw, boat for boat, by 41 minutes. Police Car and Impetuous, Two Tonners both, each finished ahead of Aries, never mind the smaller Imp. Only one of the Irish boats made it to the finish and she was well down.

On corrected time, Impetuous, Police Car and Ragamuffin finished third, fourth and thirteenth and this easily took them into first place. Afterwards the Australians made light of the storm that had cost so many lives. Aboard Impetuous they claimed that the most serious

Preceding pages. *Ragamuffin, the Peterson design, finished well at Plymouth.*
Opposite. *Aries suffers at the height of the storm.*

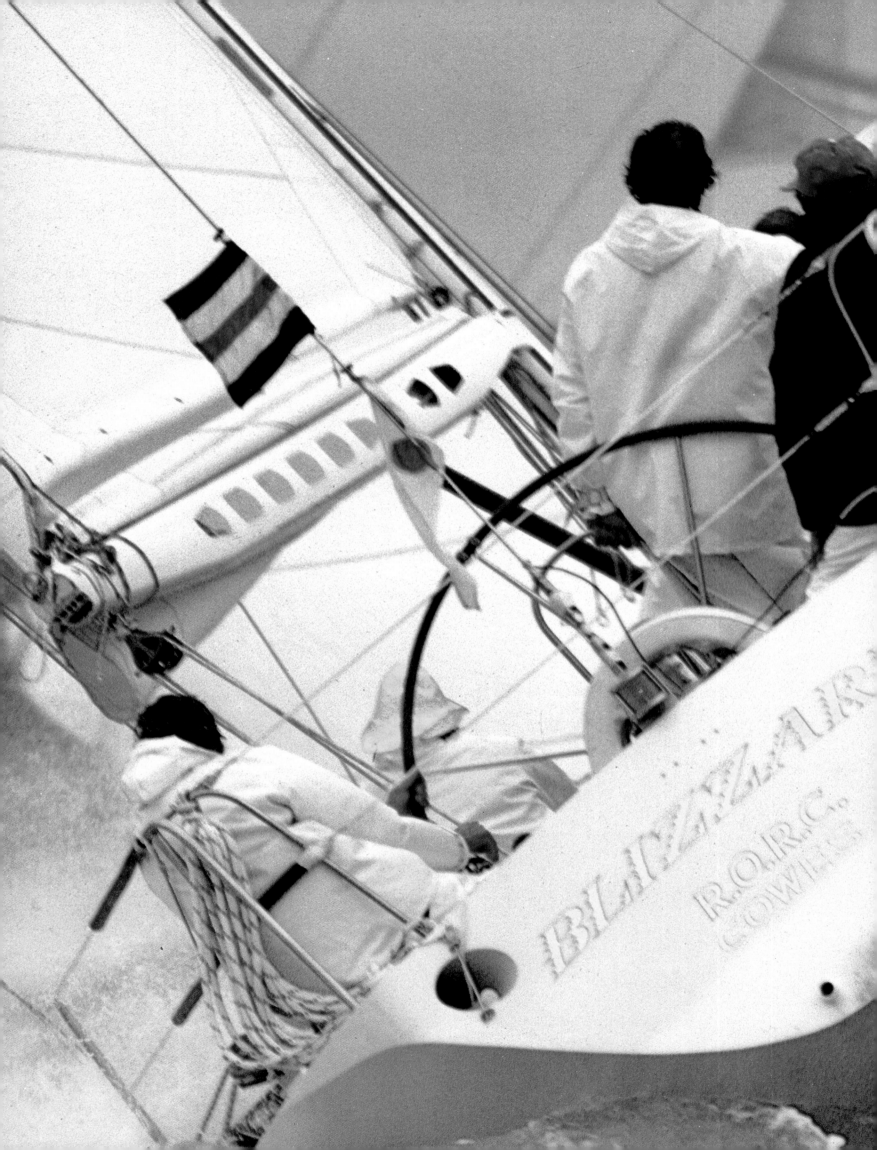

accident had been to Hugh Treharne's thumb – pricked by a needle when repairing a torn sail. Team Captain Syd Fischer, a one time surf-rower and lifeguard and still a strapping man, said that the conditions had been nothing to get excited about. They had often encountered much the same in their own Bass Straits, in fact in the 1977 Sydney Hobart the bad weather had gone on for much longer.

There was little doubt that the Australian team was better equipped, mentally and physically, to cope with the storm even if, from a purely racing point of view, their boats were a degree or so below par. To that extent it can be said that the storm did some good – it put the seamanship back into offshore racing.

More surprising perhaps was the good showing of the Italian team. Their Vanina, Jean and Rrose Selavy all finished in good order to claim 10th, 12th and 17th places. Vanina, now without her Californian expert Dick Deaver, had always been particularly well placed,turning the Rock in the first group and finishing fourth among the Admirals yachts. France too fared well. But for Accanito's broken rudder she might have matched the Australians. As it was, Revolution and Jubilé VI came 7th and 2nd.

Britain's Eclipse was best of the Admirals yachts, beating Jubilé VI by 35 minutes on handicap. She had gained by approaching the Rock to the west of the rhumb line, which meant she was high as the wind began to head. When the wind began to shriek, she was able to drop down to no more than a storm jib and then she was able to reach into Point Clear before tacking and reaching back to the west of and hence to windward of the Rock. Imp meanwhile, had been caught low by the heading wind and was unable to use her storm jib because of breaking the baby stay on which it is normally set. Once around the Rock, Eclipse's dedicated crew made the most of the easily driven shape of their boat. They were able to maintain ten knot surfing speeds under a scrap of sail. Earlier in the race, Imp had headed them. During the storm they got back on to equal terms with her and finally they finished just six minutes behind her to beat the American yacht by more than 50 minutes on handicap.

The race would have seen unusual, even without the storm. To begin with, there was the Solent style bunching around Portland Bill on the first night. The tide had turned before almost anybody could get past the Bill. So everybody tried to cheat the tidal race by short-tacking around the headland from rock to rock. Many touched rocks here. Most, after trying to short tack, later tried their luck further offshore. Then some, Eclipse included, came back for a second bout of rock dodging. Tenacious was caught here but she eventually got clear by sailing through the bumpy race itself.

The honour of being first to the Rock, to take the Elizabeth Mc Caw Cup, fell to Jim Kilroy's mighty Kialoa. She turned at 1250 on Monday in hardly more than a moderate breeze. She was then sixty-seven minutes ahead of Bob Bell's Condor which, before the recent Transatlantic race to Ireland, had been given a new mast by Hood which was even taller than the one Hood had not so long before bestowed upon Kialoa.

The fifteen foot shorter Tenacious did not round till 1830 on Monday evening and by that time the wind had risen enough to call for a reef in the main as they turned.

Just as the Australians won by driving harder all the way home, so Condor, crewed mainly by seasoned New Zealanders who had raced her around the world in the last Whitbread Race, got past Kialoa by dint of harder driving. By the Bishop, which they rounded inside the tidal overfalls, Condor was abreast of Kialoa (though neither crew could see the other in the poor visibility). By the Plymouth finish Condor was half an hour up. Kialoa had been slowed by a broken starboard runner and by cracked ribs sustained by Jim Kilroy himself when thrown to the deck by a sea. After reaching the comparative shelter of the Lizard, Condor's crew did not relax, they dared to hoist an old spinnaker. After that, the knot meter only dropped below fourteen knots when they broached. One way and another, you could say that Condor's new course record of 71 hours, 25 minutes and 23 seconds had been earned the hard way. It was a tribute to her original builders and to the Derektor yard of Mamaroneck N.Y. who had most recently modified her, that Condor broke nothing more serious than a genoa sheet turning block. She finished at 1355 on Tuesday, eight and a half hours ahead of the eventual handicap winner (by three clear hours) Tenacious. At one time even the indestructible Tenacious had been down to nothing but a storm jib.

Everything else about the 1979 Admirals Cup season pales when compared to the Fastnet. The other four races were hardly more than the sounds made by an orchestra as it tunes up. Yet it should be recorded here that the first race was won by Britain's Blizzard, a sister of Acadia, with Hong Kong picking up the team points lead. Williwaw came second and La Pantera, (Hong Kong but Japanese built, Peterson designed and rating 32.4ft) third. This race was started from a committee boat line which was not square to the wind.

The second race, started from the Squadron's fixed line which was, funnily enough, pretty square, was won by Ireland's very low rated Regardless. Golden Apple also for Ireland, also Ron Holland designed was second but since their third boat, Inishanier, was delayed by close to half an hour because of a bad accident to her helmsman Harvey Bagnall following a broach, Hong Kong kept her points lead.

In retrospect it can be seen that the outcome of the Channel Race depended upon how the yachts approached and turned the CH1 buoy off Cherbourg. Regardless won again but this time the French, sailing on local waters, earned the most team points, the wonderful old Revolution come second, Accanito seventh and Jubilé VI thirteenth. Since Morning Cloud broke her rudder and Blizzard finished well down, France was now ahead of Britain, the first time this had happened in an Admirals Cup.

The fourth race, sailed as part of Cowes Week was won by Williwaw. This was a happy event for her skipper because this had been named The Champagne Race in deference to the sponsor of the Admirals Cup, Mumm Champagne. As part of the prize, the winning skipper, in this case Dennis Conner, was to receive his weight in Mumm Champagne and Conner weighed in at over one hundred kilos. With Aries second and Australia's Police Car awarded a 20 % penalty, the USA came up to a challenging second on points.

Pages 54-55. *A symphony in white on Ernest Juer's Blizzard, a German Frers design.*
Inset. *Revolution, the highest-scoring French boat and Eclipse (right) the Contessa 39 built and sailed by Jeremy Rogers to Doug Peterson's design – Eclipse was the top scorer of all the boats in the Admiral's Cup.*
Left-hand page. *Camargue : eight crew were rescued.*
Right, top. *A horrifying record of the Fastnet tragedy. This man died from exposure.*
Opposite. *The rescue services saved 136 yachtsmen.*

Cowes Week too sprang its surprises. It began mildly enough with the wind so light on the opening Saturday that few completed the cruiser courses within the time limits. A few days later came sheeting rain and later still, on the Thursday came a full bore Force 8 gale. All but the cruiser classes were cancelled and even the cruisers needed the help of the Navy helicopters, one man aboard Incisif being injured and the Irish Moon Duster losing her rudder of Portsmouth. Several masts were broken or ruptured and the 14 metre long Marionette dug her bow so deep below a Solent wave that she lost her pulpit and lifelines.

Ashore, arsonists – French sailors were strongly suspected but no charges were brought – burned down refreshment tents at the main marina and at the nearby Cowes Corinthian Yacht Club.

The main event of the week, the Britannia Cup which had been presented by King George VI in memory of his yachtsman father King George V, which is always raced for by the big cruisers, was won by Ted Turner and his Tenacious. The same boat had won the day before too, though on that occasion most of the best boats were racing in the fourth Admiral Cup event. Nick Girdis' Marloo won the New York Yacht Club Cup, second only to the Britannia in prestige, which took place during Thursday's gale. That was another Australian storm victory.

In terms of trends and fashions, Cowes Week '79 deserves to be remembered as the time that the Offshore One Designs were brought in from the cold. The Nicholson designed SCODs (South Coast One Designs) had been racing in the Week for years of course, whilst the Contessa 32s had become prominent over the past three years. But in 1979 they were joined by formal classes of the new Peterson designed OOD34s, the 28ft long Impalas and 22ft long Sonatas, both designed by David Thomas, the slender and elegant 101s from the Danish firm of Elvstrom and Kjaerulf and the sporty little J24s from the USA.

Such classes as these, offering an obvious alternative to handicap racing under the IOR rule with all the snags implicit in that over-developed form of the sport, seem bound to become a notable part of future Cowes Weeks.□

Preceding pages. *Bob Bell's Condor of Bermuda beat the Fastnet record established by American Eagle in 1971.*
Opposite, top to bottom. *Ted Turner's Tenacious, a Stephens design, was overall winner of the 1979 Fastnet. The maxi-rater Siska, owned by the Australian skipper Rolly Tasker, and the German boat Roland van Bremen suffered serious gear damage.*

The Offshore Yacht Races

Sydney-Hobart

Sweet revenge of the veterans

by Peter Campbell

December 26th, 1978. Australia

Emerging from the shadow of IOR obsolescence, two of Australia's most seasoned ocean racers, Love and War and Margaret Rintoul II, fought out the 34th Sydney-Hobart Race, the slowest in ten years. Their performance, gaining first and second overall and in Division A, gave a great boost to the International Offshore Racing Council's two basic principles : encouragement of a dual-purpose boat, and preservation of the existing fleet.

The first objective demands a strong boat with adequate scantlings. The second requires development of Mark IIIA ratings to compensate boats which have been out-designed or overtaken by technological development.

The results of the 1978-79 Hitachi Sydney-Hobart Race underlined both principals, being dominated by conventional cruiser/racers which make up the bulk of the Australian and world offshore fleets. Overall winner and placegetters and all but one of the four division winners, fell into the moderate displacement, stoutly-built cruiser/racer category. All but three of the divisional placegetters were designed or built before 1974.

At least three of the new, lightweight boats suffered gear failures on the way to Hobart. Apart from Deception, a 1978 Peterson ex-One Tonner, none of the lightweights got anywhere near the top placings.

Although Australia has not yet introduced the IOR Mark IIIA ratings (and in fact has deferred this until after the coming 1979-80 season) it has

its own, well-proven Age Allowance system which is worked into the Time Correction Factor method of achieving corrected times. All yachts in the Australian ocean racing fleet are rated under IOR Mark III. The Age Allowance does not effect the rating but is calculated as a reduction of the Time Correction Factor (TCF) providing for a reduction of 0.4 per cent in a yacht's TCF after three years for each year of her design age, up to a maximum of 15 years.

Love and War and Margaret Rintoul II, first and second in the 34th Sydney-Hobart Race, are classic examples of how older yachts, well geared, brilliantly sailed and taking full advantage of their age allowance, can outsail the very latest offshore racing machines. Love and War, designed by Sparkman and Stephens, was launched in 1973 for Sydney yachtsman Peter Kurts who won his way on to the Australian Admiral's Cup team that year. She is a sister ship to the German yacht Saudade, the top individual pointscorer of the 1973 Admiral's Cup and also the English boat Prospect of Whitby, although she carries more sail area than both. She is built of timber, using the cold-mould system. The following year, the 47ft 6in (14.47 metre) yacht sailed a brilliant race to win her first Sydney-Hobart, beating a top quality fleet which included Admiral's Cup team contenders Bumblebee 3 and Mercedes IV.

For the 1978 race, Love and War had a five-year age allowance and owner Kurts gave the boat a new suit of sails and recruited a crack crew, including five of those who had sailed the

boat to victory in 1974. By removing 158 kg of lead and going to a slightly larger mainsail to improve light weather performance, Love and War finished with an IOR Mark III rating of 35.4ft.

This would have given her a TCF of .8520, but with the age allowance Love and War's TCF came down to .8358 – in effect a reduction in her rating of 1.9ft to a highly competitive 33.5ft for a 47–footer of her known ability.

In fact, she would still have won the 1978 Sydney-Hobart on corrected time without an age allowance – a tribute to this particular S&S design and to the skill with which Peter Kurts and his crew sailed her to Hobart. Among the crew, incidentally, was John Anderson who also sailed in 1974 and who, with Dave Forbes, won the Star class gold medal at the Olympics at Kiel in 1972.

Runner-up Margaret Rintoul's age allowance was even greater. She is Syd Fischer's original Ragamuffin, an S&S designed 49-footer launched in 1967 and undoubtedly one of the greatest ocean racing yachts ever built in Australia.

As Ragamuffin, she represented Australia a record three times in the Admiral's Cups of 1969, 1971 and 1973. In the 1971 series she also became the only Australian yacht to win the famous Fastnet Race.

Although Margaret Rintoul II is 10 years old, alterations to her hull in 1973 cut three years off her age allowance. But seven years was a mighty boon to a yacht of her remarkable ability, particularly going to windward in a fresh breeze. Her IOR Mark III rating is 38.1ft but allowance reduced her TCF from .8744 to .8499, in effect a remarkable cut of 3ft to an effective rating of 35,1ft.

With this advantage her present owner Stan Edwards of Sydney (who renamed the yacht after the original Margaret Rintoul which his father sailed to a record in the Sydney-Hobart in 1951) decided to « set » the boat for the 1978 Sidney Hobart. He bought new sails, modernised the rig and got together a topline crew under Graeme Freeman, the former sailing master of Bumblebee 3.

So both Love and War and Margaret Rintoul II went into the Sydney-Hobart Race with new sails and gear. Between them they had probably two of the finest crews one could possibly assemble for a Hobart Race, yachtsmen with great skill and tremendous competitive spirit who were certain to extract every last fraction of a knot out of the two veteran yachts throughout the 630 nautical-mile race.

Under the time-on-time basis for corrected time used in Australia, the longer the race lasted the more time Margaret Rintoul had to give Love and War. After four days (96 hours) of sailing, Margaret Rintoul had to give Love and War 85 minutes time, and for every hour after that just under one minute had to be added.

Tonner which still rates close to 27.5ft. Streaker.

When Margaret Rintoul II crossed the finish line off Castray Esplanade on the Derwent River at Hobart behind Apollo and Helsal after almost four days and five hours sailing, the time differential was around 90 minutes. When Love and War swept across the line later that afternoon she was 25 minutes inside the time limit to win the race.

Love and War is the first boat to win two Hobarts since the famous Freya completed her unique hat-trick of wins in 1965.

Third overall was another former Ragamuffin – Constellation. She was the number three boat of that name built by Syd Fischer, a 49ft (14.9 metres) aluminium boat designed by German Frers which represented Australia in the 1977 Admiral's Cup and in the 1978 inaugural Clipper Cup in Hawaii when she was in the winning Australian team. After that series Fischer sold her to Sydney yachtsman John Garner who after the Sydney-Hobart sold her to Geoff Blok who renamed her again as Mary Muffin.

The 1978 Sydney-Hobart was an unusual one in that calms in Bass Strait, followed by a fresh change from the south-west, split the fleet into two distinct groups. The « first fleet » of seven yachts took the top line honors positions and also filled the first three placings in Division A and overall on corrected time. Between them and the « second fleet » of 90 yachts was a gap of some 17 hours, a distance at times of up to 80 miles.

Line honors were also fought out by two veteran yachts, the 11-year-old, 59ft timber boat Apollo and the 72ft Helsal which, when launched in 1973, was the first maxi yacht built from ferrocement. Apollo, skippered by colorful poker-machine millionaire Jack Rooklyn, took line honors with an elapsed time of 4 days 2 hours 23 minutes 35 seconds, just on an hour ahead of Helsal, skippered by Dr Tony Fisher.

The line honors success was the second for Rooklyn who previously sailed his 72ft maxi Ballyhoo first home in 1976. It was a remarkable performance by the ageing Bob Miller– designed Apollo which reached Sydney only in the early hours of the morning of the start, on December 26, after sailing back across the Pacific from the US West Coast. She was provisioned, underwent a safety check, had her bottom scrubbed by divers, and several sheets and halyards replaced between her return to Sydney Harbor at 3am and the start at 12 noon.

Division B went to the « new » boat Deception, which led the « second fleet » accross the finish line. Built in 1978, she is a

Doug Peterson–designed lightweight One Tonner-plus. She began on the designer's board as a centre-board One Tonner but ended with a fixed keel and a rating under the revised IOR of nearly a foot above One Ton.

Division C went to an older Peterson One

previously owned by Hood Sail's top man and former world One Ton champion, Chris Bouzaid. She is now owned by Bart Ryan of Sydney and turned in an excellent performance, finishing only three minutes behind Deception across the line and ending up fourth overall on corrected time.

Division D winner was the South Australian Half Tonner Peacock, a Peter Cole designed production 31-footer skippered by 65-year-old Keith Adams, an Englishman now living in Adelaide.

The disappointment of the race was the short-lived effort of the former American champion Two Tonner Williwaw, which America's Cup challenger Alan Bond bought as a contender for the Australian Admiral's Cup team in 1979 (and missed out on). Renamed Apollo IV and with an ace crew aboard, she broke her steering less than three hours out of Sydney Harbor.

And Syd Fischer, sailing the chartered boat Superstar while waiting for the launching of his latest Ragamuffin, pulled out halfway through the race while his two former Ragamuffins went on to finish second and third overall.

For a large section of the Australian public, however, the 34th Sydney-Hobart will be remembered as the ocean classic which was not won – but in their minds should have been – by the 77ft red-hulled maxi sloop Siska.

Siska, a super-sloop designed, built and skippered by Perth sailmaker and former Olympic silver medallist and world Flying Dutchman champion Rolly Tasker, was the victim of a series of circumstances which resulted in her not being accepted as a starter in the Sydney-Hobart.

Launched only in late October 1978 and sailed more than 2000 nautical miles from the West Coast of Australia, Siska's entry was refused because she did not have a valid IOR rating certificate at the time of the start. This was due to a combination of Tasker's failure to follow-through with the measurements, the distance the yacht had to travel, some official bureaucracy, and the unavailability of a computer on Christmas Eve to assess some late changes.

Tasker, in a defiant gesture, sailed across the starting line in Sydney Harbor five minutes before the official start for the fleet of 97. Siska went on to sail the course and crossed the official finish line in Hobart after 3 days 6 hours 19 minutes – flying a protest flag – and more than 200 miles in front of the leaders in the Sydney-Hobart fleet.

Had she had her rating, 68.5ft, there is no doubt she would have won the double of line honors and first overall on corrected time. But she did not rank as a starter and the line honors victory went to Apollo with Love and War first overall on corrected time – two well deserved wins for two older but extremely well-sailed yachts. □

Pages 62-63. Forty miles from Hobart, the fleet has to turn past the cliffs of Tasmania.
Page 64. Constellation, ex-Ragamuffin III, finished third, thanks to the efforts of Geoff Blok. She is a Frers design in aluminium.
Page 65. Siska, the 77-footer designed, built and steered by Rolly Tasker, finished first but she was not an official starter.
Above. At Hobart, celebrations for the winners : Graeme Freeman, skipper of Margaret Rintoul II, an S and S design built in 1967 ; and Peter Kurts, double winner of the Sydney-Hobart in 1974 and 1979 with the Stephens-designed Love and War. Centre. Jack Rooklyn, skipper of Apollo.
Opposite. Deception, class B winner.

S.O.R.C.

A sad start to the new season

by Jack Knights

January-February, East Coast, U.S.A.

1978 contained evil omens for the safety of offshore crews and no sooner had 1979 begun than these threats were sadly realised. During 1978 yachts were lost in no less than three of the **Ton Cups. In September in Italy, the Mini** Tonner Molecule overturned after broaching and having its ballasted centre-board slide back into its trunking. She soon sank and her crew were lucky to be rescued by a competitor following behind.

Soon after, a well-found One Tonner was lost hardly two miles away from the course rhumb line when it hit hard sand during the series which was being held from Flensberg in North Germany.

In Japan, in an exceptionally tough Quarter Ton Cup, a crewman was nearly drowned – he had to be given artificial respiration – after his **centre-board yacht capsized to windward following a sudden wind-shift and he was pinned down** to the lee rail by his life-line. Then in the long race, Paradice, another centre-boarder, rolled over and sank soon after its ballasted board had fallen out. If one crewman had not been able to dive into the cabin to retrieve the liferaft they would all have drowned, for they were not picked up till several hours later and then by a passing coaster.

These were bad accidents that pointed inescapably to the increasing danger of racing offshore under IOR rules. Sheer good luck and human resilience alone prevented loss of life.

Then, in the 1979 Southern Circuit, in warmer waters, lives were lost in separate accidents in the second and third races. The real tragedy was that both could so easily have been avoided. These deaths marred a series that would otherwise have been the best for several years.

In the longest of the five races, the 400 miles from St. Petersburg on Florida's west coast to Fort Lauderdale on the east, the new 46 ft Obsession, designed by Sparkman & Stephens and beautifully built by Minnefords, was running around the Rebecca shoals that guard the southern tip of Florida and, as commonly happens when the modern IOR style yacht is over-driven, Obsession was rolling savagely. This was partly due to the size of her modern **masthead spinnaker, partly to the building sea** and partly to the extremely wide and hence unbalanced shape of her typical IOR hull. And here it should be noted that Obsession is wider in proportion to her length than any of her rivals.

Bearing off on the face of a sea to avoid a windward broach, Obsession's helmsman over-corrected so that the boat rolled far to windward and then the hull bore off on a leeward broach. The main boom, held down firmly by the now customary hydraulic vang, but not otherwise held in check by any preventer rigged forward, scythed across the flush deck in a crash gybe. Everybody but Tom Curtis managed to duck

in time. He caught the boom on the side of his head and the injury he received at that instant proved fatal in spite of the best efforts of fellow crewmen who had only recently undergone a course in emergency first aid.

In 1977, in the Channel, a similar accident **had happened in a two tonner in the British Admiral's Cup trials. On that occasion the victim was knocked overboard and drowned, but it was reckoned he was gravely injured before entering the water.**

In the very next race of the series, the Ocean Triangle, conducted between Florida's eastern seaboard and the Bahama Bank, Tom Curnow, as thoroughly experienced offshore as Tom

Curtis, fell overboard from the husky Great Lakes cutter Pirana. It was shortly after dusk, the wind was up to twenty knots and since it was blowing counter to the Gulf Stream, the sea was confused. Curnow was kept in sight, life-belts with drogues and lights were speedily thrown towards him, the head-sail was dropped, the motor started and portable searchlight rigged. Yet within seven minutes of going over, Curnow had slipped beneath the waves.

When two passes had failed to recover him, Pirana's navigator Nils Muench jumped overboard and he did get to Curnow but he couldn't hold both him and the life-line. Pirana's motor had meanwhile been stalled when one of several lines thrown to Curnow fouled the propellor.

Two men lost for no very good reason. Though the cooling drinks flowed as freely as ever in the Miamarina and elsewhere, the party was already over, because any conversation no matter how it started, would inevitably come around, sooner or later to these tragic accidents.

As is the custom of man in all his activities, life continued as usual. The show went on. Obsession even competed in the very next race.

The 1979 Circuit saw some changes, all of them beneficial. Once again everybody raced on an equal footing. The experiment of encouraging older boats by putting them in their own A Division and hiving off the new boats in B Division was now admitted to be a failure. The « old boat » division had failed to become popular and since January 1st and the adoption of radical changes to the IOR rule, the old boats were well looked after, rating wise. On top of that, the Circuit organisers added their own age allowance, starting with the year 1977 – it actually aided such hot modern yachts as Imp, the most successful offshore yacht of that year.

Stemming from the decision to race all boats together – though they were subdivided by size, into six classes – it was decided to count overall, as well as class, positions and once again to announce a single overall Circuit Champion. This was welcomed by the sailors and especially by the press, since everybody loves a winner.

The yacht that accumulated most points overall – meaning placings in each race in fleet, not class, was Williwaw. A Williwaw, also owned by New Jersey businessman Seymore Sinett had been generally acclaimed the unofficial overall winner in 1978 but this Williwaw was all new, though from the same stable and with the same team as before. Again Doug Peterson was the designer, again Dennis Conner was the sailing master and Conner gathered his regulars which included navigator Ben Mitchell and most times, sailmaker Lowell North.

Centre. *The master-sailor Ted Hood won class F with his Robin, a centreboarder built in 1972.*
Opposite. *Dennis Conner skippered the happy crew on Williwaw, the overall winner.*

Even though the rulemakers, by their changes, were trying to bring back a heavier, less scowlike type, this new Williwaw was even wider than before – 14 ft (4,268 m) maximum on a waterline of 37'2" (11.33 m) and a length overall of 45 ft (13,72 m). And she only displaces 21,700 lb (9,864 kg) of which just over half is in the deep lead keel. Displacement to length ratio is 189.

Proportions are full and fair, with plenty of free-board and a clean simple flush deck in the now familiar Peterson style. There is considerably less distortion than in many recent Holland designs, in the area of the stern and the latter is wide and powerful looking.

This new Williwaw, built as before in alloy with Stearns spars and North sails, was intended not as a new break-through but one more small step forward. Sinett and Conner are above all conservative. They reckon that if they have as good a yacht as the others, they will be able to race it to its fair share of prizes. When you analyse her results you begin to see that Williwaw did not win because of superior speed, but because of her crew's consistency and because nothing was broken not even their fancy new life-line stanchions of carbon fibre – the same material was used for the bunk frames.

Williwaw won, most of all, because in the final race, the short 27 mile olympic course for the Nassau Cup, Conner did a magnificent job on his nearest rival, Burt Keenan, owner and helmsman of the 1978 Frers designed Acadia. Last year Acadia had had John Marshall aboard and one reckons he would have realised what Conner was up to when he began herding Acadia away from the line before this final start. It seems that Keenan was over his head. So when the starting cannon fired Williwaw was away to a clean start whereas Acadia was back in the third row with dirty wind from other boats.

She did catch up fast later, but Williwaw finished eighteenth in fleet and Acadia ended up twenty-second. This determined the championship.

The pair were second and third in class in this race. The boat that beat them both was Mike Swerdlow's Aries, a new 46-footer by Ron Holland. She had also beaten both handsomely in the preceding race, the Miami Nassau. Aries

had also beaten Williwaw in the Ocean Triangle. The main reason she did not win overall was that she broke her carbon fibre rudder in the vital – because biggest points scoring – race from Saint-Petersburg to Fort Lauderdale. The 79 Circuit should be remembered as the time of broken rudders. Imp broke hers and so did the interesting new English two tonner, Winsome Gold.

Aries had power-reached straight past Williwaw on the second leg of the Miami Nassau. This was probably due to the greater power and stability conferred by Aries' considerably heavier displacement of 26,000lb (1182kg), slightly larger rig and higher displacement-to-length ratio of 239.

In other conditions – upwind in light and square downwind in anything, the extra lightness and fairness of Williwaw should give her the edge.

Williwaw had two firsts, two seconds and a ninth in class. Acadia, which this year had been « bumped » and was using shorter spinnaker poles for a rating reduction, had a second, two thirds, two fourths and a thirteenth. Aries claimed two firsts, third, seventh, thirteenth and a retirement.

This was in Class B. Class A for the largest saw the return of Kialoa with her new one-hundred-foot high sloop rig. Owner Jim Kilroy was most enthusiastic. He said that removing the mizzen and its associated gear was like removing a VW car suspended twelve feet above his deck. George Coumantaros brought along his new 64 ft Derektor designed and built Boomerang. Lloyd Ecclestone had his new Frers 62 ft Volcano. There was the superlight Circus Maximus and her newer, smaller sister Desperado. Also Mistress Quickly, ex Ballyhoo, the Bob Miller designed 66 footer, Heritage, the ex Twelve Metre, and Bob Bell's wooden maxi Condor, from England.

Two vintage S&S designed cutters of around sixty feet, dating from the beginning of the seventies – Al Van Metre's Running Tide and Ted Turner's Tenacious made the running here. With the rule changes and the local old age allowance these two had ratings so low as to be virtually unbeatable, given that they were both well sailed. Tenacious prevailed, taking four firsts a second and a fifth in class and winning the Miami Nassau overall. Tide missed the first two races then managed a first, third, fourth and fifth in class.

Class C for those of Two Ton size and above was headed by a Swede, the same Holland designed Midnight Sun which a few months before had come near to winning the Two Ton

Pages 68-69. *Bill Power's 44-footer High Roler, which finished fourth in Class B, is a Peterson design.*
Left-hand page, above. *Obsession, saddened by the loss of crewman Tom Curtis, heaves to.*
Below. *Midnight Sun, winner of Class C.*
Under. *Jack Knife, Jack Greenberg's Holland designed 41 footer.*
Opposite. *Ariès, the moral victor.*

designer Bill Cook and the New Zealand experts sailing an imported Bruce Farr One Tonner. Bill Cook returned this time with two rather heavier and larger designs. He sailed one himself – Celebration – and the other, Fire Water, was in the hands of sailmaker Bob Barton. They ended a clear first and second in class with the Peterson 37, Gold Dust third.

An older, larger and heavier One Tonner than any of these found herself racing in Class F simply because she now rates so low. This was Ted Hood's old centre-board Robin, known as Abino Robin before he bought it back for his own use. For much of the series Robin and Hood looked the likely overall champs. The surprising thing was that their two fleet first places were achieved in the toughest races, the Saint-Petersburg - Fort-Lauderdale and the Ocean Triangle, which should have favoured the largest yachts. Robin was also second overall in the Nassau Cup. Unfortunately, Ted Hood got the Lipton Cup race wrong tactically. Even so he and his old boat wound up third overall, beaten only by

Cup. She had Pelle Petterson aboard. Second and third were two of Suns near sisters, Tom Greenwalt's Secret Affair and Bob Aron's Tabasco. This was a clean sweep for Holland, but Winsome Gold, designed by the young Englishman Ed Dubois, was fourth in spite of breaking that rudder.

Class D, for those rating under Two Ton, should really have been won by Dave Allen's famous Imp (also Holland). Unfortunately, in their zeal to find still more speed, Kiwi Boats had given her a new superlight, heavily balanced rudder of carbon fibre and this gave up the ghost during the Ocean Triangle. Otherwise Imp, without too much opposition in her class, scored four class firsts and a second.

Infinity actually took the class. She is a slightly larger Imp, also by Holland and Kiwi Boats, and owned by John Tomsen. Then came Imp, then the C&C 40ft Amazing Grace V from Canada.

Class E last year had seen some tight racing and bitter protesting between the American

Williwaw and Acadia. Second in Class F was a neat new Ragnar Hawkensen designed, Kiwi Boats built, half tonner named Illusion and third a well-sailed – by John Kolius – example of the new J30 one design.

As often happens, the series got off to a dismal start. The new day race from St Pete, out of the bay and around some marks and then back in again, took place in very cold weather with clammy fog coming down in the middle. In this fog, Heritage and Desperado both ran aground on hard sand. Heritage lost her lofty rig and the other damaged her hull in the keel area. Neither were able to compete again. Results were a poor indicator of form.

The 400 mile race around Florida's toe to Fort-Lauderdale was a good tough one, though with more running than usual, the only windward work being the final leg northwards. Little Robin's win was all the more remarkable as she broke her main boom.

The Ocean Triangle, something over 150 miles, started mildly enough with a spinnaker

reach on port tack to Great Isaac Light. Then came a beat north west in rising wind to a mark off Palm Beach. This leg was a real boat shaker, as the wind blew counter to the Gulf Stream. Strangely, it paid to tack east away from the helpful Stream itself. Robin won overall again.

Pages 72-72. *Williwaw, a traditionnal Doug Peterson design won the SORC.*
Inset. *Nassau, Bahamas, the arrival of the SORC.*
Previous. *Acadia, a German Frers design, allowed the laurels to slip from her grasp in the 27 mile race.*
Above. *Tenacious, « king » Ted Turner's boat, dominated class. A with four wins.*
Following pages. *Kialoa, a Sparkman and Stephens design, was the biggest boat in the series. Now that she has been re-rigged as a sloop, Jim Kilroy was able to sail her into second place in Class A.*

The Lipton Cup, over a similar length course, was sailed in the lightest conditions of an otherwise brisk series. This was a Solent style, knob-dodging, tide-cheating exercise. Obsession won this overall.

The 200 mile Miami Nassau was an exercise in fresh air reaching. The steady veer in wind direction, by making the smaller boats stay hard on the wind longer, favoured the larger tonnage. This was Tenacious' race.

The shortest race of all was the 27 mile Nassau Cup. Yet because it was sailed in a rock steady wind and because the Olympic course was well and truly laid, this was probably the best boat form indicator of the whole series. The smallest came out comfortably best, Illusion winning from Robin.

Altogether, eighty-four yachts raced in one or more races. The largest entry was for the smallest class – F. It would have been the best Circuit for several years were it not for those two untimely deaths. □

Opposite, top to bottom. *Infinity and Imp always raced together in Class D. Of these two Holland designs John Tomsen's Infinity was unable to put it over Dave Allen's famous Imp because of a broken rudder.*
Robin, Ted Hood's incredible one-tonner, was supreme in class F. But she was unlucky to miss the overall honours behind Williawaw and Acadia.
Double win for designer Bill Cook in Class E : his own Celebration won the class from her sister-ship Bob Barton's Firewater.

Trade Wind Race

Relax ! It's a fun race

by Christian Février

March 24th-April 2nd, St Maarten

` Let her pass, young'uns. But look at what a magnificent boat she is ! We've got 150 miles to catch her in. You've been conditioned by those stupid IOR races round the cans ! '

It was, of course, Phil Weld speaking, standing at the wheel of Rogue Wave. Weld, the great apostle of multihulls, talking to his three French crewmen at the start of the first leg of the Trade Winds Race, while Peter Spronk's catamaran Tsje-Tsja (pronounced Cha-cha) slipped by on the wind in silence. And, to our surprise, Phil had no intention of luffing up his rival. He just watched her pass with evident satisfaction and obvious delight in those eyes screwed up against the sun. To luff a rival isn't quite the done thing in the Trade Winds Race. At most, you might just take his wind. 'Don't try shouting « starboard ». Some of them don't know the rules of the road around here' Phil had warned us.

The race is really only a good excuse for a lot of good chums to meet up, sail at more than 20 knots for a week under the roasting Caribbean sun and make the acquaintance of other multihull fanatics. Yes, there is a handicap rule, dreamed up by Peter Spronk, who also originated the race itself, based on an old idea of Dick Newick's when they used to work together in Saint Croix. But the rule is so complex that nobody ever really talks about handicaps. Some say that it favours Spronk's own catamarans outrageously and is less than kind to Newick-designed trimarans. That could be right : Rogue Wave is required to sail two miles an hour faster than the two other boats which are the same overall length – El Tigre and Tsje-Tsja. An impossible handicap to make up. 'That's a big compliment for Dick Newick ' roars Weld in a great burst of laughter.

For its fifth running, the race attracted a fleet of 15 multihulls. Keel boats had also been invited, but the fear of arriving a long way behind, clearly dampened their enthusiasm. The course will be in three legs and the whole thing takes about ten days. The hardest part is undoubtedly the parties ashore. Thankfully, there are the races in between for respite. The first leg, of 143 miles, goes from Saint Martin to Virgin Gorda, leaving the island of Sombrero to port. The second takes the fleet to Fort de France leaving Saint Croix to port. That one is 350 miles, which is also the length of the third leg, from Saint Anne in Martinique, leaving Dominica and Desirade to port, passing round the top of Guadeloupe and leaving Montserrat and Saint Christopher to starboard before returning to Saint Martin.

This year's race was notable both for the variety of size among the boats and the number of designers represented. Rogue Wave, winner last time, was the boat to beat. Many of the Americans couldn't understand why, this time,

Phil Weld had recruited his crew from so far away. Just think of it, three Frenchmen ! Phil explained that it was, in fact, the response to an invitation he made at the Royal Minquiers Yacht Club at Saint-Malo before the start of the Route du Rhum race. Three commodores at one go. They wouldn't falter in the rounds of rum punches, that's for sure. It's a foolish man who underestimates three Bretons.

Elsewhere in the fleet, despite the overall contraction of boat numbers, there were scarcely any inexperienced men in the crews. On El Tigre, the day-charter catamaran skippered by Malcolm Maidwell, they'd asked one sail-trimming specialist to join them all the way from New York ! On Tsje-Tsja, Peter Spronk's boat, the crew included Jim Brown, the American designer of the Searunner cats, cruising boats that are found all over the place. And on the second leg the Spronk family warmly welcomed

Daniel Forster, the young Swiss photographer, who put his knowledge of light airs sailing to very good use – they won the leg. And then there was Daniel Charles, note-book in one hand, mainsheet in the other, who joined the El Tigre crew for the last leg.

Tsje-Tsja, painted canary yellow, is the floating home of the whole family Spronk. Moored in the Simpson Lagoon at Saint Martin, the boat normally accommodates 12 people throughout the year. But then, do you know of another sailing boat which provides five double bedrooms, two singles, a saloon, a navigation cabin, a bathroom, 250 square metres of deck for sunbathing – and which can still bowl along at 25 knots on the open seas ?

Peter Spronk's wife Myrna, a great friend of Phil Weld's is actually the moving spirit of the whole race. ` We would very much like to see you in the lead at Fort de France, madame ' said Marc Berthier, gallantly. ` Then you can reserve a table at the restaurant for us. ' And she did.

Tsje-Tsja is certainly the most elegant multihull built so far. The Tulip bows, so beloved of Peter Spronk, the fine ends to the hulls aft, the absence of any disruptive construction across the deck ; they all combine to give a sleek and elegant line to the latest creations of the Saint Martin resident : Ppalu, Maho, El Tigre, Tsje-Tsja. The two 60-footers are built in wood, cold-moulded and covered with epoxy resin. El Tigre is clinker built and rigged as a ketch to make her easier to handle. Tsje-Tsja is smooth-hulled with sloop rig. She points better on the wind, but El Tigre uses her low but full sail area to go very well downwind.

Besides the three big multihulls, there were plenty of Peter Spronk catamarans in the fleet. Blue Crane, belonging to Jean Marc Gouyer, was the first to be built – in 1965 at Grenada, measuring 48 feet overall, she displaces 4.5 tons. Yvon Fauconnier was crewing on her. Blue Beard, sister-ship of Blue Crane, was skippered by Frik Potgeiter. Kaya, a third 48-footer by Spronk, is rigged as a ketch for John Westmoreland, and normally sails on charter for the rest of the year. Jacques Belier, previous owner of Kaya and also of British Oxygen, had come to race on Gang Busters, a sort of outsize cruising Tornado, built by MacGregor in California. Made in polyester, this catamaran is collapsible and can be towed behind a car. She has a single rudder in one of the hulls. She took a very good third place in the second leg of this race, behind Rogue Wave.

Fortuna Syntofil, the Lock Crowther design which had been seen in the Route du Rhum, was

Above. *Peter Spronk, designer, boatbuilder and winner of the race on corrected time.*
Below. *Phil Weld relives the capsizing of Gulf Streamer.*

entered by Bruno and Xavier Desplanques, who had been on the organising team of the Route du Rhum. Charis, skippered by the very friendly, bearded Nick Brian-Brown, is one of the first trimarans built by Dick Newick at Saint Croix, and a sister ship of Trice. She was to be sailed remarkably well throughout the race. Her ripped mainsail was repaired in Martinique, thanks to the rapid intervention of Yvon Fauconnier, who rallied helpers from the Club Mediterranée at Saint Anne. She was to break her rudder in strong winds but still manage to cross the line and finish the leg, sailed simply by adjusting the rig. Then she turned away and put out to sea again, waiting for the wind to go down before asking for a tow in. Such concern not to cause problems for the boats at anchor is not common and this should be well noted by yachtsmen. As a result of this, Charis received a special prize at the end. Phil Weld was very pleased to see the entry of Trumpeter, his old Derek Kelsall trimaran, which he sailed in the Observer Singlehanded in 1972. Ruffian, another 40 foot trimaran, designed by Lock Crowther (who also did Spirit of America) and Edith, a Val 31 by Newick, like Mike Birch's The Third Turtle, were also there at the start. But the most praiseworthy three multihulls contesting a course of more than 1 000 miles must certainly be Jzero, a tiny proa 10 metres long, Sunburst, a catamaran of the same length by Spronk and the Atlantic proa sailed by Nick Clifton, Azulao II.

Russ Brown, son of designer Jim Brown, had built Jzero when he was scarcely 16 years old in his father's garage. She keeps an outrigger to windward, like all Pacific proas, skimming just on the surface of the water. Russ adjusts the balance of the boat according to the wind by filling or emptying water containers. The Pacific proa is undoubtedly the ideal boat, offering minimum weight and wetted surface, but it requires exceptional skill to sail it. Russ and his crewman were to put up an astonishing performance in the second leg of the race,

arriving just behind Gang Busters, Rogue Wave and Tsje-Tsja ! But faced with the 25 knots of wind expected on the third leg, they wisely decided not to go.

Sunburst is a catamaran built at Spronk's yard from the left-over pieces of wood which clutter up the corners. Hence her original name, Bits and Pieces. The helmsman steers this red and yellow machine with a little round tiller sitting comfortably on canvas strips stretched across the central platform. Azulao II, Nick Clifton's Atlantic proa, was to join the fleet at the start of the second leg. This is a type of boat much liked by Dick Newick, who actually put

hydrofoils on to a multihull – like Paul Ricard – 20 years ago. But he gave up the idea, finding that the foils were too complicated and added little to the boat's speed. Clifton's previous yacht was a Kelsall trimaran which he sailed in the 1976 Observer Singlehanded. ' I really frightened myself with that thing ' Clifton confided. He had been hoping to enter the Route du Rhum. He will certainly be at the start of the Observer race in 1980. The outrigger of his new boat is as long as the main hull. It is constructed of foam sandwich. Unlike the Russ Brown proa, Azulao keeps her outrigger to leeward. The two equal masts are made from highway lamp stanchions cut down. By comparison with Tsje-Tsja the living space aboard is very small and one wonders how two men could possibly live in such a tiny boat. Displacing only 1 1/2 tons, Azulao can skim along at 11 knots on the wind and scoot up to 18 downwind. Finally, RTL-Timex, Alain Gliksman's big trimaran, decided to take part in the first leg of the race on its way to New York – where it was never to arrive.

Taking the point of the interest created by the loop around Guadeloupe in the Route du Rhum race, Martin Court, technical director of the Trade Wind Race, made the fleet complete a circuit of the island before setting off for Sombrero. The total population of Saint Martin followed the race on transistor radios and there was some hilarity at the commentary about the misadventures of the spinnaker sock on Rogue Wave. Weld's three Breton crewmen suggested to him that he could do away with the sock which he used when he was sailing singlehanded so that the kite could be hoisted more quickly. ' My sock works perfectly now, gentlemen ' replied Weld. So we kept the sock. But what Weld and his crew were not to know was that the internal halyard designed to deploy the spinnaker by pulling up the sock had twisted two or three times inside the spinnaker. At the leeward mark, Pierre Lenormand and Marc Berthier both pulled at the halyard. Despair : nothing happened. Anger of the two Frenchmen, quite used to the 350 square metre spinnaker on Gitana VI. Heated words between the foredeck and the cockpit. American logic : refusal to accept that something has gone wrong. ' Try to use a little intelligence ' says Phil patiently, convinced that they are pulling on the

wrong string. 'Do that yourself' responds one of his distinguished crewmen. With such exchanges of verbal courtesies, the spinnaker could no longer resist and broke out.

Timex and Tsje-Tsja had escaped. We were to repass them on the wind – the point of sailing which suits Rogue Wave very well, especially in a chop. She pitches less because of her low aspect ratio rig. But the second time we needed to hoist the spinnaker it was the same comedy all over again. Timex took nearly three miles out of us. We were to repass her at Dog Island by using our splendid monster reacher sail. The breeze was light and no boat that day could possibly have done the 25 knots described by one journalist – in Paris.

The arrival at the tricky navigation through Round Rock Passage to Virgin Gorda, a channel between two close islands, was made on a really black night. Peter Spronk prudently dropped his spinnaker beforehand. Rogue Wave kept hers and overtook Tsje-Tsja in the channel, A lively gust whistled Rogue Wave up to 17 knots at the finishing line, to beat Tsje-Tsja by several minutes and Timex by quarter of an hour. El Tigre finished fourth, a lot further back and well to the south of the ideal course. After a very enjoyable party on the Marina Cay, the fleet set out next day on the second leg. Gliksman left us on his way to the Bermudas. We were never to see the old Three Legs of Mann II again. Clifton arrived at the very last moment, buttonholed Peter Spronk and demanded authority to enter the race – and got it. He was allowed in – are you listening RORC ? – and trimming his sheets, he left all the rest of the fleet standing, with the exception of Rogue Wave who had already escaped. Then came the light airs. Worrying about getting caught in the williwaw from the Pelee mountain at the north end of Martinique, Rogue Wave went a little too far out and altered course too late around Martinique. Taking a much longer route robbed her of first place which was taken by Tsje-Tsja with three hours to spare. Gang Busters, Jacques Belier's boat, finished a quarter of an hour behind Rogue Wave, and the astonishing little Jzero, sailed by Russ Brown, took fourth place. El Tigre was to arrive 18 hours after Tsje-Tsja, after some pretty frustrating sailing in the light airs. But it was undoubtedly the start from Saint Anne, several days later, which will become the best memory of the fifth Trade Winds Race, because it was very much in the tradition of this friendly, happy event. Ten minutes from the start, it was obvious that nobody was much inclined to go. Phil Weld established the general feeling by turning around his mooring under the eyes of the crowd amassed on the wharf. Definitely on form, Phil issued his orders while getting under way very very slowly. But a fresher gust pushed Rogue Wave towards the mooring of Belier's catamaran. Gang Busters took up the slack on her mooring and caught the elegant aft section of Rogue Wave's rear cabin. The distinguished old correspondent of the New York Herald Tribune in Paris let out a fearsome oath. Gang Busters broke her mooring and lost her anchor. Still concerned about the incident, Phil Weld had not noticed that Rogue Wave was now bearing down on the committee boat, which was also moored. Manned by careful race officers, like all committee boats, she hastily weighed anchor so as not to be involved in another collision with Rogue Wave. At the other end of the line El Tigre carried away the outer mark while making a trial run on the wind. The fifth Trade Winds Race no longer had a starting line and everybody started talking at once on the VHF !

It was a fast course this time. The trade winds appeared on cue, blowing between 20 and

30 knots. Despite some 80 miles of beating in a pretty rough chop, Rogue Wave covered the 350 miles in 28 hours and 30 minutes – that is to say at more than 11 knots average. To disabuse any readers with oher ideas, I should point out that all this was done while wearing shorts, under a splendid sun, with glass of beer at hand. Who could possibly want to go back to single-hulled racing after that ? On the choppy waters between Nevis and St Kitts, the multihulls were spread over quite a large area. El Tigre, hot in pursuit of Rogue Wave, frequently lifted a hull, but right from the start the big Newick tri – even without a spinnaker – kept on extending her lead. The last five miles to the line were covered at between 20 and 23 knots, with the huge triple-huller literally flying over the water – all in just 30 knots of wind. At 23 knots I had a curious feeling of lightness on the helm. For one or two seconds there was nothing but air around the rudder – and no feeling at the wheel at all. El Tigre arrived three quarters of an hour later and Tsje-Tsja an hour and a half after that. For the Royal Minquier Yacht Squadron contingent, honour had been served.

To Phil Weld, we gave a little souvenir of our passage. A small packet, specially designed to modify his sytem of deploying the spinnaker. When he opened it – at a party of course – he was to find three socks in the colours of the French

tricolor and carrying the names of his three crewmen. A huge 'protest-party' was organised by Rogue Wave's skipper for the following night. Everyone had to protest his neighbour or his skipper for some totally futile reason. All serious protests were systematically thrown out. The two big Spronk catamarans were moored together with Blue Beard, thus giving birth to a 'sextamaran', as it was called by Charles Chiodi, the director of the magazine Multihulls. Phil chaired the debates with an oratorical talent and indefatigable fervour. As the effects of the punch bowl took hold, it became more and more difficult after several hours to distinguish the plaintiffs from the judges and the advocates from the witnesses. And that was that. The Trade Winds Race of 1979 had plenty of warmth, friendship, happy meetings of yachtsmen, fantastic fast sailing under the star-studded Caribbean sky, and an incedibly beautiful course. Oh Lord, but RORC races are going to seem rather drab from now on ! □

Preceding pages. *Rogue Wave hard on the wind.*
Left hand page, above. *The Val class Edith.*
Below. *El Tigre leaps in the swell under 25 knots of wind.*
Above, top. *Sunburst, built from scrap wood in the boatyard.*
Below. *Azulao II, Nick Clifton's new proa. Dick Newick's secret hope for the Observer Singlehanded ?*

Transat en double

Deceptive revenge of the multihulls

by Jean-Michel Barrault

May 26th, Lorient, France

They say that multihulls are fragile and dangerous : but they took the first three places in the Transat en Double. Does this mean that single-hulled boats are out of date for long races with limited crews ? A close study of the 6,000 miles Transat en Double indicates that the truth is probably somewhat hidden by appearances.

A stiff breeze from the south-west, a sharp chop and a grey sky ; those were the conditions on May 26th at 1.30 in the afternoon when the 40 entrants for the race made a start between Lorient and Groix, in the event organised by the magazine Le Point, the yachting journal Neptune-Nautisme and the radio station Europe 1. Ahead lay 6,000 miles of ocean, two crossings of the Atlantic with a turn round a buoy to the east of the Bermuda islands.

Who was favourite to carry off this first Transat en Double, contested by boats with crews of two ? Some of the best short-handed sailors in the world were there, sailing some astonishing craft. The winner ? The hydrofoil trimaran of Eric Tabarly, only recently launched, barely through her sea trials, seemed too complicated. Her ability to sail upwind was poor, so all the experts agreed in predicting an early return for this one. VSD, another trimaran, appeared to be too light and fragile. And everybody knows that Eugene Riguidel, her skipper, has a reputation for stirring up the worst of luck. Télé-7 Jours was an old design, which was reputed to show only moderate performance, but those excellent navigators Birch and Vidal could just give this 16 metre tri a chance, if she didn't break first . The other multis seemed to be too old, too small or too vulnerable to be serious contenders for honours. So logic inevitably led to the conclusion that victory would go to a monohull. If the wind proved strong and on the nose, then Kriter V, well sailed by Malinovsky and Lenormand, could well take a decisive lead on the first half of the course. If the conditions were really severe, then the two tough men on Fernande, a new ketch measuring 21 metres and displacing 21 tons, could do well. But they would be sadly outpaced in downhill conditions on the way back to France.

That southwesterly breeze blew like a trumpet call for revenge in the ears of those who had suffered bad luck or shipwreck in the Route du Rhum : the old master Tabarly, who had been absent, sadly, from that race, but was there to see the almost unbelievable finish of the first French-organised singlehanded trans-Atlantic race ; Pajot, who had been forced to abandon his catamaran ; Kersauson, beaten in the race and

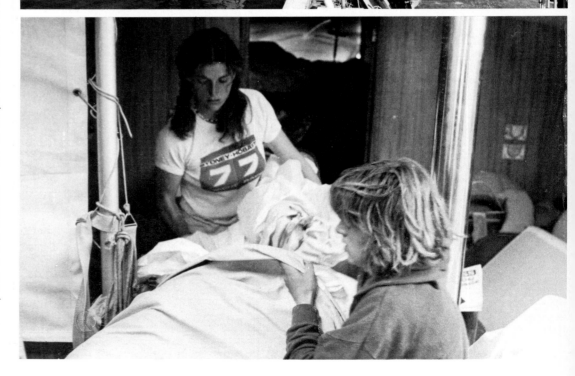

Above. *200,000 spectators watched the start from Lorient !*
Below. *Florence Arthaud and Catherine Hermann finished tenth in their Biotherm, a 48-footer.*
Right-and page. *VSD weighed only 4,40 tons.*

since then forced to leave his splendid trimaran in the middle of the Atlantic with a broken outrigger; Gliksman, unlucky twice over, had barely escaped from a shipwreck. These last two, like unsaddled horsemen who line up once again for an obstacle, were setting out in monohulls. Perhaps they were saying to themselves that these sleek and rapid boats against the wind, provided they are well sailed, might be preferable to fragile trimarans. After all, hadn't Birch chosen a longer trimaran, in theory much faster than his little Olympus, in order to beat these star sailors, despite the fact that his smaller boat had proved good enough to beat the rest in the Route du Rhum? But actually that boat had been bought by one of the rum-makers on the island. Malinovsky had no wish to relive the finish of that race, when he was beaten by the tiniest margin of 98 seconds after 4,000 miles of sailing.

On one point all the pundits were agreed: we would never see another finish like that one at the end of an ocean race – a finish which would go down in yachting history. And certainly not in this Transat en Double, with its 6,000 miles of North Atlantic sailing, its storms and its ferocious head winds in which those long single-hulled craft like Kriter V should certainly show their superiority. And logic seemed to be triumphing. Against that force five wind, on the passage from Groix, the monohulls took the lead: Kriter V, Kriter VI and Avi 3000. It looked as though Paul Ricard was having a bad time: with one float submerged in the sea, the outrigger arm plunging in at intervals and the windward arm creating enormous windage. The Tabarly-Pajot trimaran was certainly going quickly at around 11 knots, but she was having to sail way off the wind. Her course, compared with the monos, did not encourage any illusions about her chances of success.

So began the deceptive trans-Atlantic race. To start with, two fierce squalls decimated the fleet: at the end of one week there were a dozen crippled craft which had turned for home, put into port, headed off for the Azores, were hobbling on as best they could or had simply sunk. On the list of those having to give up were Anaho (her skipper suffering a slipped disc; Capri and Muratti (rigging failures); Josephine (who restarted after her boom had been repaired); Spirit of Delft (a crewman injured by a big sea) and Club Francais du Sport (dismasted). The trimarans, as was feared, had been suffering too. Roger Marthe Video was dismasted, Great Britain IV had broken her chain-plates, Prisunic was taking a lot of water but pushed on to the Bermuda islands to make a stop there, and carry on for a bit more afterwards, the enormous Charles Heidsieck (27 metres long) simply fell apart, Hydrofolie broke one of her foil supports. As for VSD, she lost the foils which descend from her main hull and suffered some small leaks which could well have become much worse; the fairing of the starboard outrigger arm ripped off and the resulting loss of hydrodynamic efficiency slowed the boat down; then the boom broke. The same old Riguidel bad luck: the white trimaran with its rainbow stripes hadn't a chance now. Still, Eugene and Gilles pushed on, making course for the Bermudas, still a very long way off. But for them all hopes of victory had flown.

Then came a surprise: two days after the start, despite the solid beating conditions Malinovsky and Lenormand made out the strange silhouette of Paul Ricard through the drizzle. So despite the headwind, strong as it

Opposite. *Eric Tabarly experimented on Paul Ricard a swivelling mast with a very aerodynamic section. It worked well, but turned out to be very heavy.*

was, the clumsy hydrofoil had kept pace with the long monohull, even managing to compensate for her inability to point. And that despite the problems with the furling jib which had obliged Tabarly and Pajot to turn themselves into trapeze artists at the top of the mast, where there was very little support and not much to hold on to.

Then logic seemed to take over again. At the end of the first week of the race, Kriter V was in the lead from Kriter IV. But, astonishingly, the multihulls were not far away. Paul Ricard had pulled up to third place, VSD, despite all her problems, was in fifth, Tele-7 Jours was seventh. Less than 100 nautical miles separated the first seven. The monos, in conditions which really suited them, had not pulled out any real advantage. The trimarans were close up, lying in wait. And Paul Ricard had not broken. The depressions, which had only been really severe for certain boats, moved away. An anticyclone settled in and with it, calms. The seventh of June most of the fleet lay motionless on an oily sea. Kriter V could cover only 50 miles in 24 hours; Fernande took four days to log 250 miles. Tabarly had swung away to the south. « I had three reasons for doing that » he explained to me on the radio. « I wanted to avoid the counter current of the Gulf Sream, to skirt the anti-cyclone which had been forecast by the weather service and finally to arrive at Bermuda from the south-east because there are frequently winds from the south-west in that area ». The gamble paid off. Under a covered sky from which a gentle drizzle descended, the strange aluminium monster arrived on the night of 13/14th June, jolting from one float to the other. Eric, in his yellow oil-skin, was at the tiller. Marc, wearing a blue sweater, was on the deck making an adjustment to the trim. Apart from the fairing to the starboard outrigger, ripped off, the hydrofoil trimaran had suffered no damage. The swivelling mast was working perfectly. The only real problem: two of the four spinnakers were useless. But, despite this handicap, nobody could see how Paul Ricard, first after the section of the course which was least suited to it, could be caught under the following winds of the return trip. Everbody agreed that, barring accident, Tabarly and Pajot had won the Transat en Double.

But then an astonishing second arrived: Kriter VI. On this monohull of 16,4 metres the Kersauson-Dijkstra team had put up a fantastic performance, with Olivier constantly steering and trimming while Gerard found the best possible courses according to the weather. They were only 22 hours behind Paul Ricard and 4 hours and 25 minutes ahead of Tele-7 Jours. Mike and Jean-Marie were surging along in clouds of flying spray which filled their cockpit. The wind was fresh. Almost without a shout or a wave they turned the buoy as if it were a race round the cans, and they were crewing a Tornado on an Olympic course. The old Quest – now Tele-7 Jours – had 26 1/2 hours to pull back: it looked a difficult task. It seemed even more improbable for Kriter V, which had 45 hours to make up on the hydrofoil, not to mention the crippled VSD, which only arrived at the buoy when the leader had been round and gone 51 1/2 hours. Under sail, the little trimaran entered the narrow strait to the harbour entrance in the middle of the night and sailed down the Saint George channel. A motor boat was there, ready to tow her. It was 2 a.m., at the weekend.

Above. *In Cherbourg, Eric Tabarly checks the jacks which control the foils on Paul Ricard.*
Opposite. *Charles Heidsieck (81 foot long) fell apart. Her crew could be rescued.*

But the staff of the yard were standing by, ready to work and all prepared to get the boat on to the slip as soon as possible. By flood-light, and supervised by Alain Barberet, the repairs were soon started, with plenty of willing helpers and despite the teeming rain. The leaks from the foils were stopped up, a new fairing was fitted on the outrigger, the rudder was changed for a better one, the rigging checked and fresh food supplies put aboard. Eugene and Gilles devoured double breakfasts of steaks and omelettes, buttered toast and ice cream. The repairs were finished and I helped Gilles to bag up the sails, coil the ropes and sheets, and get everything ready on deck. I might just have saved them five or six minutes...

When VSD rounded the buoy a second time, she had lost another 13 hours and was now 62 hours and 40 minutes behind Paul Ricard. In a fresh south-westerly, she flew away and our little motor boats were hard pressed to keep pace with her as she sped along eagerly at 15 knots with the spray flying all around.

Pages 88-89. *Second ! Eric Tabarly and Marc Pajot kill their spinnaker, the sail they had most need of on the way back from Bermuda.*
Above, top. *Fernande took only four minutes more than VSD for the return leg from Bermuda.*
Below. *Tele-7-Jours had to be content with third place, despite the endeavours of Mike Birch.*
Right-hand page. *On the way back, the monohull Kriter V regained the consolation margin of 31 hours and 32 minutes from the hydrofoil trimaran Paul Ricard.*

Riguidel and Gahinet had just one target : the prize for the fastest passage from Bermuda to Lorient. As for catching Tabarly, they had no illusions that that was at all possible.

Fernande reached Bermuda in a disappointing seventh place. Like Kriter V, she had lost time in the calms along the northern route . She had even been overtaken, about half-way along the leg, by the 13 metre long monohull Serenissima, a very light design with the Italian-French crew of Bruno Bacilieri and Marc Vallin, which beat her to the buoy by 10 minutes.

So, at half-distance, all the forecasts had been turned on their heads. In the bad weather of the first week the trimarans lost very little ground to the monohulls. In the calms and light airs they had been able to make up their slight disadvantage. If Paul Ricard was not to go under to all the misfortunes predicted for her, there seemed no way that she could be stopped from flying away from the rest of the fleet, followed by the well-sailed Tele-7 Jours. Neither Kriter VI, too small, nor Kriter V, too far behind, had a hope. And certainly not VSD even further behind.

That was the scene set for the most amazing pursuit in the history of sailing. When Paul Ricard and her pursuers had turned the buoy, the wind was against them ; but when VSD eased her sheets, the breeze had turned and she was able to make a direct course, straight downwind. In two days she had made up a lot of leeway and from 18 June she was no more than 130 miles in arrears. Tabarly was following the most direct course along the great circle route ;

Riguidel and Gahinet chose to head off north. The distance was greater but they found better winds up there. All the luck went with them. During two weeks the wind blew sweetly over the North Atlantic and the weather was just what every cruising yachsman dreams of : a kindly, good breeze and a flat sea.

Tabarly and Pajot were in despair : their secret weapon, a light spinnaker, had disintegrated inside an hour. Their medium spinnaker had jammed in the block and shredded ; they were only able to bring shreds of sail back on to the deck. For the remaining 3,000 miles of downwind sailing they had just two chutes at their disposal, one heavy and one very light. But the wind was always too strong to risk the light one and not strong enough to use the heavy one to best advantage. « We lost a knot at least » said Eric afterwards. There was another maddened crew, too. Michel Malinovsky knew that with a following wind, Kriter V would go as fast as the trimarans ; as long as the breeze was strong enough. It would even go faster than the multis if the helmsman of a tri, worrying about breaking gear or pitch-poling, should feel it necessary to reduce sail. But the wind was never strong enough for that. VSD is very light : 4 tons, as against the 8 tons of Paul Ricard, and it has to be remembered that the two trimarans have similar sail areas. They are like two cars with the same engine cubic capacity but with one weighing half what the other does. They said that VSD was fragile. But how would it be likely to break, with the wind following and the sea flat ?

On 20 and 21 June, VSD logged two straight days of more than 300 miles each, an average

speed of 12 knots, thanks to some fierce surfs at 15 and 16 knots. She overtook Kriter VI, unexpectedly gone off to the south, to find nothing but calms down there ; then Tele-7 Jours, which didn't have her turn of speed, and in no time she was on the heels of Kriter V. The weather became cold, wet and drizzly. But the overcast sky couldn't put a cloud on the jubilation of the brothers-in-arms from Morbihan : they could see a glowing sun through the grey, a gleam which seemed to whisper to them : « Just suppose we could actually catch the Apollo capsule ? » That's the name Gahinet had given to Paul Ricard. Eugene Riguidel, red-headed, headstrong, scruffy, and Gilles Gahinet, tough, humorous : they had both won the Aurore singlehanded race in the past, and they both knew what it takes to sail a fiercely-contested solo race – nights at the tiller and constant sail changes. On the 22 June they passed Malinovsky and Lenormand. Riguidel yelled into the radio « We're going like a bomb ». There was 1,800 miles to go, and Paul Ricard was only 90 miles away. But Tabarly and Pajot had no intention of being overtaken ! They could now pick up the French radio stations, so they knew that VSD was catching up fast. Eric volunteered to mend the medium-weight spinnaker, patching up the cloth, sewing the long strips together and filling up the holes with sticking plaster. It took 48 hours of constant work, and by now Eric and Marc were regretting that they hadn't put a sewing machine on the boat, or any supply of spare cloth. Come to that, they must have wished that they had stopped at Bermuda long enough to put two or three spare chutes aboard (if they

had had a radio transmitter strong enough, they could have asked for them in advance and put them on with the minimum delay). Failing that, they had to « make do », which mainly meant using the heavy spinnaker as much as possible – a red and white one, solidly put together but really too small.

Trying to make up the leeway, Gahinet fished the light chute out of the sail locker. The lads on VSD weren't any happier with this sail than those on Paul Ricard. Sure enough, it ripped within a few hours and they sailed over it. All they could recover was a mass of rags and tatters, and long strips of cloth which they had to unravel.

This let Paul Ricard pull out a little more lead – a mere eight miles. Not much, but at this stage every hundred metres could make the vital difference between victory and defeat.

The gap closed to 60 miles on 24 June. Marc and Eric decided to chance their arms and sent up the light spinnaker – it gave them an advantage of nine miles. But the light cloth ripped apart after 12 hours. VSD kept on clawing back miles day after day. The gap on 27 June was 40 miles ; on the 28th it was 35 miles – and the finish line was only 250 miles away. Riguidel and Gahinet realised that by heading off to the north they might get some help from a current flowing down the French coast. At dawn on 29 June they rounded the buoy at Ar-Men, going like a train.

The wind eased, a steamy mist settled on the sea. « Suddenly », Marc Pajot told me over the radio, « we saw VSD loom up 300 metres away, just as we were going about ». We were able to pull away from her again, but we knew she couldn't be far away. That was off Pen-March, just 40 miles from the finish. From the bridge of the motor boat Le Henaff, superbly navigated, we could look over to the hydrofoil tri as the wind freshend to force 4 – the most it had been since they left Bermuda, Eric told us.

Under her old faithful red and white chute, Paul Ricard was surging along at 11 knots. Eric, dressed in a blue sweater and red trousers, smiled into his month-old beard. Marc was giving us the thumbs up. The finish was very close and with it a famous victory, it seemed. Because where was VSD ? We had searched for her in vain.

Then suddenly there she was, under genoa and main, about a mile to windward of Paul Ricard ! The two boats began to sail against each other as if they were in some weekend regatta, as they drew closer to Basse Jaune. At the helm, Riguidel luffed up, passed behind Paul Ricard and sat on her wind. The two boats were neck and neck just 500 metres apart. Then the wind went light and Gahinet went up on deck to hoist the spinnaker. But the sail got snagged and precious time was lost. When the beautiful multi-coloured chute eventually opened out, the Tabarly flying machine had pulled out another 500 metres. But now she had a lot more sail area, the little white trimaran really began to fly. She suddenly accelerated and plumes of spray began to fly up from her floats. She was going at least a knot faster than her rival, and Groix was now in sight, so the line was very close. Marc Pajot had taken over the helm of Paul Ricard. Eric Tabarly, arms crossed at the foot of the mast looked up at the sails and rigging, wondering how he could possibly make her go faster. Like a dinghy sailor, Marc Pajot luffed up on VSD to take her wind and cover her. But the other boat was quick ; VSD cut under the stern of Paul Ricard. It was 7.16 p.m, and Tabarly and Pajot were desperate. As a last resort they hoisted their patched up spinnaker. Too late ! VSD had taken a lead of 100 metres, then 200 metres. Just 45 minutes from the finish Tabarly and Pajot saw their lead blown away, having held it by such herculean efforts almost from the very start of this marathon of sailing. At one minute past eight in the evening Riguidel and Gahinet, the men nobody had given a chance, won the Transat en Double. They had clawed back from Tabarly and Pajot no less than 62 hours, 5 minutes and 42 seconds since leaving Bermuda. Paul Ricard lost by less than 6 minutes, at the end of 34 days of sailing, twice across the Atlantic.

And another trimaran took third place : Tele-7 Jours. Although too heavy, she had still taken 19 hours out of Paul Ricard on the return trip. One illusion shattered : despite her lead all the way to Bermuda, Paul Ricard had proved to be not all that fast. Despite the hydrofoils, the boat did not rise on to plane in following winds. Tabarly knew it. He had already decided on several improvements for the prototype : the floats will be altered in shape, the cross-arms lightened, the hydraulics strengthened, the steering simplified and the swivelling mast system thoroughly examined. On certain points which had seemed odd before the start, such as the dihedral angle of the cross arms, Eric said, frankly and without bitterness : « It was my fault. I was the one who wanted it like that. » For all that, the boat's performance was astonishing for a very audacious new design. And, for the British Observer Singlehanded race in 1980, the modified machine must start favourite.

Three multihulls in the first three places. The first mono took fourth. So, are classic yachts now outdated ? It has to be admitted, as it was by Malinosky, a little sadly, « Multihulls are the future. I suppose I shall just have to get into them myself ». But let's look a little closer, behind the superficial appearances. On the outward journey, in a smallish single-hulled craft, Kersauson and Dijkstra had been very nearly as quick as Paul Ricard. On the way back, the monohull Kriter V had regained the consolation margin of 31 hours and 32 minutes from the hydrofoil trimaran. And the heavy but beautiful ketch Fernande had completed the Bermuda-Lorient passage in exactly the same time as VSD, to within four minutes – and that in

conditions ideal for a light trimaran. Serenissima, deserved winner of the class for monohulls less than 15 metres, finished well ahead of the small trimaran Elle, while the other small multihulls had sunk or been dismasted.

So, in a race which had been marked by light winds most of the time, the superiority of the multihulls, despite the appearances, was not actually overwhelming.

Another illusion to dissipate : the tough men of ocean sailing, the gorillas at the winches, the « macho » men of the sea : they are not really the great champions of the sport. The women did almost as well, and sometimes better. Biotherm, just 15 metres long, was originally designed to sail in the Admiral's Cup with a crew of a dozen muscular yachties. They were saying that two girls couldn't possibly master her. But Florence Arthaud, after her superb performance in the Route du Rhum, and Catherine Hermann, who is well used to sailing on the 15 metre boat Petrouchka, decided to take her on. From the first week they settled into tenth place overall, and they gave it up only momentarily, despite plenty of problems. A leaking hull and loss of fuel oil transformed their deck into a skating rink, polluting their clothes and food ; they

suffered broken gear and a dud motor prevented them from charging their batteries. The stop-over in Bermuda allowed them to settle some of these problems, but even so a breakdown in the gas system meant they had to eat cold food, a twisted spinnaker forced Florence to spend four hours in the rigging, knife in hand. Their nearest rivals profited from their setbacks. Biotherm dropped four places, only four days before the finish. But by sailing all out, using tactics like dinghy sailors, pushing themselves all through the long nights, Florence and Catherine gradually clawed back the miles – especially encouraged by the professional observers who put a softer note in their hard Breton voices when they spoke to the girls over the radio. And they regained their tenth place, beating by four hours the Cape Horner and yachting specialist Alain Gliksman in Timex – a 17,50 metre boat. They also beat another Cape Horner in Philippe Bougoin in his Meridien. And the experienced Jean-Pierre Millet in his very attractive 15 metre sloop Casavian.

Not only that, behind Arthaud and Hermann, Marie-Noelle Dedienne and Catherine Vaton completed a very commendable race despite rigging failures and the constant risk that a cracked chain plate would break and send their mast crashing on their pretty heads.

The other great victor of the Transat en Double is called Argos. The small transmitters fitted on each boat in the race sent out constant coded signals which were picked up by a satellite and retransmitted to the French Centre of Space Studies and then sent on again to the race organisers. This Argos system showed itself to be dependable and able to enhance the interest of the race. Twice a day at least, the position of each boat was recorded with absolute precision. This made a great contribution to the safety of the event, because when there was an accident the rescue forces could be directed exactly to the spot : and that happened with Charles Heidsieck, Prisunic, and Runaround. The last two also used their distress beacons.

Additionally, Argos made a vital difference to the news services for the race. It was possible to follow, almost hour by hour, the progress of the boats, their courses, the incredible overtaking passage of Riguidel and Gahinet. It's sometimes said that the French are not natural sailors and yachting is not a spectacular sport. But with this race being followed with passionate interest by the general public, that must be the greatest illusion shattered by this surprise package called the Transat en Double. □

Preceding pages. *At the helm of Paul Ricard, Marc Pajot tries to take the wind of his rival – as if they were sailing in a dinghy race. But it's too late – VSD is sailing 2 or 3 knots faster and escapes from under the Tabarly-Pajot boat.*
Left-hand page, top to bottom. *Three views of the dramatic denouement of the race, fought out between VSD and Paul Ricard.*
Above, top. *Michel Malinovsky, fourth to finish, seems to be wondering "Is it time I gave up sailing monohulls ?"*
Opposite. *Gilles Gahinet (left) and Eugene Riguidel relax after their victory.*

Los Angeles-Ensenada Race

The Tequila Derby

by Robert Payne

April 21st, USA/Mexico.

Southern Californians, perhaps because of their relationship with Hollywood, seem to have the knack for turning mundane events into grand spectacles. The Newport Harbor to Ensenada International Yacht Race is just such an event.

As a test of ocean racing skills, this race – sometimes called the Tequila Derby – is not much. True enough, all 125 miles of the straight-as-an-arrow course are in the open waters of the Pacific Ocean ; but in April, when the race is held, they are waters which are normally barely alive with any kind of breeze. The greatest dangers a boat usually faces is that the crew will fall asleep during the calms or that the navigator will get bored and set a course for Tahiti.

Yet despite a lack of the ten-foot-seas-in-the-galley-sink, who-got-seasick-in-my-seaboots, is-that-our-rudder-off-to-leeward, kind of excitement found in offshore classics like the Sydney Hobart and the Fastnet – or perhaps because of it – the organizers of the Ensenada race claim it is the largest open water, offshore racing event in the world. This year 554 boats crossed the starting line.

With over 500 boats (at least that many have started in every race for the past decade) divided into classes that cross the line in rapid succession, a normal start is one in which pandemonium reigns. Collisions occur with a regularity that hasn't been seen since the days of Mediterranean war galleys. Yawls instantly and unwillingly become sloops, ventilation ports appear in the hull where moments before there were none.

The fleet is such a collector's album of designs, racing under so many different rules, that many of the starters take their racing less than seriously. At the end of the race many of them don't known who won in their class, and don't much care. For them, the race is an excuse to get to the party in Ensenada.

For those who do attempt to race, tactics are sometimes unorthodox, to say the least. Some crews, taking advantage of the sure knowledge that many of their rivals have broken out the beer and tequila in an attempt to get themselves in the right frame of mind for the big bash in Ensenada, send panic through the fleet by filling the night air with recorded shoreside sounds – like those of a freight train. Another tactic is to project pornographic films into the sails in the hope that the boats coming up from astern will

have no interest in passing until the show is over.

Participants have even developed tactics to help win the much-coveted Last to Finish trophy. In 1961 one of the contendors for the trophy threw his hands up in the air near the finish line and lowered his sails. Black exhaust smoke was seen puffing out from astern, seeming to indicate that he had given up and was motoring in. His rival, seeing this, sailed on across the line. Only then did the rival notice that the « exhaust » was coming from a charcol grill. The skipper upped canvas and sailed across to become the last-place winner.

For those who do take their racing seriously, one of the liveliest rivalries is between the multihulls and the big monohulls for first-to-finish honors. This year the prize went to the 59-foot catamaran Double Bullet, which finished in an elapsed time of 15 hrs 35 mins 47 secs. That was well behind the 14 hrs 01 min 07 secs record set by Rudy Choy's 46-foot catamaran Akane in 1957, and slower than Double Bullet's winning time last year ; but it was fast enough to beat the second place finisher, Machete, a 36-foot catamaran by more than two hours, and the first monohull, Fred Preiss's 84-foot IOR maxi-boat Christine by two and a half hours. The monohull record was set by the 96-foot ketch Morning Star in 1953. Her time was 14 hrs 20 mins 30 secs.

Double Bullet's skipper, Robert Hanel, who has sailed the race six time – all in multihulls – said his strategy is always the same. « A lot of guys go way out in the ocean, where the wind usually blows stronger at night ; others stay close to the shore so they can cut inside of the Coronado Islands and save a couple of miles. I

just sail as fast as I can during the day (the race starts at noon on a Saturday) then decide which side of the Coronados to go on when the sun sets. »

This year the wind carried him on a beam reach away from the land, until at dark he found

The Los Angeles-Ensenada race is not exactly a fierce test of the seamanship of its participants such as these on the ex-12 metre yacht Ji Serena.
Left-hand page. *In the 1979 race. 554 yachts crossed the start line at Newport Harbour (Right-hand page).*

himself about a mile outside of the Coronados. Another mile outside of him was the much smaller Machete. Normally, the bigger boat would have been in trouble, because the night breeze usually favors the seaward boat. But this year Double Bullet was able to hold her breeze all night and long before sun-up was first to smell the garbage dumps of Ensenada.

Double Bullet was designed by Hanel for just this kind of downwind slide. The cabinless cutter has a 30-foot beam, a 70-foot mast which can carry 2,360 square feet of sail, and a displacement of 13,000 pounds. She has won 13 of the 17 races she has entered and was leading the Multihull Transpac fleet this year when her rudder broke 80 miles from the start.

A 20 knot north wind which blew up late Sunday morning sent the tail end of the fleet scooting into Ensenada under surfing conditions and sunk the big boats to the bottom of their classes on corrected time. Jerry Wetzler's catamaran Freestyle won the 16-boat Ocean Racing Catamaran Association division on corrected time for the second year in a row. In the 76-boat Ocean Racing division (where the IOR boats are) Charles Cook's North American 40 Slicker topped Class A. In Class B it was Bingo, a CF 37, owned by Bert Gardner; and in C, Lebaron, a San Juan 24 owned by McSwain/Wagoner.

In any other fleet, 76 boats would be considered a sign of glowing health; but in the Ensenada race the IOR is dying. It has been overtaken and continues to be pushed aside by the Performance Handicap Racing Fleet (PHRF) rule. Some 435 boats raced in the PHRF division this year.

Basically, the PHRF is an arbitrary handicapping system by which a committee of experienced sailors adjust the handicaps of competing boats based on their performances against similar boats. And if the committee is wrong or a boat's performance improves, the committee can readjust the rating at its pleasure. The success of the system rests with the confidence the participants have in the race committee – just one of a long list of things detractors see as wrong with the system – but it has a great following on the West Coast, and is spreading to all parts of the United States.

There were eight classes in the PHRF division this year. First in class on correct time were: A - Oblio, Olson 30, James Betts; B - Redhead, Cal 40, Larry Maio; C - Blue Blazes, 37-foot sloop, Eugene Pennell; D - Tyche, Apache 37, J.S. Peterson; E - Mini B, Ericson 2-32, William Wilson; F - Holo Kiki, Ranger 26, Richard Raff; G - Puffer, 25-foot sloop, G. Woody Sanders; H - Capriccio, 28-foot sloop, Peter Noteboom. Redhead and Blue Blazes both won their classes last year.

Organizing all these boats into their respective classes and doing all the other administrative work that makes the Ensenada Race posssible are the 40 to 50 people on the various committees of the Newport Ocean Sailing Association. The NOSA was formed in 1947 to promote cruising races. They'd run a couple to nearby Catalina Island when someone suggested what they really needed was a race south of the border. The first one was held in 1948 and would probably have lived forever under the very mundane name of Governor's Cup Race, except that California Governor Earl Warren never showed up in Ensenada. So the name was quickly changed to the Newport Harbor to Ensenada International Yacht Race.

Unlike many of the participants, the NOSA's 40 to 50 committee members take their role in the race very seriously. They insist, for instance, that only boats with an overall lenght of at least 24 feet and a waterline lenght of 20 feet may enter. They insist that each boat have a valid measurement certificate. They insist that the number of crew members under 18 be restricted. And they insist that each boat be subject to a safety inspection to see that it has proper offshore equipment.

On the few times the gentle Pacific has kicked up, their insistence has paid off. It paid off in 1977 when the 150 boats that dropped out, the three that were dismasted, the two that collided, and the one that capsized had the committee to thank that their mishaps were no more serious than they were.

But no committee is perfect. Which is why when a starter who decided to spend the weekend on Catalina Island once telegramed the race committee asking them to tell his family not to make the long trip south, the committee tacked up the message on the bulletin board in Ensenada.

Although Ensenada was a sleepy little fishing village that probably had no bulletin board when the first marineros norteamericanos first sailed into Todos Santos Bay, they were not the first outsiders to visit in large numbers. In the late 1800 s a rumor of gold turned what until then had been home for three permanent residents into a boom town. The boom turned out to be hollow – no gold – but one of the things the prospectors left behind was Hussong's Cantina. Today, it is yachtsmen in search of silver who have made Hussong's their number one watering hole. It is a nondescript, usually quiet little bar where during race weekend people have been known to ride horses in the door and motorcycles out the window.

Until recently, the yachtsmen were joined in Hussong's by Mexicans celebrating a national holiday and by « heepies » from north of the border. The resulting mixture was so explosive that a whole lot of people – both the innocent and the guilty – spent part of their Mexican holiday in jail. One year, the overall corrected time winner in the ocean racing division was behind bars when he received a telegram of congratulations from the President of Mexico.

By 1973 conditions had become so riotous that the race dates for the following year were changed so that the sailors wouldn't arrive in town on the weekend. Much of the hell raising that had gone on had been blamed on the « heepies » who Mexican officials seemed to dislike even more than their American counterparts did. However, it is no coincidence that the change in dates coincided with a decline in the number of entrants. In 1973, 581 boats entered the race. There has not been as many since.

One of the reasons is that many of the Ensenada Race crews came to raise hell. After all, what is a race if you can't try to see how many margaritas you can drink before passing out, or how many senoritas you can hustle into believing you are a boat owner when in reality you are only a friend of the owner's son, or how many Federales you can convince that riding a horse into Hussong's should not be a jail offense. Whatever it may be, it is not the Tequila Derby. □

Pages 98-99. *The Los Angelese-Ensenada fleet contained quite a few, of the big boats of the United States west coast fleet, such as Fred Preiss's Christine* (top left) *as well as old-fashioned craft such as Tioass del Mar* (below, left) *and Newsboy* (right).
Left-hand page, above. *The winner receives the Cup from the American President.*
Below. *The course down the coast is well-stuited to a catamaran like Kat's Paw - above, right.*
This is the beautiful cup presented by the American Goastguard.

Transpacific Race

It's a long way to Paradise

by Jay Broze

June 30th-July 12th, U.S.A.
The 1979 Transpac could hardy have been à bigger contrast to the 1979 Fastnet. Where the British race was raked by ferocious winds and ravaged by gigantic seas, the Pacific event was a drifting match - the slowest in its history since 1939, when Blitzen finished in a little under 11 1/2 days.

They say that the sight of the Hawaiian islands rising out of the ocean in the middle of a black night is one of the most memorable experiences of off-shore yachting. There were plenty in the TransPac fleet this time who had more than enough time to relish that sight as they drifted interminably towards the finish.

Il was the 30th TransPac, and its early history was largely centred on the Biltmore Hotel in downtown Los Angeles. There, a couple of days before the off, at the end of June, most of the 1,200 or so participants gathered to drink, talk, boast and compare crew shirts. Everyone was wearing flowers, and feelings of bonhomie and good fellowship permeated the whole gathering. It was more like a fun outing than a serious ocean race.

The racing craft weve scattered down the Pacific coast's profusion of marinas, and on

June 29th the hangovers were worked off in every one of them as crewmen sweated to load up the boats, carry out last-minute maintenance, flake sails, sort charts, lubricate blocks, charge batteries and fill water tanks.

There are 80 yachts entered for the race, 24 of them built since the last TransPac in 1977. Together they make up a very varied armada, with ten or more venerable Cal 40 s the rump of the fleet. Jader, à huge 79 footer designed by Sparkman and Stephens, is the East Coast favourite of the big boats. Her crew are immaculately turned out in blue and white, her fenders are evenly spaced as she nudges into Marina del Ray, her whole appearance « Bristol fashion ».

By contrast, Warrior lies close by, epitomising the West Coast approach. She is a 50-foot

Opposite. *Dennis Choate, the winning skipper of Arriba.*
Below. *The start from Los Angeles.*
Right-hand page. *At long last Jader, an 80-foot Stephens design, sails into the Ala Waï lagoon.*
Inset. *Terri Clapp, the 21-year-old skipper of the all-female entry Concubine, which was such an attraction to all the photographers.*

cutter designed by Britton Chance, and she has three times recorded high places in the TransPac. Her crew of motley-clad hangers-on sit sipping beers and watching the drilled manœuvres on Jader with amusement.

Perhaps the most extraordinary-looking yacht in the fleet is Bruce Farr's new design Zamazaam, a very broad-beamed 57-footer. Also close by is the old campaigner Sorcery, in the last stages of a refit and repaint. It is difficult to believe she will actually get under way the next day. At Long Beach, there are plenty of stories for the media men. Concubine, one of the oldest of the Cal 40s, has been chartered by an all-woman crew. They are having to play host to an endless stream of writers and photographers, while still trying to get their last-minute jobs completed. Also there is Nomi II, a Japenese-built Peterson 42 and Ragtime, the boat which has twice taken line honours in the TransPac.

She'll be rivalled this time by Drifter, the 69 foot very light displacement boat which lost by minutes two years before to Marlin.

The day of the start, June 30th, dawns with plenty of smog down the Californian coast and a light northerly breeze trying to disperse it. The fleet gets away on time and heads out through the vast armada of spectator craft. Warrior, determined as ever, heads straight offshore, while Christine makes a monster tack through the small boats full of watchers. Zamazaaam has a man up forward to bellow at every piece of small fry in her path.

As the fleet separates out, the camp followers stick with their own favourites. Ragtime, Merlin, Sunset Boulevard, Warrior and Windward Passage all have devoted followers. By the time Chutzpah, twice a winner, clears the area the spectators boats have thinned out.

In the early stages, the leading boats are beating into a 20-knot breeze, reefing and shortening sail as they go. At that stage it looks as though it will be a good, brisk race. But by the 3rd July the calms have settled over the fleet. Windward Passage and Jader are still just about ahead, but there is little in it. Drifter and Merlin, keen at first to watch each other carefully, have drifted far apart.

The next day there is no relief. the skippers who thought better of the temptation to dump unwanted water over the side the first night out are now thanking their stars. The forecast is uncertain, but one thing is sure, the little boats are ahead of the big boys on handicap. The Peterson two-Tonner High Roler is particularly well placed.

With just five knots of wind, navigational decisions are shots in the dark. Miakadori III, a 54-foot sloop from Japan, decides to break away south. Ragtime starts to edge down too. So it goes on, after day.

In Honolulu, the waiting wives, girl friends and followers meet in the Hawaii Yacht Club, where shorts and T-shirts are much more common than blue blazers and ties. While their men drift on under the Pacific high, they bask in the sun or scour the shops of Waikiki.

But the move to the south is beginning to pay off for some yachts. The high runs along the rhumb line and Merlin and Windward Passage are virtually stationary. But further down Ragtime has actually managed to complete 200 miles in 24 hours. The Japanese boat is gaining too. Mitakadori III is inexorably closing the gap on High Roler. The smaller boats are still stuck in a pack, but Jader is doing well among the bigger boys.

When the time of the course record is passed the leading boats are still 600 miles away and most of the fleet are barely half-way across.

What progress they are able to make is largely from the current rather than the wind.

By July 10th there is no wind in the island. Drifter has drifted south to cover Ragtime, while Arriba and Zamazaam have dropped down in search of some breeze, too. In the smaller boats, still well to the east, they are beginning to count the stores carefully.

But there is plenty of food in Hawaii. Too much, in fact. The first big party is planned to come off soon, with dozens of pigs to be spit roasted. Will there be any yachtsmen there to enjoy them ?

On the 11th, Drifter is off Makapuu Head, her sails lifeless. Marlin is moving slowly, further off, and Ragtime and Jader are out there somewhere, too.That night the optimistic welcomers are sitting in a small flotilla of boats on the finish line. Nobody sleeps, and yet there is nothing to keep them awake. As the sun rises on the 12th, the sea is still flat and still, but there are deceptive trade-wind clouds on the horizon, turning bright pink with the advancing sun.

And then, at last, Harry Moloscho and the crew of Drifter, bring their boat over the line at five past four in the morning, in a manner true to her name. Behind her, the biggest boats in the fleet are still whistling for the non-existent trade winds.

But 36 hours after Drifter arrivés they come back again, and the rest of the fleet are scooting home in winds of 15 to 25 knots. As so often happens in a race where the wind is fickle, the handicap computations stood the results list on its head. Arriba, a Bruce King 48 emerged as overall winner, from Miyakadori III and Secret Love, a Swan 44. Drifter wasn't even in the first ten. □

Left-hand page, top. *Drifter, Harry Moloscho's 70-footer, glides gently towards the finish line.*
Under. *Arriba, a Bruce King 48-footer, was the smallest of the Class B boats to take the southern route and get the help of the trade winds after the big boats had finished.*
Opposite. *Windward Passage had the most numerous devoted followers.*

Sjaelland Rundt

The most popular race in the world

by Jack Knights

June 22nd, Denmark

To Denmark must surely go the honour of running the greatest yacht race in the world. In 1979, one thousand seven hundred and eighty yachts, from open trimarans to large motor sailers, were entered for the Round Zealand Race organised as always by the Amateur Sailing Club of Elsinore.

Nearly one thousand seven hundred actually started over the long course of 233 nautical miles.

Zealand is the most easterly of the islands which, together with the peninsula of Jutland, make up Denmark. It is actually closer to Sweden than to the rest of Denmark and at the place where the race is started, in the straits between Halsingor (Elsinore) and Sweden's Halsingborg it is closest of all, only four miles distant.

Elsinore is famous for its Kronborg castle, chosen by Shakespeare as the « mise en scène » for his Hamlet. Copenhagen is on Zealand, some twenty five miles to the south.

Nothing succeeds like success, in yacht race organization as in everything else. The Round Zealand prospers now because no self-respecting owner of a sailing boat in Denmark would want to be seen not entering this annual event. Yet going deeper there have to be other reasons.

One, probably the main one, must be the variety offered by the course. The great armada circulates anti-clockwise from the Elsinore start.

This means an initial open sea passage across the Kattegat, westwards towards the lights on the dangerous Zealand Reef. Happily the race always takes place in the exact middle of summer and therefore the Kattegat, which at other times can be hard on those who go to sea in small boats, is almost always on its best behaviour.

The choice of date is almost certainly another reason for the race's popularity. Scandinavians attach a mystical significance to mid-summer's night. They like to mark its passing in some special and memorable way – what better way than to spend it racing ?

Once the Zealand Reef is rounded, the fleet begins to head south for the first time, entering the Great Belt as it does so. This is the recognised deep water channel into the Baltic from the North. Jutland is somewhere out of sight beyond the western horizon. So too is the small island of Samsoe. Then bit by bit as the yachts progress into the funnel, the island of Fyn (pronounced « foon ») glimmers into view. Gradually open sea becomes protected waterway and inexperienced family crews can begin to relax a bit.

From time to time, the water opens out again and the land recedes beneath the horizon, but this openness is now illusory for one soon discovers that to wander far beyond the narrow marked channels is to invite grounding. The coastal waters run anything but deep.

Slowly, as the circumnavigation continues, a south easterly and finally an easterly course is shaped. The island of Lolland grows out of the haze on the starboard hand and then, much closer, the smaller Falster.

A rigid line across the horizon, obviously drawn by man, grows into the road bridge joining Zealand with Falster and later with Lolland. This bridge creates, better than any rule, the upper size limit for the race, for if your mast is more than 25 metres above water, you will not be able to pass beneath the bridge – no « ifs » or « buts » or exceptions.

East of the bridge, the channel tapers to a canal and even though it widens once more, the channel itself remains canal-like. Wander from it when short tacking and you will almost certainly ground. Here again there is a premium on smallness. After the bridge the course divides, the smaller, later starters taking the port hand channel which leads to the north west of the island of Moen. Those in front are required to circle Moen as well as Zealand, thus adding eight miles, usually against the wind, to the course. When the big boats do finally emerge into the open Baltic after tacking down the

Centre. *No yacht worthy of the name in the whole of Denmark would miss the Round Sjaelland event. Certainly not this Aphrodite 101.*
Opposite. *Elsinore Castle, overlooks the start.*

channel, far out to sea before being able to bear off for the north east cape of Moen, they are nearer to East Germany than to Copenhagen.

When the cape is finally weathered, a northwards course can be shaped, through the Baltic and up into the Oresund which divides Denmark from Sweden. Once again the land closes in. On the port hand is the drone of Copenhagen airport. Around one are the fortified islands which Nelson successfully eluded. Forts and lighthouses have an elegance of architecture that is almost sad in buildings that are seen by so few.

North of Copenhagen come the expensive residential districts each one, Hellerup, Skovshoved and Rungstedt with its own marina. The direct course leads away from the Danish coast and towards the little Swedish island of Hven (pronounced « veen ») made famous, many moons ago by the astronomer Tycho Brahe.

From Hven to the Elsinore finish is but a short and easy sail. Slowly the copper roofs and turrets of Kronborg build against the northern sky. This great edifice is more like a French château than a fortification in the massive, monolithic British sense of a castle.

The finish is around the corner and out of sight. But once you cross it, if you are a winner, you are in for a welcome you will not easily forget.

Your writer was fortunate to find himself a winner on his very first Sjaelland Rundt in 1979. He had been invited to crew a new boat, named Bianca Aphrodite, the first of the 414 class, which as its name suggests, is a 41.4 feet long version of the well established 101 class. This boat had been very fully fitted with sails by Elvstrom and Hood. It had Stearns spars and Navtec hydraulics and Signet electronics and Lewmar winches – the best of everything that money can buy. A few weeks back it had been launched with considerable publicity by Denmark's Prince Henri and then, ironically it had failed in its first race – the Fyn Rundt.

Now designer skipper Jan Kjaerulff and his mate Ib Anderson (an ace offshore sailor who now runs Elvstrom Sails) were determined to make their mark.

And make our mark we did. The race is divided into divisions according to speed. The fastest now go first in order to avoid the frustrating log jams of boats which used to form at various windless points around the course. First away at 1300 on Friday June 22, were nine multihulls, all of them quite small. Multihulls are not popular in these cold waters.

We left one hour later with about three hundred of the faster IOR and stet handicap boats. Other starts would take place on the hour, every hour, till 2000.

At the finish we were second in fleet, half an hour ahead of the next keelboat, having overtaken all but one of the multihulls which had started an hour ahead of us. The only boat with a better elapsed time than ours was the little trimaran Fleur 7, about 26ft long and devoid of creature comforts which had been skippered by the redoubtable Paul Elvstrom. Her elapsed time : 43 hours, 5 minutes 23 seconds. Our time : 44.01.29. The next best was also the best Scandicap boat. This was Gry IV, looking like a Farr One Tonner, 36ft long but actually the prototype of the Ravage 36 class designed by the 23-year-old Dane, Niels Jepperson and obviously calculated to blast a hole right through the naive Scandicap rules. She was sailed by tigers from the Elvstrom loft. Her time : 44.32.23. Then

came the Peterson Contessa 43 Pinguin which at one stage had drawn slightly ahead of us. Her time : 44.40.43. The American owned Swan 441 Defiance returned 44.54.07.

Paul Elvstrom has an obsession about this race. He cannot leave the course alone. Once upon a time, he won regularly with an open Soling. Quite recently he almost drowned himself when attempting to lower the course record. It was late November when his frail trimaran broke up in the open Baltic. The American liferaft he was carrying failed to inflate properly and for some time he and his two crewmen were clinging to flotsam in the icy water before being picked up by a passing ship.

At first we looked set to take the IOR award also, but then the significance of a small asterisk against our name was pointed out. We had failed to lodge our rating certificate within the deadline. In any event the first and second IOR boats turned out, much later to be two Manzanita Quarter Tonners designed by Ron Holland.

The results service is one of the wonders of this surprising race. You wander over, after your finish to the Datema shed and give your boat name to an operator. Within seconds you receive a print-out giving the up-to-date status of your boat together with the names and times of all your nearest rivals. During the race corrected time situation reports are given at all the main headlands.

The entry list looks like a medium size telephone directory. From it, you begin to grasp the heart and soul of the race which lies in the dozens of separate classes made up of production boats and one designs. There are pages of Nordic Folkboats (which must have found it slow going without spinnakers). There are scores of Ballads and Maxis (divided further into their sub species). Molich ten Metres and B10s and 101s and Granadas and Scampis and Commanders and Grindes and Vindoes and even two classes of motor sailer.

To do well in this race, you need a large and ever alert crew and a handy and adaptable boat. One weather condition hardly lasts for more than ten minutes. Sails must be trimmed or even changed unceasingly. During our race we had calm, fresh and light winds on the nose, fresh and light winds from behind and some two sail close reaching. We gained several times by keeping very close to the rhumb line. After all, the shortest distance around an island is the one closest to the shore.

Following our victory celebrations at the dockside at Elsinore which included the presentation to each crew member of a chilled bottle of Veuve Clicquot and the recitation of speeches, we slowly wended our way southwards to our home port of Skovshoved. En route we noticed further out to sea a thin skein of later finishers, all running under spinnakers in the now fresher afternoon breeze.

Hours later that same night, dining in the yacht club which fronts the sea, we could just pick out on the now grey horizon the indistinct blots of further spinnakers, further finishers.

The next morning I had occasion to drive along the sea front, and out to sea I spied more spinnakers and they were even thicker than the day before. The boats were to continue on their grand procession for hours and even days yet.

Is there anywhere, another race like the Sjaelland Rundt ? □

Above. *Jan Kjaerulff and Jack Knights in their Bianca 414 places second in the real time behind Fleur 7.*
Middle. *Paul Elvström and team-mates Kjeld Espensen and Mogens Asmussen are enthusiastically welcomed at the quay in Elsinore.*

The Ton Cups

Two Ton

Poole belongs to the French — and German Frers

by Jack Knights

July 24th-28th, Poole, England

A French crew captured the Two Ton Cup in 1979 from the biggest and best fleet that had ever gathered to contest it. The funny thing is that if Baron Edmond de Rothschild, the owner of Gitana VII the winning boat, had had his way, she would have been sold before the Cup races and so not made the trip to Poole in England.

The Baron had wanted his regular crew to win a place in France's Admirals Cup team. Since his Gitana VI was too large to be eligible, a finished hull to the design of German Frers Jr and similar to the yacht which had come a close second in the 1978 Two Ton Cup was purchased 'off the shelf' from the British alloy building yard of Martland Marine, builders of Ted Heath's present Morning Cloud.

Unfortunately, the plans did not work. There were problems in having Gitana finished and fitted out. There were problems in getting her to measure and rate within the necessary 32ft Two Ton limit. Because of this, she was still without an official rating certificate when the selection trial races began. The final blow came when, rated at last, she broke her rudder in one of the trial races.

Who could blame the selectors for passing over Gitana VII and choosing instead the '78 Peterson designed Jubilé, (ex Jena), the famous old Revolution and the lightweight Accanito designed in the Farr style by Michel Joubert? But when the Baron found his boys were out of the Admirals Cup he promptly put his newest yacht on the secondhand market.

Failing to find a buyer and with Two Ton Cup time approaching, it was decided to recruit a crew under the captaincy of Ghislain Pillet and to take the ill-starred Gitana VII to Poole after all. The eventual crew which included Jean-Louis Fabry the highly experienced owner skipper of Revolution, was by no means bad... there was Bernard Louvray and François Boucher and Bruno de la Sablière, Daniel Andrien, Jean-Baptiste Le Vaivant and P.-H. Pallude la Barrière*.

From the opening minutes of the opening Two Ton race, sailed in a good steady breeze over a well-laid, thirty-mile Olympic course in Poole Bay, opposite Bournemouth, it quickly became apparent that the three yachts racing which were designed by Frers – Madrugada representing Brazil, Sur for Argentina and Gitana VII were in with an excellent chance. Each was big in both hull and rig. Yet they were so lively they were amongst the first to heel and require sail reduction. And on that opening

windward beat they appeared to be sailing at least one degree closer to the wind than the others whilst moving through the water at least as fast.

Sur turned the first mark first followed by Gitana. Gitana, by dint of superior handling soon took the lead and later on, Britain's Winsome Gold, designed by the up-and-coming, twenty seven-year-old Lymington designer Ed Dubois, overtook Sur.

In the second Olympic course race the next day, which took place in a freshening wind, Sur and Gitana were again in front. Then, as the wind freshened, Winsome Gold and another, more extreme Ed Dubois design named Police Car from Perth came surfing up. When the two Frers boats were slow to set spinnakers (Gitana had broken the fitting which holds the spinnaker pole to the mast), Police Car and Winsome Gold took the lead. After the finish, Police Car was

Left-hand page. *Winsome Gold, an Ed Dubois design owed by David May, gybes at the leeward in front of another Bristish entry, Lancer V. Winsome Gold finished third overall.*

Right. *The Australian boat Police Car, skippered by Peter Cantwell, is another Ed Dubois design, but a more extreme conception..*

penalised on a controversial protest lodged by Sur.

Madrugada was less well-handled than the other two Frerss designs, partly because of practise time lost before the series when her fragile wooden hull was in Lymington yard being repaired after having been damaged in transit from Brazil.

Dugenou, an older sistership of Accanito, sailed for France under Yves Pajot, took the third race, over an offshore course of 150 miles. This had started in a heavy wind which had soon after eased but Dugen ou made the most of the offwind legs. Before the series had started she had survived enquiries and protests concerning her stern lifelines. Gitana, well sailed as always and with Jean-Louis Fabry providing the Channel expertise, came second to preserve her points lead.

The fourth race, over another thirty-mile Olympic course, was started before the wind had settled down for the day. Madrugada quickly established an unassailable lead by being first into the incoming sea breeze which most appeared to sail away from. Later, Madrugada and Germany's Champagne turned the wrong

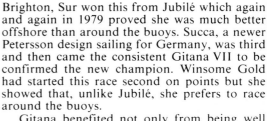

mark (the race committee were guilty of some deception here) and retired. More French yachts quickly seized their opportunity and Accanito won from Jubilé (ex Jena). Then came Sur and then the Australian Ron Holland designed Impetuous.

With the wind easing progressively as the week wore on, the final race, a marathon, around the Channel, of 254 miless became long drawn out. By encountering a hepful wind streak when en route between Cherbourg's CH1 buoy and the Portobello sewer buoy to the east of Brighton, Sur won this from Jubilé which again and again in 1979 proved she was much better offshore than around the buoys. Succa, a newer Petersson design sailing for Germany, was third and then came the consistent Gitana VII to be confirmed the new champion. Winsome Gold had started this race second on points but she showed that, unlike Jubilé, she prefers to race around the buoys.

Gitana benefited not only from being well handled by an experienced group but from finally being rated at the exact Two Ton limit of 32ft. Most of her rivals, even Sur, were appreciably below this figure sincce their owners were concentrating on the Admirals Cup which was to start two weeks later. Thus Impetuous was always well sailed, yet at a rating of 31.5ft she probably lacked about 0.05 % of the necessary ultimate speed. Sur weighed in at 31.6ft, Winsome Gold was 31.8ft, Accanito 31.5ft.

It was noticeable that all three Frers designs were 'bumped' at the main measurement points with quite abrupt blisters intended to increase the helpful depth and width measurements. Some measurers might have taken exception to them but on this occasion they met with approval.

As with all Frers designs, Gitana VII is handsome and 'conservative' in the sense that she has no really radical features. She is shaped more like a Peterson design than a Holland or a Farr but Frers appears to have the knack of drawing hulls which balance slightly better and hence retain their speed, when heeled to 25 degrees or so. He also does hulls which rate well and hence may be given big sail areas, though in this case it is possible that his Two Ton design is just a fraction on the big side.

Had it been a windier week, it is more than likely that the much lighter, three quarter rigged Police Car would have prevailed. She had been well tuned in her home waters by the New Zealand Half Ton Cup winner Tony Bouzaid and just when some of the others were beginning to look over-powered, Police Car began to look at her best. Bust she was giving away too much sail for the lighter winds that came with the end of the week. Her near sister Winsome Gold was a better all-rounder but lost points offshore.

None of the many Holland and Peterson designs, new and old, made much of an impact. The most successful was Impetuous which had America''s Cup challenger Jim Hardy at her helm. Yet she looked just that fraction small in hull and rig. Like the celebrated Imp, it appeared that she had been designed to rate below the Two Ton mark. One of the biggest ccompetitors and the only one apart from Gitana, to rate 32ft dead, was the Japanese designed and built Koteru Teru 2. Frankly, she was a disappointment, proving difficult to control in fresh breezes downwind and yet appearing to lacck liveliness in light conditions. Yet she had the tallest mast and biggest rig of the fleet.

The series was excellently organised by a hardworking team from the Royal Thames Yacht Club under Chief Race Officer R. Hamilton Parks and everybody appeared to enjoy the facilities of the Poole Harbour Yacht Club Marina. Not everybody agreed with every decision of the international jury however. □

Preceding pages. *The winning boat Gitana VII is a Frers design bought in haste by Baron Edmond de Rotschild in the hope of getting into the Admiral's Cup. She benefited from an excellent crew.*
Above. *Ghislain Pillet, Gitana's skipper, with his wife.*
Centre. *Sur, the Frers design owned by Diego Peralta from Argentina, a finished second, thanks to her victory in the 254 mile race in the Channel.*
Below. *Accanito and Dugenou are sister-ships designed by Michel Joubert and Bernard Nivelt. Each of them won a race.*

One Ton

Won by and overgrown Three Quarter Tonner

by Rob de Wijk

September 10th-13th, Newport, U.S.A.

The American John MacLaurin achieved a singular victory in this year's One Ton Cup at Newport, Rhode Island. Having taken the laurels in the Three Quarter Ton Cup with his yacht Pendragon last year, he won the One Ton Cup for 1979 with the same boat. A number of modifications converted the yacht to One Ton rating – and made her very quick too. She took the lead in the very first race of the series and was never seriously threatened.

Pendragon was designed by Laurie Davidson in 1978. And it was Davidson who made the modifications to her. The hull itself was not changed ; 'the main modification was the increase in sail-area' said the New Zealand designer. 'We pushed it up by 20 per cent by fitting a longer mast and a short bow-sprit. We also put more weight in the bottom and made the centre board wider and heavier'. In fact, Pendragon was the only centreboarder in the fleet at Newport, and this proved a great advantage, especially on the reaches and runs. By lifting the board she achieved a noticeable increase in speed downwind. Skipper MacLaurin has strong views about centreboards. 'I am a dinghy-sailor and I don't like keels' he says. A boat like this should sail like a dinghy and you should handle it the way you would a dinghy'. So MacLaurin won't hear of things like hydraulic back and headstays ; he uses powerful tackles. 'It gives me more feeling ; I want direct and simple control of my tuning possibilities.'

Most of the competitors took Pendragon for a typical light-weather boat. Many of them thought she could not have achieved any real success if there had been light to medium weather for the Cup. As it was, the predominance of very light going suited her exactly.

Two British-owned boats were at Newport for the Cup, which was staged between September 1 and 13. Oystercatcher '79, a Stephen Jones design, is flush-decked and elaborately equipped. She had a very successful Cowes Week before being shipped to the States and her owner Bob Matthews was hoping to take her on to glory. The mast of this boat was particularly striking, with mast bend controlled by three running back-stays. The other British boat was Graham Walker's Indulgence, a Ron Holland design. Thought to be the fastest boat in the fleet, she was crewed by some of the top names in the sport, including Butch Dalrymple-Smith of Holland's ; Lowell North, who made the sails ; and Tim Stern, whose Stern Sailing Systems built her spars and rigging, including the very thin section mast with a very complicated system of tuning.

From Germany came last year's champion boat Tilsalg-Flensburg, skippered by Klaus Lange. She is also a Holland design and her eventual tenth place was a disappointment. She clearly needed more wind.

The third country in the lists was South Africa, with two Lavranos designs, Spirit of Mainstay and Archangel. Both these boats had mast-head rigs, unlike the rest of the fleet.

The achievements of Bill Donovan's Not by Bread Alone, a Contessa production boat built in 1974, were remarkable, considering her age. She actually scored a second place in the short off-shore race. A lot of her success must be attributed to her canny navigator Maura McNally – it was thanks to her good work that Bread took home the prize for the best production boat in the fleet.

It was a pity that only 12 yachts from four countries contested the Cup. The Brazilians withdrew very late in the day and there were no boats from those strong One Ton Cup countries, New Zealand and Australia. But the cost of transporting boats is becoming a very serious deterrent these days. The series was supposed to have five races : three short courses plus a medium and a long-distance course. But the remains of hurricane David tore those plans apart.

The first short race on an Olympic course was sailed in very light airs and fog. The race committee decided to shorten it, much to the annoyance of some competing boats. But the conditions suited Pendragon perfectly and her navigating was better than on most of the yachts. She came from behind on the last leg to win, followed in by two Bill Cook designs sailed by American crews, Celebration and Firewater. Indulgence had been leading, but she proved slow downwind and lost her chance to recapture the lead when the race was shortened.

Pendragon's good luck on the water was compounded by her fortune at the dockside. A spot inspection showed that she had too many headsails on board, an oversight by the crew when they were loading them aboard. But the jury accepted the accidental circumstances and levied no penalty. On the other hand, the German crew of Tilsalg-Flensburg were penalised five points for a starting line incident.

The second race on an Olympic course was blown away by David. The Race Committee elected not to race the rather fragile fleet when the wind was gusting to 40 knots and there were threats of worse to come. The question arises : shouldn't the best of off-shore racing craft be able to race in gale-force winds in proctected waters ? Opinions varied : some thought racing in Narrgansett Bay, with little searoom, was worse than taking the fleet out into the ocean. Others said they were ready to go but doubted if some boats in the fleet could handle that amount of wind. It seems plain that the Race Committee was concerned about the extent of their liability and the recent Fastnet Race disaster was almost certainly a major factor in their decision. But without a lay day, the committee could not reschedule the race, so the series was now down to four races. The medium-distance race scheduled for the next day, also had its problems. The fleet sailed 135 miles for nothing :

Below, left. *Skipper John Mac Laurin : « a onetonner should sail like a dinghy and you should sail like a dinghy and you should handle it the way you would a dinghy. »*
Right Pendragon, the Laurie Davidson – designed quarter – tonner sailed by John Mac Laurin.

the results were thrown out and the race ordered to be re-sailed. Problem was that the gale had set adrift the last mark of the course, a sea buoy 25 miles off Newport. It finished up five to six miles from its scheduled position. Most boats actually saw the mark because it was drifting on the rhumbline of the previous leg. Some navigators assumed that it was in its proper position and ignored their own dead reckoning position. That put them five miles wrong when they tried to find the leeward mark off No Man's Land.

In the resailed race, local knowledge – particularly which way to sail round Block Island – proved crucial. Not By Bread Alone chose the right course, the South African entry Archangel was wise enough to follow. Result : a win for the South Africans, with Bread a good second, and Pendragon third.

The final race of the series was the longest – a 245 miler which seemed to favour Graham Walker's Indulgence. By the last mark of the race Indulgence was nearly one hour ahead with just 30 miles to go to the finish. But she was very aware that she had to finish at least two places up on Pendragon to clinch victory in the cup. So the crew decided to go on a Pendragon hunt. When they found the American boat, they sat on her wind and tried to insinuate two yachts between them. But this dubious tactic failed to pay off : Indulgence won the race by barely four minutes and Pendragon got through to take second place – and the One Ton Cup. Lowell North admits that it was his idea to seek out Pendragon and sit on her. It was a tactic which raised some queries about what constituts fair sailing. In the end, it was probably a good thing for all concerned that Pendragon could not be shaken off and took her just rewards.

After the race a protest was brought in because Pendragon was alleged to have no navigation lights. Her crew replied that they had experienced battery problems. Once again the protest committee accepted the Pendragon explanation.

So in the end, only three races with a sadly-depleted fleet were run. It seemed to take some of the credit out of what should have been a longer series with many more boats to make a true world championship series. Some commentators had plenty of opinions to air after the Cup had been decided, both about Pendragon's 'luck' and the general organization of the regatta. Klaus Lange, the deposed champion, was outspoken in his criticisms. 'That Pendragon should certainly have been properly inspected' he said. 'In my opinion the boat is out of rule. They told us they trusted everyone to take care that his own boat was within the rules. The committee talked about a 'gentleman's agreement'. This should not happen in a world championship.'

At the final prize-giving, after everyone had praised everyone else for their fantastic work, some one from the organising club said they were certainly willing to organize this event again. But the Tilsalg crew quickly made it clear that they didn't think that was at all a good idea. It was a painful way to end a competition which had brought a lot of pain to a lot of people. □

Preceding pages. *Bill Cook's design, Celebration. Only three races were possible at Newport, which was close to the path of Hurricane David.*
Centre. *Oystercatcher, a Stephen Jones design, finished fifth.*
Below. *The South African entry Archangel, a masthead rig design by Lavranos, was the winner of the 125 mile race.*
Top and right. *Indulgence, Graham Walker's boat which was designed by Ron Holland races against Pendragon, the Laurie Davidson – designed quarter – tonner sailed by John MacLaurin.*

Three Quarter Ton

Triumph for Sweden and a third title for Peter Norlin

by François Richard

August 16th-19th, Denmark

Originally staged at La Rochelle in 1977, then organised at Victoria in British Columbia in 1978, the Three Quarter Ton Cup was held at Hundested in Denmark in 1979.

As in the previous years, the number of participants was rather disappointing. The rival claims of the Half Ton Cup, the Quarter Ton Cup, and above all of the Admiral's Cup undoubtedly weakened interest in this event. The Cup therefore resolved into a struggle between the Scandinavians, with additional contributions from the lively visitors from Holland and, particularly, from Britain. Hundested, a little fishing port and pleasure resort, played host to 38 competing boats. The town had already organised the Half Ton Cup some years previously. It lies about 40 miles from Copenhagen, facing on to the open waters of the Kattegat, that channel which separates the Danish kingdom from Norway. As this area is obviously much more suitable for open water regattas than the confined waters around Copenhagen, the Kongelish Dansk Yacht Klub, which was organising the series, transferred its headquarters to Hundested for the 15 days of the event.

One of the most famous Danish champions, Ib Ussing Andersen, who is actually manager of the Elvstrom sail-loft, was competing aboard Messina, a boat designed by Christian Rode. But Andersen was never able to put together one good race before giving up the struggle. Of the whole fleet, where quite a number of prototype boats were racing side by side with series production yachts, the British soon became the most serious aspirants to the world title which Lowell North had not come to defend himself.

The first race on an Olympic-type course, which was staged in very light airs, almost could not be finished within the time limit. The first three boats crossed the line virtually side by side, just making way against a strong tidal current in an almost total absence of wind. Regnbagen, designed and helmed by the Swede Peter Norlin, took the honours, just ahead of the other Swedish boat 32 AN, belonging to Ingmar Boding. Third in this race was the British boat Gunsmoke, who gained her revenge for the defeat she suffered on the second day, when the breeze held up much better. She was a clear winner of that race ahead of Hans Kure, skipper of Buccaneer. Gunsmoke belongs to the very enthusiastic sailor from London, Harrison.

Included in his crew was the fiery and bearded Stephen Jones, one of the rising young boat designers on the English scene. This boat had been specially prepared for this Three Quarter Ton Cup and, after their original trials in the spring, the eight members of the Gunsmoke team were really hoping to make a big impact on the competition. And half-way

Half Ton

Waverider... just makes it

by François Richard

July 9th-22nd, Netherlands.

Tony Bouzaid and his crew, for the second year running, sailed their Wawerider to victory in the Half Ton Cup. The Kiwis, however, achieved this just reward only at the end of a difficult series, where the struggle for first place continued right to the very last minute. Fifteen miles from the finish of the final race, the four leading crews were still neck and neck. And in the final classification they were only four points apart. Before the start, Wawerider, holder of the 1978 title, was automatically the favorite. She had been modified to suit the IOR rule for 1979, with an altered rudder and more ballast. Besides the three-year-old boat, New Zealand was also looking for success from Swuzzlebubble. Wawerider was skippered by Tony Bouzaid, a master sail-maker with Hoods in Auckland. Swuzzlebubble, belonging to Ian Gibbs, was equally strongly crewed by Murray Roos and Andy Ball. These two Flying Dutchman specialists, already famous for their sailing expertise, made Swuzzlebubble the most threatening boat at the start of the championship. But from the beginning, Wawerider was successful – taking the first Olympic course race of 30 miles in a light wind. Then, on an identical course but in even lighter airs, it was the Frenchman Moureau who brought his Jina through to victory. Wawerider was still there in second place.

In the third race, 180 miles long, a massive

Left-hand page, top. The French entry Jina, spoilt her chances by a premature start. She finished under fourth.
Below. The tactical crew work under Tony Bouzaid helped Waverider's retain the Quarter Ton Cup. She is a Laurie Davidson design.
Under. Entered as Kiwifruit, Bouzaid's boat reverted with disqualification for breaking the advertising rules.
Right. Swuzzlebubble drawn by Bruce Farr and sailed by Murray Ross and Andy Bell, turned out to be fast but inconsistent.

blunder by Waverider's crew relegated her to 20th position. Jina, with a penalty of 10 per cent of her time for having crossed the line at the start in the last minute, found herself dropped to eighth. Swuzzlebubble carried off this race majestically in front of the Dutchman Lamstraal Van Kats. These two boats went to the top of the overall classification and it looked like the turning point of the whole championship. However, the third Olympic-type course was to put Bouzaid and his crew back on top. In the usual Dutch drizzle, with very strong North sea currents, and thanks to a good force five breeze, Waverider went scuttling through to a second win in ideal conditions. Swuzzlebubble, third at this time, had some bad luck. She missed one mark because of the current, and in turning it refused to give way on a port-and-starboard.

The New Zealanders, penalised for their mistake, lost about ten places by this difficult manœuvre. In the following winds, they vainly struggled to catch up with Waverider and the British team, among which Roller Coaster had a very good race to take second place. Jina, held up by a tactical error, finished in the middle of the fleet.

Before the start of the long final race, five teams actually had a chance to take overall honours. The long course of 280 miles was made up of a rectangle described within the North Sea. Setting off from Scheveningen, the 35 boats were set a long beat towards the English coast, then travelled along that coast under spinnaker, turned a mark off the Essex coast to return down-wind to the Dutch buoy Texel and finish off La Haye.

Waverider, Swuzzlebubble and Jina set off at electrifying speed. When the wind dropped during the night, Jina caught up with her rivals while behind them Roller Coaster and Jaunal were engaged in another duel. At the Texel buoy it was impossible to forecast the final order. Roller Coaster, lying fourth, seemed to have the overall series in her pocket. But then she was passed by the French Jaunac and losing that

place meant that overall victory would go to Waverider. Winner of three of the five races in this 1979 Half Ton Cup, Tony Bouzaid and his crew fully deserved their title. But their victory was undoubtedly the result of both experience and technical superiority. On the question of boat design, the two New Zealand craft and the French boat Jina were very similarly built. Bruce Farr, Laurie Davidson and Michel Joubert all design hulls with flat aftersections, very wide, with a U-shaped forward section. These hulls, designed to go well down-wind, also worked well to windward thanks to very sophisticated rigs. Waverider used an aluminium mast by Yacht Spar with an oval section. Bouzaid reckons that this mast was probably the main reason for his success. He admitted that he had spent a lot of time getting the rig right and he thought that both Swuzzlebubble and Jina lost out by not having a similar set-up. Roller Coaster, on the other hand, was unusual in that she was much more of a cruising style design by the Englishman Rob Humphreys. Very good to windward, this yacht was rather tender down-wind. Once she had been selected as the British entry, she took Eric Duchemin and David Howlett into her crew – two very experienced Olympic class sailors – Flying Dutchman for Duchemin, Finn and Star for Howlett.

In the team table, the French were first, ahead of the British and the Dutch teams. The outstanding characteristic of the 1979 Half Ton Cup was that the competing boats were so alike in design that we often had the impression that we were witnessing a battle of one-designs. □

*Above. The Dutchman Lamstraal Van Kats was fifth overall but finished second in the 180 mile race.
Below. The British entry Roller Coaster was a production boat from the board of Rob Humphreys. Sailed by Eric Duchemin and David Howlett, she was just beaten in the long final race and had to give best to Waverider.*

Quarter Ton

Fauroux beats Elvström

by François Richard

September 11th-23rd, San Remo, Italy

After an excursion to the coasts of Japan in October of 1978, the Quarter Ton Cup returned to European waters in 1979 and was staged at San Remo in Italy at the beginning of September. The teams of the Land of the Rising Sun, which had performed so well in the previous year were, sadly, absent this time. Among the favourites, the Australian and New Zealand teams looked to be very dangerous indeed. But in fact the championship was largely disputed by the Europeans. The French and the Italians, used to the weather conditions of the Mediterranean, were strongly favoured by those trying to predict the outcome. The Italians have always put a lot of time and energy both in design and sailing expertis einto events run under the IOR rule. This year, they had almost 60 boats vying for selection for the national team. The best helmsmen, designers and boat builders made it a point of honour to prepare thoroughly for this Quarter Ton Cup and their elimination trials had taken place at San Remo on the same waters as the ultimate competition at the beginning of August.

The French also organised open selection trials and this led ultimately to Bullit's final Quarter Ton Cup victory. This totally new design by Jacques Fauroux made a very big impression there and the boat went to San Remo as the favourite to win at the beginning of September

Unfortunately, the position of favourite is not the most comfortable one and maybe that had something to do with a certain nervousness on the part of Jacques Fauroux, skipper of Bullit. On the very first race, round an Olympic course, Fauroux was over the line early and had to turn back and so lost several precious minutes. But he was still quick enough to get up from 30th place to finish 8th. The Italian Piccola finished first, but he was disqualified for being over the line at the start, so the honour of being provisional leader went to Son of a Gun, an Italian team steered by the celebrated Danish helmsman Paul Elvstrom, The quadruple Olympic champion was to give ample proof of his enormous skill in the following races.

The young Italian crew on Free Way had failed to get into the official Italian team and so they were competing for England in this cup. Sailing very competitively, they took two of the short Olympic course races. In a very light and unpredictable wind, Free Way was first across the line in the second race just in front of Son of a Gun, steered by Paul Elvstrom. For the 100 mile race, the conditions were scarcely any better: the wind varied between a light breeze and nothing at all, and sailing close to the land turned out to be a hazardous affair for some boats which had initially been well placed. The Frenchman Dupuis, skipper of Bigouden Ex-

press, won the 100 mile race ahead of Paola 5, an Italian boat sailing for West Germany. This time Paul Elvstrom and his Italian crew, consistent as ever, finished 9th, just beating Bullit, the best of the French

In both the 2nd and the 3rd races Bullit made bad starts. Worrying about breaking the line too early Jacques Fauroux and Dominique Caparros often showed themselves far too careful and were therefore badly placed in the early stages of the race. But, blessed with a very high boat speed and choosing the right side of the course, as a rule, they still put together some very good results, finishing 5th and 9th in those 2 races. So before the 4th race they were nicely placed in 3rd position overall. That 4th race was on an Olympic type course of 30 miles and it turned out to be one of the most interesting in the series. Starting with a weak breeze and beneath a diffident sun, the conditions seemed absolutely made for Paul Elvstrom, who made a splendid start at the end of the line and quickly gained several boat lengths - enough to cross the whole fleet of 56 boats. But Elvstrom was soon to realise that he had started on the wrong side of the first beat. He then tried to catch up with his

main rivals, who had gone off on the far side of the course right from the start - the side where the wind was much more favourable. Free way and Bullit were on that side and the race became a duel between them. Around the marks they were seldom separated by more than a few metres. The wind got up progressively during the race until it was close to force 4 and behind the two leaders Paul Elvstrom made the most of the speed of his boat. Son of a Gun recaptured several places on each leg and finished in 3rd position. With more than 10 points advantage over Jacques Fauroux, Paul Elvstrom seemed very well placed when it came to the final race. This was a long course of 180 miles which would normally have gone around the Giraglia rock to the north of Corsica, but the wind conditions

Below. *On the Italian Riviera, the 1979 Quarter Ton Cup was mainly fought out by Italian and French one-off designs - boats which were lightly-built but still able to go well in a blow.*

were so strong and the frequent rain so persistent that the organisers decided to lay a course along the coast, close to both the French and Italian Rivieras. From the start at San Remo, the contesting boats rounded the rock of Gallinara, close to Alassio. And at this point Elvstrom was in the lead. He held on to first place when they turned the Lion de Mer rock off St. Raphael in France, but he was very closely followed by several good Italian boats, Bullit and some other French yachts, which had made up ground on the second beat. The return towards San Remo turned out to be a beat against an easterly wind, and then turned into a reach with northerly winds coming off the coast. Naturally Elvstrom and Fauroux were covering each other and several other yachts close enough were trying their hardest to carry off this final honour. The French crew on Mister Magoo chose to go further out to sea and were able to overtake the pack of leaders which had stayed close to the coast. But they all came together again close to the finish.

A thousand metres from the line, Fauroux on Bullit, Albarelli on Lisa and Langlois on Mister Magoo found themselves virtually neck and neck. The outcome was always uncertain, because it was effected by very local gusts which helped first one boat then another. The first to benefit was Jacques Fauroux. He crossed the line just a minute ahead of Langlois on Mister Magoo but thankfully 8 places ahead of Elvstrom. Having let two more boats get past him, Paul Elvstrom lost the chance of yet another world championship and Jacques Fauroux took his first title under the IOR rule. He had previously been one of the best Moth international sailors in the world.

At 33, Jacques Fauroux is an up and coming boat designer. Trained in science and mathematics, he has always been one of the best sailors and technicians in France. This Quarter Ton Cup victory was a kind of revenge for him, because he had been up against Paul Elvstrom in the Finn singlehander at the beginning of the 70's. At that time the Scandinavian champion beat Fauroux at a very memorable Ski-Yachting event at Hyeres.

Even though the Quarter Ton Cup was largely sailed in light winds, the two boats which finished in the lead overall, certainly showed themselves to be able to go fast in any conditions. Designed by Jacques Fauroux and built in glass fibre, Bullit follows the general trend in design these days. She was very fast downwind, no matter what the sea state. Son of a Gun is a new design by Fontana, Maletto and Navone, the young Italian designers from Milan who won the Mini Ton Cup with their Wahoo. Their boat is quite broad and shows very good seakeeping qualities as well as speed. Nevertheless it has to be said that Paul Elvstrom's sailing skill contributed a lot to the Italian boat's performance. On a technical note, one must mention the French designer Alain Jezequel who drew the lines of 10 of the best yachts in the fleet, notably Lisa, Los Angeles and Free Way, three of the outstanding boats at San Remo. Not very habitable overall, the 1979 crop of Quarter Tonners are really stripped-out racing machines, made as light as possible, yet they have proved themselves quite tough in a breeze. □

Left-hand page. *Bullit rides the rollers.*
Right, top to bottom. Son of a Gun *designed by the three Italians seen here - Fontana, Maletto and Navone. Paul Elvstrom and Jacques Fauroux, designer and skipper of Bullit - two famous dinghy champions who took the first two places.*
Los Angeles *designed by the Frenchman Alain Jezequel, as were the other two boats seen here, Lisa and Free Way.*

Mini Ton

Wahoo does it again

by Paul-Gerard Pasols

September 3rd-4th, Estartit, Spain

Originated in 1977 by the Cercle de la Voile de Paris, on the same lines as the One Ton Cup, The Mini Ton Cup, was won the first time by the French one-off design Jaunac, to the designs of Berret, at La Rochelle. The second time it was staged at Porto Ercole in Italy in 1978 it was given the status of a world championship. As a result, the quality and the quantity of the contestants improved noticeably, but at the same time an element of dishonesty crept into the competition too. For example, it was possible to witness certain unscrupulous yachtsmen making alterations to their boats between two races, in defiance of all the regulations.

Thankfully these benders of the rules had nothing to do with the victory of the Italian one-off design Wahoo. Steered by the star helmsman from Austria, Hubert Raudaschl, Wahoo wa designed on the lakes of Lake Como by three very talented youngsters ; Franck Fontana, Claudio Maletto and Flaviano Navone. Remember these names well, because Wahoo this year again took the Mini Ton Cup and made everybody who saw the victory realise that we shall certainly hear a lot more of these.

The win was all the more remarkable in that it was achieved against yachts designed by the top names in the business, notably Ron Holland and Gary Mull, who until this year were strangers to the competition. And Wahoo also won for the second time against some outstanding helmsmen – people like John Kolins, who had represented the United States at the Olympic Games in the Soling class, and the Spaniard Abascal, one of the top flying Dutchmen sailors in the world.

As for the rest of the fleet in this Ton Cup, just as in other world championships of off-shore sailing, the 1979 modifications to the IOR rule brought about the eclipse of lifting keel boats, which are now far too heavily penalised. On the other hand, 7/8 rigs, adopted by some other categories of Ton Cup yachts, seemed to have become the rule amongst Tonners. At Estartit in Spain, which was the scene of the Mini Ton Cup in 1979, there was not one of the 43 boats in the fleet with a masthead rig, yet all of them were within the new IOR rule, duly verified by an armada of measurers sent by the Offshore Rating Council to make sure that the chicaneries of 1978 were not repeated.

As a result, the only aspects of this regatta that one might criticise were the winds which, in September, around the Costa Brava just as along most coasts of the Mediterranean, were as fickle as any woman in any of the many proverbs propagated by misogynistic men. And talking of misogyny, though frequently seen on big boats it was not to be found in the Mini Ton Cup. On small cruising yachts of this size – about 7 meters overall – a woman can steer just as easily as a man and it is hardly necessary to say that several young women were seen in the crews of Estartit.

One entirely feminine crew attracted a lot of attention, mainly because of the identity of the skipper. The green painted Mini Tonner Wind Jammer which carried the colours of Ireland was actually skippered by Laurel Holland, wife of the designer Ron Holland, and she was backed up by two well-known regulars of the Crosshaven Yacht Club, Pauline McKechnie and Kate Casey. Taking part in the competition on a boat which was, of course, drawn by Ron Holland and which the Astilleros Garriga had lent them the day before the competition began, these three ladies finished the Cup in 33rd place, leaving ten all-male crews trailing in their wake.

A sister ship of Wind Jammer, built in the same shipyard in Barcelona, was the American Honey Moon. This was the only contestant to seriously challenge the Italian supremecy in the Cup. As it turned out, the only race which was not taken by an Italian yacht was the 3rd Olympic triangle course, during which the wind quite unexpectedly got up to force 5.

Even so, the victory of Honey Moon must have been connected with the failure of the rudder on Folletto, a sister ship to Wahoo and the Italian champion of the Mini Ton class, which was doing very well up until this setback.

At the start of the last race, a 54 miles course, Wahoo looked very strong on paper. She only had to finish directly behind Honey Moon to take the Mini Ton Cup for the second time. But she wasn't favourite on the water for long, because at the first windward mark at the end of a 2 mile beat, Honey Moon was in the lead and

Wahoo was lying 19th.

At the following marks, the American boat was constantly extending her advantage and by twilight John Kolins, the helmsman of Honey Moon, his compatriot By Baldrige and their Spanish crew man Umberto Gastos, believed that they had the Mini Ton Cup in their pocket. Sadly for them, the wind fell as the day died, and the following dawn discovered them imprisoned in a calm while Wahoo, crewed by Tiziano Nava, Mauro Mosetti and Claudio Maletto, one of her designers, pressed irresistibly towards her second triumph.

In the final classification Honey Moon was

2nd, followed by a Spanish sister ship Gargio VI. This boat was sailed brilliantly and it illustrates the emergence of yachting in Spain, where there has been lots of enthusiastic action in these last two years both in dinghies and in Quarter and Mini Tonners.

The German Boat Keule, to the design of Judel Vrolijk, slipped into 6th place, among a crowd of Italian and Spanish craft. She was a Pop Corn, a production Mini Tonner built in Switzerland by the Portier yard and, of all the boats at Estartit, was one of those most like a conventional family cruising yacht. The best French entry, Clementine, was a veteran craft. She is the very first Mini Tonner designed by Jean-Marie Finot and despite all the typically Breton energy of the Elies brothers and their chum Legomidec, who crewed her, this boat was outclassed by the more recent designs in certain wind conditions, particularly in ligth airs. The

first English boat in the list was Shaved Fish, designed by Julian Everitt and she finished 16th. Her crew made a number of tactical errors but the unusual shape of the hull, which has a kind of bulbous expansion beneath the water line, seems to make her just as fast as the others.

It's pretty sure that in 1980, when the next Mini Ton Cup will be staged in Scotland, the British Isles will be better represented than this year. □

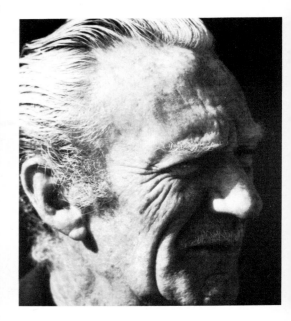

Page 130. *The Guardia Civil keeps an eye on the mini-tonners.*
Page 131, top. *Wahoo, a Fontana, Maletto and Navone design, kept the Cup for Italy. Ron Holland's design Honeymoon, steered by Jon Kolius (below) ran aground in the last race of the series.*
Above, left to right. *Tiziano Nava, the skipper of Wahoo, with Mauro Mosetti. Claudio Maletto, with his co-designers Frank Fontana and Flaviano Navone, not only created Wahoo but also Son of a Gun, second in the Quarter Ton Cup. Enano Saltarin, Organiser of the event.*
Below, left. *John Kolius, helmsman on Honeymoon, is an ex-champion of America in the Soling class.*
Below. *Wind Jammer, a sister ship of Honeymoon, was entrusted by Ron Holland to his wife Laurel (at the helm).*

The major regattas

12 m. J.I. Championship

Lionheart wins the oddest World Championship

by Jack Knights

September 15th-29th, Brighton, Great Britain

Has there ever been a stranger world sailing championship than the one that ended in style on Saturday September 29th with a banquet in Brighton's opulent Metropole Hotel ?

Only six yachts competed and only two of these met current class rules. Three of the six were crewed by British. Of the other three, one came from Sweden, one from Holland and one from Australia. Yet the event called for a budget of £ 100,000, a budget which in the modern manner was probably exceeded.

Two full weeks were set aside for racing, yet on only three days was a full programme completed. Though the yachts were well over sixty feet long and cost a quarter of a million pounds each, it seems they were insufficiently seaworthy to be raced safely longshore in the British Channel in a wind of more than twenty knots. This is a velocity that is often exceeded in late September in Britain.

Another oddity : though thirty three races were started and finished only one involved all six yachts together. The other thirty-two took the form of two-boat duels, duels so short that several were no longer than the races for the Finn Gold Cup which were being concluded seventy-five miles to the westward as this remarkable event was beginning.

We are not finished with the unusual even yet, for the organising club, the Royal Southern Yacht Club was conducting the event on waters quite strange to it, over forty miles away from its familiar River Hamble. It chose the two-boat

match pattern as well as the twenty knot upper limit because of the long shadow cast by The America's Cup.

This, the very first World Twelve Metre Class Championship would not have come about if the most famous of all yachting trophies was not being put up for grabs, once again, in 1980.

It was the America's Cup which inspired this championship and the America's Cup which came close to being its downfall. When the regatta was first planned, emissaries were dispatched to recruit participants. At least one good American Twelve seemed essential and when the group now racing the 1977 Defense trialist Independence was signed up, this condition appeared to have been met. Agreement was only achieved after the organisers had promised to pay the transport costs, but agreed it was – and then came the clump clump of the heavy feet of the New York Yacht Club. Even before 1902 when the prosper Bostonian, Thomas Lawson deemed it necessary to set the record straight by publishing his own history of the America's Cup, the NYYC had shown that in hanging onto its cherished cup it would sacrifice much including, if necessary, good sportsmanship. Now, in 1979, it has made this sacrifice once again.

From the NYYC came a stern warning... no American Twelve Metre crew which offered comfort to the enemy by attending the World Twelve Metre Championship need think about competing in next year's Cup defense trials.

At that final Brighton banquet, David Wilson,

the chairman of Southern Television, the championship's sponsors said « I'm so sorry the Americans were kept away... I think that is the best way I can put it ».

By the time Russ Long had withdrawn Independence, the championshop was a couple of months away and other overseas Twelves- Sverige from Sweden and Gordon Ingate's Gretel 11 from Sydney were committeed to competing. Soon after that, a group in Holland, having just lost Constellation to the British, bought Chanceggar from Baron Bich. Their original intention was to convert her for charter work but then they thought it would be fun to race her first in her present form. So it came about that Windrose, ex Chanceggar was entered for Brighton.

Baron Bich himself, having this time been easily the best organised of all the 1980 challengers was well ahead with his own plans and these did not allow for a trip to Brighton. (But it does seem that, at the last minute, the Baron came to regret not sending one boat, France 1 for instance, to join in the fun.)

With Britain's Lionheart and her pacer Constellation, five yachts were now assured but this was an unfortunate number since one would always be waiting while the other four were duelling. Britain's John Caulcutt saved the day ; he phoned a few friends and scratched together sufficient backing to charter Columbia from the now defunct group which had set out to build a record French Twelve for 1980. Then they went off to La Rochelle, got the old lady into some semblance of racing condition and sailed her to Brighton.

And so it came about that the first World Twelve Metre Championship opened off Bright- on's new marina on sunny Saturday September 15th with the first of two all-in practise races.

And how long has it been since as many as six Twelves crossed a starting line, more or less together ?

The time limit ran out on this race before the leader, Sverige, could make it to the finish but before we get into the racing one final oddity which casts light, not only on the regatta, but upon the times in which we live, must be mentioned.

Though the Chairman and Managing Director of Southern Television are true yachting enthusiasts, the decision to spend £ 100,000 on a few yacht races was not taken on completely uncommercial grounds. It was foreseen that by dint of widescale promotion, public interest in this event would be awakened and having been

Preceding pages. *The British challenger Lionheart finishes the championship unvanquished.*
Opposite. *32 races in the Brighton regatta, matched the 12 m. J.I. against each other, two by two, with an eye to the America's Cup.*
Right page. *Bridge design for Lionheart (top) and twin steering on Gretel II (below).*

136

awakened this interest would then be assuaged by coverage on Britain's, TV screens, which would be brought exclusively by Southern Television.

Nobody had allowed for British trade unionsim. For some weeks before the championship and all through the championship, for a period, so far of eight weeks, the Association of Cinematograph and Television Technicians had darkened Britain's single commercial television channel. Southern Television was unable to publicize their bold event, in the way they understood best, beforehand. They were prevented from recording it as it happened and they even had some difficulty in getting together an ad hoc crew prepared to focus any kind of camera lens upon it. So far as the public was concerned, the First World Twelve Metre Championship might have been taking place inside a bank of Channel fog. Few Brighton promenaders could have appreciated why the flags were hung out.

The first, frustrated practice was followed the day after, by another. Sailed in perfect conditions this was won by an emphatic four minutes and more by Lionheart from Sverige. Constellation steered by Guy Gurney was third and Gretel 11, steered by Graham Newland was fourth. For Sverige it could be said, that she was still tuning the new mast that Proctors had delivered to Brighton. For Gretel one could only suggest that perhaps some of her young crew were short of practise.

Lionheart proceeded to win the event. She was not once headed across a finish line. Once she retired before she got as far as that but she won even this race since that same evening, skipper John Oakeley successfully protested his adversary for failing to respond to a luff. Sverige's disqualification was one point worse than Lionheart's retirement.

Lionheart was acclaimed champion. Sverige's crew went home with only one trophy – for winning the match race series inside the marina which was staged in Topper dinghies on the third consecutive day that the wind exceeded twenty knots. Yet the British success had a slightly hollow sound and not only because of the absence of the best boats from the USA, France and Australia.

The morning after the completed practice race, Lionheart despatched her pacer Constellation by 3 1/2 minutes, Sverige beat Gretel 11 by close to three minutes and Columbia beat Windrose by nearly two minutes. In the afternoon Lionheart was matched against Sverige and the watchers drew up their chairs.

The Swedes won the start, Lionheart was powering through to windward and then Sverige's new mast tumbled over the side. It was discovered afterwards that a lower shroud had come adrift from its internal seating, probably because that seating had been insecurely held to the mast wall. While Sverige was towed back to harbour, Lionheart was awarded a sail over.

The pair next came together the following Sunday afternoon. By this time it was crystal clear that neither Gretel 11 nor any of the others could match their speed in anything but freak conditions. This time the wind could not have been far short of twenty knots and Sverige was setting a short footed jib on her original mast. Once again Pelle Petterson outmanœuvred John Oakeley coming into the line and eventually both crossed near the Committee Boat on port tack with Sverige to windward and ahead.

Top to bottom. *Constellation was skippered by Guy Gurney (left). The 21-year-old Columbia was refitted by John Caulcutt and Windrose, ex Chancegger, by Tjerk Romke de Vries.*

Above. *The Swedish 12 m. Sverige, second at Brighton, had the advantage of Pelle Petterson's skill at the helm, but suffered from problems with her rigging.*
Following pages. At the helm of France III, Baron Bich seems more determined than ever.
Inset. France tries an Intrepid sail.

Within minutes Lionheart had thrust through the other's lee to such effect that the Swedes were forced to tack away. Lionheart soon followed and when Sverige tacked back, Lionheart coossed her. Lionheart led by 29 seconds at the first mark and by 34 at the gybe. On the second reach Sverige held high, Lionheart stayed low and lost all but nine seconds of her lead. There was more sea on the second beat but though Lionheart appeared to pitch more and ·have more forestay sag and sideways mast bend she had little trouble getting further ahead. As she did so she got out of phase with Sverige's tacks. Approaching the mark the latter picked up a nice shift and gained to within 11 seconds at the turn.

Starting the run so close it was hardly surprising that Sverige drew abreast. Halfway along it appears there was contact following a luff by Lionheart. The pair continued to the lee mark with Sverige always the inside boat then, coming into the turn, Oakeley misjudged either his own speed or the slowing of Sverige as her spinnaker was taken off and the British bow ran up on the Swedish stern. Lionheart retired and Sverige now finished alone but as we know, one more shot remained in the British locker and this was fired with effect at the protest that evening.

Would Lionheart have pulled through to win had the boats not touched? From the evidence of the first two beats this certainly appears probable but we cannot be certain. Sverige had more bad luck that evening for in a second protest, her morning victory over Gretel was

reversed as the result of another buoy rounding argument. Sverige might well have survived both protests, according to one jury member, had she defended them differently.

Lionheart and Sverige came together once more in the very last match of the series, by which time the British were already sure of the trophy. This final heat should have taken place on Thursday September 27th but Sverige asked for extra time in which to step the Proctor mast which had that day been returned, repaired, to Brighton.

On Friday morning, Lionheart came from behind Constellation to beat her by nearly two and a half minutes and Windrose reversed a 43 seconds deficit against Columbia at the first mark to win by 86 seconds. Gretel 11 meanwhile, had bowed out, explaining that the yacht had to be aboard a ship at Tilbury that weekend. In the inner basin of Brighton Marina the morning was spent in stepping and fitting Sverige's repaired mast.

At 1400 Sverige locked out for her final tilt at a yacht which in a few short months had already become her greatest rival. Then with the soft low sunlight glinting off the silvery spar she sailed majestically out to sea. The start was set for 1455 the wind was blowing at around 15 mph and since it had veered from north to east was fetching up a tumble of sea. Oakeley without his usual navigator Ian Howlett, tried to avoid tangling before the start and stayed well clear of the line but Petterson after him, fastened into his stern and forced the British onto the defensive. The pair approached the line on port tack with Sverige to weather. Sverige then tacked to cross on starboard leaving Lionheart to her own devices.

Lionheart was recalled and while Sverige continued on her way the British Twelve bore off on port and came slowly back, luffing as they recrossed and then hardening up again on port. By this time Sverige had tacked into port too and now it could be seen that she was two or three hundred yards dead to windward. This was because the line had been strongly biased in favour of its port end – the end to which Sverige headed when she tacked into starboard (see diagram.)

The 71 seconds by which Sverige led at the windward mark had been nearly all accumulated at the start. For the third time running Petterson had outstarted Oakeley. Lionheart gained nine seconds on the first reach then lost four on the second. The second beat brought no change whatever. The two boats turned the lee mark 65 seconds apart and they rounded the windward mark separated by precisely 65 seconds. On this beat, Lionheart had used a lighter, compensator style jib which was too full for the windspeed. Oakeley said afterwards that faulty instruments had prevented him from gauging the windspeed before beginning the beat. But it should be borne in mind that when the best American Twelves are caught with the wrong headsail they simply change it at the first available tack.

Lionheart gained fourteen seconds on the square run and with a flatter headsail was apparently gaining on the final beat. Yet with a mile of the final 2.5 miles remaining, Sverige looked in no real danger. To gain is one thing, to overtake another.

Sverige's mast had been bending off sideways at the top and there had been quite a bit of low down fore and aft bond which showed itself in the pumping and backing of the lower part of the main. Lionheart's mast, also by Proctor but

139

John Oakeley former Flying Dutchman olympic medallist steers Lionheart.

differently constructed had shown similar characteristics but to a lesser degree. At this precise moment, with less than one half of the final leg remaining, Sverige's mast came crashing down again. This time the tube folded a foot above the lower spreader. For the second time out of three, Lionheart was left to sail over by herself.

Lionheart finished the series with two points to Sverige's eight (one loss Lionheart and two « dsq's »). Lionheart's crew could point to their clear win in the completed practice race and to their superior upwind speed in their first two brushes against Sverige.

For their part the crestfallen Swedes could return home saying that they had led the first practice till the time limit ran out and that if their Expletive Deleted mast had hung on for another ten minutes in the final heat they would have done much to restore the balance of power. They had in addition outstarted the British three times running.

Gretell 11 with nine points, came third overall but the one point difference with Sverige was misleading. At Brighton she could hardly have been as fast as she had been in 1977 or indeed when losing with such spirit to Intrepid in the America's Cup match of 1970... either that or Lionheart and Sverige are going very much faster than they were.

Gretel 11 came to Brighton with the biggest main and smallest foretriangle in the business, with a minimum of stability and with Gordon Ingate explaining that to win the Challenger trials in August, light air speed is essential. The sorry thing is that Gretel is no longer the all-rounder she once undoubtedly was. Neither did the seasoned Graham Newland enjoy much success behind her twin wheels. Some of his starts were wildly off... once she was fit and ready for the start whilst her opponent Columbia was desperately struggling to get her jib hoisted before gunfire. Yet when Columbia came reaching back into the line on port, about twenty seconds late for the gun, she was able to comfortably cross Gretel 11, starting even later on starboard tack. Gretel 11 will need to do a great deal better against Australia in the forthcoming David Brand Trophy series off Freemantle in mid November. (This series will give the British and Swedes a line on form.)

Fourth, with twelve points and four wins against Windrose and Columbia came Constel-lation with the second British crew skippered by Guy Gurney. Apart from a couple of new Hood spinnakers, Connie makes do with some very flat and well used Hood fore and aft sails. She can outpoint Lionheart but she appears to make more leeway in doing so (the same can be said of Sverige). Downwind Lionheart is clearly faster. Connie would be helping Lionheart more if she became more aggressive. Thus in their last match Connie started ahead of Lionheart and promptly tacked to keep on the other's wind when the other first tacked away. At last it looked as if we observers would be treated to one to those fifty tack, duelling legs which often enliven the American trials. But no... when Lionheart split again, Connie was about half a minute late in responding and by then Lionheart had slipped the other's backwind. Afterwards one of Connie's crew explained that they knew they couldn't hold Lionheart in a quick tack duel since their gear wasn't as good. But surely that was limp and defeatist. The only hope of staying ahead lay in staying on Lionheart's wind and that meant tacking until either they dropped or their winches seized.

In fifth place with 16 points and two wins – one against Columbia, the other against Gretel on protest for coming into the line from the wrong side of the course, was Holland's Windrose. Skippered by round the world sailor Tjerk Romke de Vries, the Dutch improved as the series progressed and they often started very well. But they remained short of boat speed.

To nobody's surprise, twenty one year old Columbia with a single win against Windrose in her very first match came last with 18 points. Yet John Caulcutt and his merry men and various guest advisers, by bringing the old lady from La Rochelle had kept the series alive. Unfortunately their lack of speed suggested a bad case of barnacles whilst helmsman Andy Cassell never got to grips with match race starting. Afterwards a Columbia crewman claimed that they had proved that amateurs could still mix it in the Twelves. I would have thought they had proved quite the reverse. Before each start they had a board count to make sure the correct number was aboard.

How fast is Lionheart ? A Twelve which can beat Sverige by over four minutes, which can beat Gretel 11 and Constellation by over five minutes and Chanceggar and Columbia by over eleven and all this over dinghy length courses in firm breezes, can be nobody's pushover She is at her best upwind, possibly in smooth water. It may be that her fine ends and big midship section by leading to a low prismatic coefficient, will limit her ultimate high wind speeds, particularly offwind and they may also increase her pitching but this at the moment remains speculation.

Preparations are under way for the America's Cup.

While Lionheart, Sverige and Gretel II were competing against each other at Brighton, the American 12 m J.Is were polishing their arms on the course which will be the battlefield for the next big challenge in September 1980, Newport, Rhode Island.

The defender 1977 title-holder Courage-ous, designed by Olin Stephens and again captained by Ted Turner, will be on the lists, after having undergone some modifications.

The Enterprise team, with helmsman Dennis Connor, has chartered Freedom, a new Stephens plan. Ted Turner and Dennis Connor : the 1979 Fastnet victor against the SORC winner !

Ted Hood, the master sailmaker, architect and skipper of Independence, eliminated by Courageous in 1977, is trying his luck again in the modified Independence.

Even France III, Baron Bich's boat has been busy practising at Newport since early summer 1979. Marcel Bich himself is directing the finishing touches to his 12 m. J.I., built in aluminium at the CNA shipyards at La Rochelle, France.

At the end of the summer, France III and Intrepid were neck and neck with 20 regatta victories each.

Using Tom Chadwick's Windmaster cloth, Oakeley had made a second compensator mainsail, which he used all the time at Brighton and one or two more headsails. While being flatter than her first sails, these are still full and twisted by the standards of the American Twelves in 1977. Oakeley is unabashed; he believes in footing rather than in pointing and he theorises that power will be needed to get his heavy boat over those big Rhode Island swells. He may be right at that but it is to be hoped that money and time will be found to enable the Lionheart team to develop in addition a stand-by, flat sail rig. Then if after getting to Newport next summer they discover that are full sails are not working out, they will have a known alternative instead of a last minute panic.

Lionheart's crew work is coming along well though it would be reassuring to see some more

beef amidships to cope with those full blooded tacking duels that she has yet to get into. And they must practice jib switching on a tack, even in a seaway and they need to hoist those spinnakers a great deal quicker.

As for starting – one of two things must come about. Either John Oakeley must greatly improve his technique and his level of aggression or a special starting helmsman must be recruited. One shudders to think what Dennis Conner will do to Oakeley on the starting lines, should the pair ever come together. It is no good having a boat designed for upwind speed if each race is started in the backwind of the adversary. The only man we can think of who would either teach Oakeley how to start and do his starting for him is Harold Cudmore. He has the twin disadvantages of being Irish and being hard to get.

Sverige came to Brighton with new sails, some of them from Hoods, made from fabric woven in Ireland, the others made by Petterson himself from Vectis cloth made by Ratseys at Cowes. Petterson preferred his own sails and spoke highly of the British cloth. His boat was really moving in that final heat even though the main, because of the spar bend, was all of a quiver. Twelves seem very sensitive to their spars.

The series was well run by the Royal Southern under the strong leadership of John Burt. The Swedes have already said they would like to hold the next World Twelve Metre Championships. In spite of the New York Yacht Club's mean-minded boycott this show is on the road. □

Above. *American Dennis Conner at the helm of Freedom, new candidat for the 1980 America's Cup. Following pages. Entreprise and Freedom, two Stephen's designs practise together.*

The 6 meter World Cup

The comeback of an elegant racer

by Jay Broze

September 4th-12th, Seattle, USA.

An observer in Seattle last summer could have been forgiven for thinking he had just stepped out of a time machine. There, arrayed at the northern end of the Shilshole Bay Marina were twenty-five racing yachts, all designed to a Rule that was first formulated nearly seventy-five years ago. Long, narrow, and low, with fractional rigs and deep full underbodies suspending huge lead fins, the Six Meter is at the same time one of the most beautiful racing classes ever, and the antithesis of 1970's yacht design.

The Six Meter was once the single most important class in international competition. The class had Olympic status, and the British-American Challenge Cup, the Seawanhaka Cup, the Scandinavian Gold Cup, and the One Ton Cup were all races in Sixes. The modern triangular race course was first formalized for the Scandinavian Gold Cup. During a Six Meter regatta in Genoa, one of the great skippers in the class' history, Sven Salen of the May Be dynasty, flew his reaching jib on a

weather leg. This innovation, first called the "Swedish Jib", was to become a standard piece of racing canvas within a few months, and it is still known as the Genoa. The same sailor was also responsible for the first work done with modern "parachute" spinnakers. The history goes on and on.

In the last ten years the class has been enjoying a bona fide renaissance, and a host of true and new believers were on hand to contribute to the process in Seattle. There were eighteen modern Sixes from the boards of seven different designers, Gary Mull, Peter Norlin, Sparkman & Stephens, Doug Peterson, Pelle Peterson, Brian Wertheimer, and Britton Chance. Four of them sailed in the regatta, and two skippered their own boats. The crews included several world and national champions in a variety of classes, plus many veterans of the Twelve Meter wars in Newport, Rhode Island. The skippers included Tom Blackaller, Malin Burham, Patrick Fredell, Hank Thayer, Ted Turner, Pelle Petterson, Scott Rohrer, and Brian Wertheimer. And, completing the time

travel tableau that confronted the unprepared observer, there was a gathering of older Sixes that numbered some of the most famous ever built, Llanoria, Goose, May Be VII and Saga, among others, all competing for a special trophy for "classic" hulls.

The World Cup for Six Meters was instituted in 1973 when a squat silver punch bowl with cups was donated to the International Six Meter Association by the Port of Seattle. The first cup was sailed in Seattle, with most of the overseas fleets represented by charters out of the large stock of older boats still racing on Puget Sound. Only Australia had a new foreign construction, the Sparkman & Stephens Pacemaker. Tom Blackaller and the St. Francis V, (US 100) ran away with the World Cup that year.

In 1975 the Cup was held in Sweden, with three American boats joining the Europeans, Toogooloowoo V, Razzle Dazzle and Poisson Soluble. After a rehearing of a protest, the title went to Patrick Fredell in the Salen's May Be X, with Gary Philbrick in Toogi V se-

cond. The 1977 World Cup in Marstand saw Pelle Petterson in Irene taking the win during a respite from his less successful Twelve Meter campaign with Sverige, while Scott Rohrer and Razzle Dazzle the placing American boat fell to third after leading most of the regatta. The truly international competition of the two Swedish World Cups, plus the new Europa Cup, also sailed in Sixes in 1978, fired the interest in the upcoming races in Seattle, as did the fifth matching for the American-Australian Challenge Cup, scheduled for a fortnight later in San Francisco.

The first European boat to arrive was Nuvolari (I-72), a new Peter Norlin designed boat from Italy. The Swedes, led by defending champion Pelle Petterson, shipped six boats to the Northwest, including a new Irene for Pelle, a new Mull boat, the eight year old S & S designed Toogie V, and three Norlin boats, including the newest May Be, number twelve in the line. Five older boats came south from Canada, all but one competing in the classic division, while the new Australian boat by Gary Mull was withdrawn when Lloyd Fallshaw and her Prince Alfred YC sponsors could not meet the scheduling deadlines.

On the American side there were new boats for Ted Turner (Ranger), Tom Blackaller (St. Francis VII), and Gayle Post (Perspicacious) all from Gary Mull's board. Doug Peterson did two new sistership, one (Ah, si si) for Malin Burnham, and Discovery for Hank Thayer. Razzle Dazzle was re-rigged and reballasted for the event, and Brian Wertheimer designed his own Six Warhorse to be built by Bob Cadranell of Seattle.

The first matchings of the new boats was the North American championship, sailed to eliminate the three slowest American boats from the field of the upcoming Cup races. In these races, sailed in light to moderate air, Warwick Tompkins, the stand-in helmsman on St. Francis VII was undefeated in four starts, and did not finish the fifth race, his throwout. Ted Turner, with Gary Mull and the core of his America's Cup crew on board, was second, while Wertheimer's brand new Warhorse was third, after winning the last race. The old US 100 took fourth and Ah Si Si fifth.

The European boats shadowed the fleet during most of the races, and from a few hundred meters away, a couple of them appeared to have the speed needed to be competitive. Luca Bassani-Antivari in Nuvolari looked very fast, and in the preparation races for the World Cup, Pelle's new Irene, the only boat that featured a bustle in the bow as well as the stern, showed some very fast legs. Irene, however, had only sailed twice before the series, and there was no indication of whether her speed was real or imagined.

The "racing" opened with a whimper, as the winds, notoriously fickle in late summer on Puget Sound, abandoned the site of the regatta for two full days. Finally the winds filled in on Saturday, September 8th, and for the first time in two decades, twenty-five Six Meters hit the starting line. The first leg was a case of "cover

the most dangerous", and Turner and Blackaller let Malin Burnham escape. Ah Si Si reached the top mark first, with the Italians close behind. In sixteen knots of air, the new Peterson boat was not to be caught, but in the fleet, positions were changing rapidly. By the next weather mark the Italians had been overhauled, and Pelle Petterson was careening up through the pack. The finish saw Burnham taking his only win of the series, followed by Irene and St. Francis VII. US 100, Warhorse and a frustrated Ranger followed in close order.

In the afternoon the order was reversed, with St. Francis just holding off Wertheimer's new boat, then Irene, Discovery, and Ranger. In the lighter second race, US 100 missed a big shift on the west side of the course and collected a dismal 10th. That afternoon Pet-

terson walked the dock like a small smiling Swedish elf with a very big secret he couldn't keep long to himself.

The day that followed saw one race started, then abandoned as the second weather leg became a very light run, and the fleet met again Monday morning, hoping to get four more races completed in just two more days. The gods answered their multilingual prayers that morning, and the winds finally filled in. After one general recall the fleet sailed into a moderate, but building, northerly. Petterson and Blackaller staged a virtual two boat regatta from dead even starts. However, the San Francisco crew, honed to their usual unbeatable match race form could not really engage Pelle's more simply equipped Irene without allowing the other top competitors to sail by on one side of the course or the other. In long-leg fleet racing Irene had a tiny speed advantage, and Blackaller had to be content to follow Petterson across the line, with the surprising US 100 in thirs. Patrick Fredell in May Be XII was fourth, and Nuvolari beat out Turner for fifth. After this day's racing and yet another sixth place Turner averred that he seemed to be " Happy as a banana, just one of the bunch", The third race was Wertheimer's turn in the barrel, however as he sailed four great legs to come from 24th to 7th after a disastrous opening beat.

The second race was started in the late afternoon, and after a general recall, it was clear that the fleet would not cross the finish until well after sunset, and perhaps after twilight. Night racing a Six may not have been what the Royal Yachting Association had in mind for the International Rule back in 1906,

but in 1979 the skippers and crews were more than willing to grope in the dark for a few minutes if it meant having a six race regatta with one throwout.

In the restart Fredell was over early, and rather than hang behind the fleet he chose to take a flyer into the beach, right under the bluffs along Puget Sound. The gamble paid off handsomely, as May Be XII nipped Pelle by half a length at the top mark, with Blackaller seconds behind. Fredell could not stove off the regatta leaders, but he did manage a third, just a step ahead of Wertheimer, whose boat looked to be gaining momentum on every leg. Fifth was Perspicacious a new brightwork Mull boat that thrived in the dark, and sixth was, of course, Turner. Burnham was DSQed in this race, ending his in-the-money hopes, and US 100 had a poor ninth.

The final day of racing was the best of all, with fifteen to twenty knots of air, and two races that finished in the daylight. It was also the day that Pelle's mainsail and Blackaller's concentration both fell down. Petterson lost his main while sitting in a strong second place behind Gary Philbrick in US 100. Figge Montan, a longtime Petterson regular, attempted unsuccessfully to climb the mast. But on the opposite tack, with a greater angle of heel, he made it to the top and retrieved the halyard. Within minutes Pelle was under full sail again, fighting his way back from sixth place. Philbrick, sailing his old boat superbly, picked his shifts and protected his lead against a very fast Wertheimer and a resurgent Ted Turner, who managed a fourth place. Pelle caught all but one of them to place second ahead of Warhorse, and Blackaller could do no better than seventh.

The fifth race was the first one in which Blackaller did not get an even, or better than even, start on the fleet. In this big a group of fast boats, the San Franciscans could not get up the speed to cut through the fleet, no matter what they tried. They were especially thwarted by Nuvolari, who beat them twice on the final day. The Italian strategy had evolved to one of match racing the nearest fast boat on any leg, and unfortunately for St. Francis VII, they were usually the nearest fastest boat.

If the first race of Tuesday was a shambles for Blackhaller, and a scramble, albeit a heroic one, for Petterson, then the second race was even worse for both. The start was nearly even between Wertheimer and Burnham. Warhorse was crossed once by Discovery, then led the way to the weather mark, and held on to the pace all the way around the track. Petterson had a mediocre start again, but then quickly dealt a crushing blow to Ah, Si Si. First he sailed through their lee, then tacked and sailed over them on a one tack beat to the weather mark. Blackaller was actually moving backwards at the start, fatally late for a "duck-in" at the pin end of the line, and blanketed by the entire fleet. He would make up a dozen hard-fought places in the course of the race, but finish a distant tenth while Wertheimer, his only likely rival for second overall, was winning the race. The two boats left the course tied in points, but with more boat-for-boat victories, Blackaller won the tie breaker for second place in the regatta.

Petterson managed to fight his way up to third behind Warhorse and Discovery, and was in the enviable position of having his "throwaway race" be a third against the best fleet of Sixes assembled in many a year. Turner, the victim of a missed flyer on the first beat, finally got back to 12th, for his worst showing of the week.

The final results in the World Cup said many things about the quality of the modern Six Meter and the kind of sailing they require. Petterson and Blackaller, first and second, sailed very different boats, one a pudgy, simply equipped fleet racer, the other a dramatically outfitted match-racing machine. The key to their success was their ability to extract the last bits of performance from the big-main small-jib rigs, an ability due in large part to the years they have spent racing Star boats and Six Meters. The Six Meter is one of the most close-winded yachts racing, and is one of the few that can actually convert a tiny increase in efficiency into a tiny increase in real velocity made good.

Among the "also-rans" the fate of Ted Turner was indicative of the competition. Turner is unquestionably a fine skipper, but it takes time and concentration to develop a winning effort in a throroughbred like a Six Meter. A Six is not a scaled down Twelve (luckily for all the non-oil sheiks of the sailing world), and even the best Twelve Meter sailors in the world cannot expect to win the first time out. Gary Mull "stopped counting" the number of sails that went on Ranger at fifteen bags, and Robbie Doyle of Hood was recutting the main for the boat every night of the World Cup. There was a surfeit of money and talent on Ranger, but not enough time to solve the problem. Ah, Si Si faced similar problems, but with a boat that was slightly slower through the water than the new Mull designs. Here too, a Twelve Meter skipper with a crew that included Olympic Medal winners, Star champions, and the reign-

ing North American Laser king didn't have the feel of the boats.

Of the European boats, only Irene and Nuvolari managed to finish in the top ten of every race. The size and quality of the fleet (Ted Turner was an also-ran) led most of the Swedes into a number of gambles that could not possibly turn out. Racing against Petterson and Blackaller, one can't rely on brief repeals of the law of averages.

The next major regatta for Sixes is the 1980 Europa Cup in Geneva, then the 75th Anniversary World Cup on Lake Constance in 1981. Already there are new boats underway, and renewed interest in the class in Australia and America as more of the old Six Meter trophies are reactivated for the class. It may be that the old fashioned and beautiful Six will again become a truly preeminent international racing machine, largely because they encompass so much of what racing has been and aspires to be. □

Previous page. *The 6m. J.I. s line up under spinnaker, on Seattle's beautiful waters.*
Left. *American Doug Peterson, one of the most famous designers of offshore racers, is responsible for two 6m J.I. sister ships, Ah Si Si and Discovery.*
Below. *Irene, designed by Gary Mull is a well-curved yacht, with a simple superstructure. Very fast, she benefits from Pelle Petterson's vast experience.*

Class boats
and Windsurfing

An olympic sailing year

by Daniel Nottet

Finn

The day of John Bertrand

The story of John Bertrand's 1979 love affair with the Finn, that pitiless Olympic single-handed dinghy, started with a set-back. Nothing can impair the ambition and the grace of this 23 year-old American who is already World Champion in both Lasers and Finns. Nothing, not even his mast! One race lost because of his broken spar, and that robbed him of victory at Hyeres despite some first-class performances. And in addition one disqualification – for being over the line at the start of a race, a misfortune which was common in Olympic fleets during this 1979 season – had a heavy effect on his classification. So, in the final analysis, history will show that Guy Liljegren, the rangy blond Swede who has dedicated his life to the Finn, which he calls 'the least onerous of the Olympic boats', was the most consistent performer and emerged as victor at Hyeres nine years after his first victory there.

After his disappointment at Hyeres, John Bertrand's victory in the Finn European Championships, which were held in Italy, had a touch of revenge about it. Gentle revenge, it should be said, since he won three of the races.

While the best Finn sailors were pitting their wits against this star of the American scene, the British Finn sailors were contesting the Weymouth Olympic Week. It was really like letting the sheep out to pasture with the wolf waiting to pounce. The wolf was Chris Law who has won the Finn Gold Cup in the past before losing some of his rhythm by entering a mad round of non-stop international competition. The tall Englishman with a deceptively nonchalant air did not race on the last day at Weymouth, which meant that the final victory of Norman Starling put him into 2nd place for the week before the veteran Belgian sailor Luc Van Keirsbilck.

What does it matter how the regatta went provided I come out of it with the spice of victory? John Bertrand might have exclaimed after the conclusion of Kiel Week. His final score was an eloquent testimony to the superiority of the American superman, for it was made up of 3 victories and 2 second places, a total of 39 points ahead of the best of his challengers, the Swede Kent Carlson. Carlson had been one of the great revelations of the Optimist class, and he finished at Kiel ahead of the Canadian Lawrence Lemieux from Edmonton.

Winners laurels again for John Bertrand at Tallinn. This time he built up his win in light airs, consolidated it in medium going, and kept it when the wind blew. He is not actually irresistible on the wind. I have even seen him make some tactical faults that Serge Maury wouldn't commit. But his mistakes only emphasise just how much he has in hand over the others. In fact it is difficult to believe that anyone can beat him. He has balance, co-ordination, a sense of attack and of tactics which are simply extraordinary. If he is in the leading group at the first mark he will be first over the line. But it shouldn't be overlooked that in order to get to this level the young Californian gives his whole life to sailing, practising all through the year more than 4 hours a day in a very helpful climate, sustained by a very wealthy club and assistedo by two coaches. The most professional of tennis players couldn't ever be easy to beat Bertrand at his own game.

On the subject of the regatta at Tallinn, the best of Bertrand's challengers were his countrymen. His runner-up was none other than Cameron Lewis, an attractive lad with a devastating smile, a kind of happy-go-lucky urchin who's always making jokes. Cameron Lewis certainly knows how to get to the front of a fleet and he doesn't pay much heed to the ambitions of John Bertrand.

There is proof of the point in the result of the last regatta of the season, which was far from being the least important. It was the Finn Gold Cup, the World Championship of the class series, which was held at Weymouth in England. Just as they had during the months when they roamed the scattered waters of Europe, covering miles and miles of beating and hours and hours of down wind planing, John and Cameron amused themselves. They were like young lions having a good time at the front of a fleet which was struggling hard. Cameron was the victor. My own verdict: the strongest challenger that the best Finn sailor of the 1979 seasons has to meet is on his own doorstep, his brother-in-arms, Cameron Lewis. Those Spring trials in America will be a real shoot-out.

Left-hand page. *The Spaniard Jose-Luis Doreste finished third overall at Tallinn in 1979.*
Below. *The two young giants of the Finn, Americans Cameron Lewis (left) and John Bertrand (right). John, 23, dominated the Finn series as easily as he did the Lasers last season. Only his friendly rival Cameron, winner of the Finn Gold Cup, was able to withstand him.*

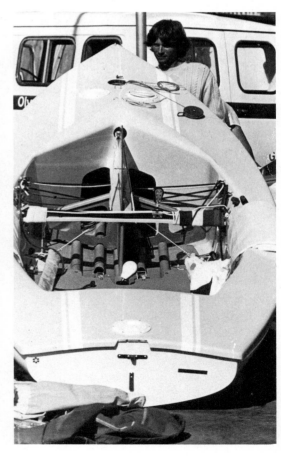

470

A contest of giants

After his remarkable visit to Hyeres week in 1978, the Canadian Tom Matthews came back in 1979 determined to avoid those poor results which blotted the copy book of the best 470 sailors. Today the competition has become so intense in this class that it is a kind of ironic fate that the boat which really should be the example of Olympic competition for all, is now the one where victory is the most difficult to achieve. It is impossible to imagine even a talented beginner competing in these very restricted regattas.

Behind Matthews and Cross, the two young Frenchmen Richer and Claude finished second,

unable to avoid the blot of a 50th place in one race. Nevertheless, it was the start of a brilliant series for them, because the two Frenchmen managed to finish in the first five at all the major regattas of the year. The French team decided to take part in Weymouth week in England. There is always something to be gleaned from the English, sometimes even a victory. Laurent Courarie-Delage and Herve Wattine had the happiness of doing just that. It was a good international scene, indeed, which saw Richer and Peponnet battling with the best in the world, such as the Israeli Brockman, the New Zealander Paterson and the East German Borowski. The Israeli pair finished 2nd, which was the first olive branch in the desert for, after their success in 1978, they had begun to feel that they had lost all their supeeriority. The performance of the English in their own waters was very uncertain, and disappointing even to those of their rivals who had a high regard for them. Perhaps it was simply that they were too heavy in a class where the combination of strength with low weight is essential.

The growing strength of the new French team was seen most dramatically at Kiel where in three races – it was too light for the results to be confirmed – Jean-François and Claire Fountaine gave the newcomers to the class a lesson in how the old stagers of the 1975-1976 campaign could perform.

The 470 European Championships were held in Denia in Spain, and were won by the Israelis, Brockman and Friedlander. Shimson and Etan were not always most dominant on the beats but they were incredibly quick under spinnaker, and that gave them an advantage over the German pairing Hunger and Korte (it seems there's always a good German boat in the main 470 championships) and the Polish pair Wrobel and Story, who proved to be excellent performers in light airs. It should also be mentioned that the French team of Alain Chourgnoz and Xavier David were the heroes of many disputes with the Committee and won some acclaim from their fellow competitors. But this really didn't do them much good when it came to clocking up results.

In the World Championships at Medemblick in Holland the forthright claims of the Japanese Kai caused some hilarity in the boat park : "I have the best boat, the most beautiful sails, and I am just as strong as you". Some thougt it rather comic. But a week later, it had to be acknowledged : Kai indeed had the best boat, the most beautiful sails, and had turned out to be the strongest of the lot ! He was Champion of the World in front of Laurent Courarie-Delage and Herve Wattine and Stephane Richer and Philippe Claude. I'll leave you to guess who was smiling ruefully after that. The French were happy as long as they could get a crew man out on the trapeze. But there was too much light air sailing in Holland : plenty of work there to be done on the basics of sailing, and the French team, with their trainer Marc Laurent, are determined to overcome this weakness.

Tallinn Week in Estonia was more or less a full dress rehearsal for the Olympic Games regatta in 1980, one year before the event. The New Zealand pairing of Mark Paterson and David Mackay proved to be the best at Russian roulette, the new game which consists of always guessing which side of the course will prove the right one. It is important not to be misled by the apparent fragility of the skinny New Zealander. He's a tough competitor who styles himself on the American David Ullman, that master sailor with the bizarre silhouette. With his face creased by concentration and the will to win, Paterson may be small in size but he is large in talent.

Previous pages. *Enthusiasm and technique from the French couple Fontaine, first at Kiel.*
Opposite, above left. *New Zealanders Mark Peterson and David Mackay top at Tallinn in 1979.*
Middle. *Miyuki Kai, master-sailor in Japan was an unexpected World Champion with team-mate Ryo Komiya.*
Below. *American Dave Ullmann, series leader in 1977 and 1978 was second in 1979.*
Right-hand page, above. *Frenchmen Richer-Claude and the Peponnet brothers were very consistent this season.*
Below. *Israelis Brockman and Friedlander became European Champions in Spain.*

Flying Dutchman

Honours even

Although sailing their 1978 boat, Albert and **Rudy Batzill** were easy winners of the Flying Dutchman class at Hyeres week. The way they managed to pick the right side of the course every time filled rivals with wonder. It also brought a sweet smile to the bearded face of the Lake Constance farmer and his brother. But Erik and Sjoerd Vollebreght never seemed to find this same happy spirit of mind, and took it very hard that they finished behind the German pairing. It was a resentment which they vented on each other, shouting backwards and forwards. And if they couldn't get the boat to go right, what seemed to please them best was to start fighting. Five minutes after the finish they were the most charming companions even towards each other. Behind these two pairs, the Italian Marco Savelli, an accomplished helmsman who has done good things in Ton cups, and the Frenchman Marc **Bouet**, who won his first race in international competition with the Flying Dutchman, took 3rd and 4th places.

It was the very experienced American, Augie Diaz, who carried off the Kiel week honours. But his tiny winning margin was achieved only in the last race shead of Marc Bouet, who seemed to have the title in his pocket. Augie and Marc have both come to the Flying Dutchman from the 470 class, a graduation which like that of the Laser to the Finn, explains how more and more world champions are emerging from the very popular small boat classes.

Immediately after Kiel week, the World Championships were held in the same waters. To the surprise of most observers, the French pair Marc Bouet and Thierry Poirey werre the winners. It is worth pointing out that these young lads from Nantes only took up **the class in the previous year. The speed of** their graduation to the upper ranks has surprised even themselves. In fact, they didn't think they were really ready for top level competition and didn't expect to be in line for major titles until 1980. Marc, the tall quiet one, who has already won national titles in the 470 and 505 classes over the last 10 years, and Thierry, the athletic blond one who has only recently taken up sailing, often did badly on their first beats, but then careered through the fleet under spinnaker, astonishing their rivals, who just could not maintain the same rhythm and balance. They beat the Spaniard Abascal by a whisker. He was the worthy winner of 3 **races when the wind blew reasonably hard, but** he could not do so well in the light airs of the first races. Abascal's crew, the gentle giant Miguel Noguer, was rather sad. Just like the Spaniards, the Vollebreght brothers, who finished third, came close to the victory which is just about the only thing missing from their roll of honour which contains so many other successes. For certain competitors, this regatta seems to be a beautiful siren cajoling sailors towards hera only to trick them at the last moment. One day the bell will ring for both Alejandro and Erik.

Erik and Sjoerd, who really put on their finest performance at Tallinn, carried off a victory that they must surely hope is a premonition for the future ; they would very much like to repeat this success on the same waters in 1980. They would dearly love to pin that medal in the right place – and we're not talking

about a jacket or even a vest. At Tallinn the Dutch twins managed to avoid the inevitable bad choice of course and they were always in touch with the ex-World Champions of the Flying Dutchman class, the East German pair Steingross and Schramme. These two were at the top of the table right through the week and took it into a dramatic battle for the final title in the last race, which was contested in light airs.

Pages 158-159. *Double Olympic champion Rodney Pattison gives Russian Leonov a good fight.*
Left-hand page, above. *World vice-champions Spaniards Alejandro Abascal and Miguel Noguer are great in a breeze, not quite so strong in light airs.*
Below. *Fighting around the buoy with Pattison, the German brothers Albert and Rudy Batzill gained a great first at Hyères and a third at Kiel.*
Opposite middle. *Dutchman Erik Vollebreght, best of the season with his twin Sjoerd, winners in particular at Tallinn.*
Above, right. *American Augie Diaz carried off Kiel Week, thanks to his F.D. experience and crew Mark Reynolds.*
Below. *Frenchman, Marc Bouet, a graduate from the 470 like Augie Diaz, became World Champion with Thierry Poirey in his second season on the Flying Dutchman.*

Tornado

The return of Reg White, the great white wolf

The Hyeres races were an oustanding success for the German Tornado teams. It was a mere formality for Tobias Neuhann and Herbert Plenk, the European Champions of the class, who finished the 5th race freewheeling over the line standing up on one hull of their catamaran, far ahead of the 2nd placed boat steered by their compatriots Spengler and Heinimann and Ettl and Visslamber. It was unnecessary for them even to go out for the last race, and that left the door open for the Russians, who were going ever more quickly, Jakov Kliver and Sergej Vegelev, solid winners of the last breezy race. There were fewer unknowns in the Tornado class than in any of the other boats sailing at Weymouth week. And yet an American, the Californian Randy Smith, won it. And with a production boat, although it should be pointed out that it was made by Reg White. Of course it is difficult to sail at Weymouth in a Tornado without coming up against a White boat. Reg, the master, the top winner of the lot in the Olympic catamaran which he knows better than anyone (hasn't he been building Tornados since they were first designed and didn't he take an active part in that

design 17 years ago ?). He is still the king at 44 years of age, and he came back into competition after voluntarily stepping down for a while. And then there is also Rob White, his son, who burns to be the best Englishman and certainly would be if his father didn't show him the way home with monotonous regularity.

Bret de Thier and Stephen Moffat came halfway around the world to win Kiel week by a nose and snatch away the title from the World Champion, the Russian Victor Potapov. Sailing or rugby, which is the top sport in New Zealand, a country whose international renown owes quite a lot to its sporting endeavour ? You must always take good account of any Kiwis in a tough international regatta. As a nation of pioneers who nowadays cover the oceans to search for victory on sailing waters, they are experts in the Ton Cups, in dinghies and of course in the Tornado.

The Kiel breeze came like a special blessing upon Reg White so that he could recapture his old title of World Champion when there was very little wind. His new plastic-hulled Tornado seemed to have little advantage over the classically constructed boats ; in any case Reg isn't really at ease in this kind of weather. In a blow, on the other hand, Reg White still keeps and shows all his superb skill and concentration, thrusting forward like the battler that he is, shoulders hunched to meet the flying spray which shoots towards him faster and harder than on any other Tornado. Tunnel (all his Tornados are called Tunnel) whips along, its bow well down. On the trapeze Steve Olle, 18 years old, does almost as well as the perfect Tornado crew, John Osborn. Out on the open water, at the height of the wind, Reg and Steve constantly push forward their infernal machine ; who could possibly overcome them in

these conditions ? Reg's tactical skill is immense and had an awful lot to do with his recapture of this title. Another facet of his personality is his tenacity. That, added to his experience and his knowledge of the limits of his craft, all contributed to this world championship success. The highlight probably came in the 3rd race, when he managed to finish in 7th place with one tiller broken, one hull taking water, after the boat had been in collision at high speed with a piece of driftwood floating between the waves.

The 1978 World Champion in the Tornado class, Victor Potapov, has never been so dominant as he was at the Olympic regatta in Tallinn. Of all the winners in the different classes, he appeared to be the most certain. He also appeared to be the only one who knew which side of the course to choose all the time, a vital decision for success in these waters. Mystifyingly quick in light airs, he was less convincing in the stronger and more erratic breezes – conditions which were much better suited to the Germans, Spengler and Schmall. These two put together their old successful partnership for this regatta. Third were White and Olle, ahead of the top class Brazilians, Axel Welter and Bjorkstrom, who turned out to be remarkably at ease in the Baltic, even if they were rather suspect in their tactical approach.

Reg White, the great white wolf, has certainly made a success of his return to the Tornado class. He took the World Cup, finishing ahead of Potapov and Spengler. And all this before he chose to put his latest Tunnel into the water.

Pages 162-63. *Englishmen Rob White-Johnson and the duel of Danes Due-Kjoergerd come up together in the breeze.*
Left page, above. *American Randy Smyth takes Red White's boat and wins at Weymouth.*
Below. *We're off. Reg White, with 18 years old Steve Olle, is again World Champion.*
Above, right. *Buddy Melges, World Champion.*
Below. *Italians Giorgio Gorla and Albio Peraboni, the most consistent in the 1979 results.*

Star
When the Americans are away, the Europeans can play

At the start of the season, the Russian Valentin Mankin made a big impact on Hyeres Week. All through the previous year he had dominated the Stars in his own class. And here it was starting all over again !... After two hazardous first races, Valentin and his giant crew man, Alexandre Muzitschenko, chalked up victories enough to cancel out any danger from the Squadra de Vela, the Italian sailing team which was headed at Hyeres by Flavio Scala. He finished 2nd. Mankin also finished well ahead of those terrible Gorosteguis, the Spaniards who had moved up from the 470 class where they had been top of the pile. Antonio and Victor Gorostegui, were always able to produce marvellous boat speed when it was necessary in a Soling or a 470 or even a Star. Also worth remembering about Hyeres was the astonishing debut of the Swiss sailor Heinz Maurer who conceded 2 races only when the well-oiled technique and tactical skill of Mankin took over.

At Weymouth, the Star fleet was thin and the strongest team was a non-English one – that of the Spanish Gorosteguis. Unfortunately for the British, the Gorosteguis were easy winners ahead of the British hope David Bowlett who, having given up the Finn for the Star, seemed to have lost some of his aggression, even if he hasn't lost his talent. He needs now to rediscover his technical mastery of a boat which is difficult to control precisely, and that seems to be his problem. Behind him the next to finish were 2 other Englishmen, two helmsmen who have known their hour of glory in the Olympics, Iain MacDonald-Smith and Alan Warren.

A strange result to Kiel week, because the Canadians Paul Louie and Chuck Lawson, who train on the West Coast of the continent at Vancouver, regularly had the better of the Italians Giorgio Gorla and Albio Peraboni. The performance of this pair shows the admirable strength and depth of a richly-endowed Italian team. We haven't heard the last of them yet.

The World Championship of the Star class was staged at Gothenburg, in Sweden, and it saw the arrival on the scene of several new actors. Stealing the limelight from everybody else was the old master Buddy Melges from America, who put up a tremendously impressive series and carried off the title for the 2nd consecutive time, in racing which was spoilt by light airs. Buddy never leaves his Wisconsin home, except on the really big occasion to sail on really top-performing boats or when the competition is so intense that it makes the enjoyment of the racing exceptional. The outstanding gifts of this American have been shown in the Soling class and the Star from time to time. They have been carefully nurtured over a long period in competition with the very best American yachtsmen in all sorts of sailing boats, from Olympic classes up to maxi-raters. At Gothenburg the personal intervention of Buddy Melges seemed to be very helpful to his compatriots. He certainly made plenty of friends amongst them, because out of the whole series the 2nd and 3rd places also went to American teams ; Wright-Cozzens and Buchan-Knight. This was a sad disappointment for the Swedes, Sundelin and Pelle Petterson, the man who will be challenging for the America's Cup at the tiller of Sverige. Likewise a disappointment for Peraboni.

Valentin Mankin, after his victory at Hyeres

week, disappeared from the scene. Is he in decline ? Probably not. His performance at the Olympic regatta at Tallin showed a definite return to form. On the Estonian waters of the Baltic it needed one of those invincible Americans and a tenacious Italian to beat him. William Buchan was the man of the hour. He has the face of a Jack London hero and the ungainly walk of a Hemingway.

But he has already been Star World Champion twice before, in 1960 and 1970, which indicates both his skill and his persistence, because he has an incredible experience accumulated over the years in nerves and muscles. And he certainly knows how to get the best out of the sleek lines of a modern Star. The tenacious Italian was Giorgio Gorla, who put together a very good series, in a boat which was not significantly faster then any other downwind, but was able to take advantage of the slightest shift on the beats to make him the victor and all the others also-rans.

So is Mankin really going down ? We shall see next year. He finished the season just as well as he started it – victoriously. He took the European Championship convincingly. This triumph was especially merited because it was acquired despite the fact that his rudder broke in one race. But he has several European challengers who dream of some day overtaking the master ; particularly the Italians Flavio Scala and Mauro Testa and Giorgio Gorla and Alfio Peraboni.

As in the 470 class, the World Cup went this year to the Star sailor showing more consistency than outright victories. On this point there are two observations which apply to all the series ; and all the classes, really. Firstly, all the regattas considered for the award of this trophy took place in Europe, that is to say, outside the normal sphere of the Americans. One the other hand, one must also remember that all the regattas are given the same value.

Previous pages. *A close race between Briton Alan Warren and Spaniards Antonio and Victor Gorostegui, as much at ease in Star as in 470 or Soling.*
Above. *Canadian Paul Louie from Vancouver, first at Kiel Week with crew Chuch Lawson.*
Below. *Other than Melges-Josenhans, the Americans have formidable representatives in Buchan-Knight.*

Soling

A toughly fought series

The Swiss Navy rules the wawes ; in the Soling class that is, and the waves of the Mediterranean during Hyeres week. Despite two breakages in the middle of the championship, the Swiss Jean-François Gorminbeuf was able to bang on to his lead acquired with some very consistent performances, ahead of the always-talented and difficult to beat Englishman Phil Crebbin. In fact Crebbin was only beaten by a disqualification and the Russian Boris Budnikow was not far behind.

The French Helmsman Patrick Haegeli went to Britain to find success at Weymouth. It was a high point in a mixed year, for the veteran Parisian took part in all the classics of the class during the season.

At Kiel week it was necessary for everybody to know the meaning of starboard, no matter what language they spoke, beacause that was the word shouted by all the best Soling helmsmen there. In the lead, the American Robert Haines, who took command of the whole regatta right from the start. He beat the Australian John Bertrand, the former Champion of the World in both Lasers and Finns (and, confusingly, the man with the same name as the Californian star of the Finns today). The 3rd man very difficult to beat at Kiel, even though he was disqualified in one race, and threatened by Budnikov and the Canadian Peter Hall, is none other than Buddy Melges, the versatile helmsman who has already been commended for his brilliance in the chapter on the Star class in this review of the 1979 season in Olympic boats.

After Kiel, Visby in Sweden was the scene of the World Championship. Something unusual these days, the Soling fleet was required to make some really flying starts, and cope with some very variable winds. In fact the crews were given plenty to do and fortunes changed rapidly. The Danes took the lead to start with, first Bandolowski and then Jensen. Then it was the turn of the Swede Stig Wennerstrom followed by a Brazilian, Vincent Brun, brother of the World Champion from 1978. But the ultimate triumph went to the Californian Robert Haines, 25 years old, who led all the way on the last race. Bobby Haines left Paul Jensen some way behind, a significant shift, considering that Jensen seemed to be the man to beat in this class after his victory at Kingston in 1976.

At Tallinn the Australian Mark Bethwaite seemed to be certain of victory on the eve of the last race. But unfortunately there was very little wind for the final clash. The wind took a long time coming, the hours went by, the wind turned and then it died. Is the start on ? Yes. No. Yes. It turned out to be a triumph for the German Willy Kuhweide who just managed to clinch overall victory with this result. So it was a disastrous regatta for Bethwaite, who has previously represented Australia in the Flying Dutchman class and was left grasping at the fickle winds for some solid recompense for his efforts. The German Richter finished 3rd, sailing the boat which used to belong to Below. It has a blood red hull and it still glides through the water just as quickly as it did when it was first launched 5 years ago.

The very consistent performances of the Frenchman Haegeli at the maximum number of European Soling regattas was rewarded with the World Cup. Haines was second. But one must remember that if the American continent was a bit closer to Europe things would be a bit different. □

Top. *West German Kuhweide snatched the victory from Australian Betwaite in the last lap at Tallinn.*
Above. *Danes Jensen-Theis-Flemming, second in the Soling World championships, remain prospects for the series.*
Opposite, right. *American Robby Haines can smile, he won with no problems in the world championships at Kiel Week.*
Pages 170-171. *the Solings re-group under spinnaker.*

Women's World Sailing Championship

A rough trip in the breeze

by Dave Perry

September 7th-15th, Rochester, USA.

The second IYRU Women's World Sailing Championship was held from Sept. 5-15, 1979, at the Rochester Yacht Club, located on the southern shore of Lake Ontario. 90 women representing 17 different countries took part in the singlehanded and doublehanded classes.

The courses were Olympic and varied from 7-9 miles in length. Due to left-over hurricane activity to the south, the winds were predominantly strong with only one race sailed in below 10 knots. The races were professionally run by the Michelob/USYRU Mobile Race Management Team, under the direction of Larry Johnson, and though the schedule called for only one race a day, most of the competitors were still completely exhausted by the end of the regatta.

In the Lasers, the Swedish, U.S., and Canadian teams placed well. Canadians Judy Lugar, Karen McRae and Annette Henderson finished eleventh, ninth and seventh respectively. For the U.S. Susie Pegel, Betsy Gelenitis and Lynne Jewell finished twelfth, fifth and fourth. Aiko Inoue from Japan jumped from 22nd last year to finish 6th this year. And last year's runner-up, Vanessa Dudley from Australia, finished third.

The most impressive showing was from the Swedish team, whose only two entrants in the regatta finished first and second in the Lasers, and only 0,7 points apart. In the last race Gunilla Berg was leading and Marit Söderstrom had to fight back from fifth to third to capture the championship. Marit is 17 years old. She stands 5'6" and weighs 135 lbs. This was her first major regatta in Lasers, being more familiar

with the Europe Moth. Her boat handling was superb, her tactics conservative and her speed good enough to hang in there. But her winning edge was her endurance, and she simply out-hiked the rest of the fleet.

In the 420s it was a two-boat battle right from the first race. Defending Champions Cathy Foster and Wendy Hilder from Great Britain shipped their Rondar hull over from England

and were using Musto & Hyde sails. U.S. Champions Nell Taylor and Charlotte Lewis were using a Vanguard hull with North sails. Throughout the series Nell and Charlotte showed better boat speed and upwind tactics, while Cathy and Wendy showed far superior team work and good downwind tactics. The pattern was for Nell to lead at the first mark, but fall prey to some team work flaw which Cathy would quickly capitalize on. Then, once ahead, Cathy would stay ahead on the runs and cover up the final beat. In fact it wasn't until the fifth race of the series that Nell and Charlotte sailed a flawless race to break Cathy's string of firsts. The two teams chose not to sail the last race, as their positions were solid, while those of their teammates were not.

Going into the sixth race, five boats could have conceivably ended up with a third overall, indicating the closeness of the racing behind the two leaders. The wind was 18-20 knots and the team of Sandy Ray and Carolyn Brodsky from the U.S. zoomed out into the lead. Dianne Groome and Charlotte de Heinrich were second, with two British women close behind. Up the last beat, Sandy's rudder bolt fell out forcing her to withdraw. This gave third overall to the British team of Mimie Currey and Jill Blake, put Sandy and Carolyn in fourth, and Dianne and Charlotte finished fifth. Jan and Pat O'Malley, from Mantoloking, N.J. finished only three points back in seventh. □

Swedes Marit Soderström (above) *and Gunilla Berg* (lower left), *first and second in the 1979 single-handed, and British crew Foster-Hilder* (below), *who carried off the doubles.*

Australia

A prelude to Olympics

by Peter Campbell

One of Australia's major problems in reaching and maintaining a top level of success in international yacht racing is distance. Distance from the major yacht racing nations of the world, particularly the Northern Hemisphere countries, but also the distances between the major yacht racing centres of the continent of Australia.

Thus the annual KB Olympic Regatta held each Easter is an event of major significance to yachtsmen who sail the Olympic classes. It brings them together at one sailing venue for one of the few times of the year, the only other time being when Australian national championships are held. Some may have to tow their boats as far as 3500 km overland.

The KB Olympic Regatta is also the major event where an Australian team of top sailors is chosen to go overseas each year to compete in world championships and international regattas.

This year's KB Regatta, held on Lake Macquarie, a coastal seawater lake about 80 km north of Sydney, had special significance in that it was used, along with results from national championships, to select a team of 24 yachtsmen, two crews from each of the six Olympic classes, to form Australia's Pre-Olympic yachting team – an important step towards selection in the 1980 Olympic group.

In 1979 the Australian Olympic Federation, supported by funds from brewers Tooth & Company and the class associations as well as donations from yacht clubs and individual yachtsmen, is spending $A 95,000 on sending the Pre-Olympic team overseas to compete in major international regattas such as Kiel Week, Travemunde Week, the Helsinki Open, the world championships for the Olympic classes in Europe, and finally the Baltic Regatta at Tallinn, Estonia, venue for the 1980 Olympic yachting.

From there they will come back to Australia's summer sailing season of 1979-80, a season of intense competition which will climax with the 1980 KB Olympic Regatta from which will be chosen the Olympic team for Tallinn. The selection trials will be sailed on Botany Bay, Sydney, and on Lake Macquarie with the theme « bring back the gold ».

In fact, the high level of competition at the 1979 Australian Olympic Regatta and the subsequent results in Europe augur well for Australia's prospects at Tallinn, particularly in the Soling, Tornado and Star classes. At Kingston, Canada, in 1976, Australians won bronze medals in the Finn and 470 dinghy classes and were unlucky not to win a medal in the Tornado class. At Kiel, Germany, in 1972 they won gold medals in the Dragon and Star classes.

The seven race series, spread over six days including the Easter weekend, was one of the most closely-fought Olympic regattas held in Australia, with less than two points – in practice, one place in the final race – determining the winners in four of the six classes.

The Solings and Stars provided champagne racing – spectacular starts, brilliant tactical sailing to windward, fine spinnaker work, and frequently race finishes with the margins a matter of a boat length or less. The end result in the Solings was a winning margin of .9 of a point, and in the Stars 1.7 points. In the Tornado class only one point separated first and second.

David Forbes, who won the gold medal in the Stars when the class was last in the Olympics – at Kiel in 1972 – won top place in the Pre–Olympic team with a narrow, one-place victory over local Lake Macquarie yachtsman Tim Owens who represented as a crew in the Stars at Tokyo in 1964. Forbes now has his 23 years old son, Stephen, sailing with him.

Two members of the 1976 team which went to Canada fought out the Soling – Mark Bethwaite, who sailed in the Flying Dutchman at Kingston, and John Bertrand, who won a bronze medal in the Finns. After a dramatic start to the regatta when both lost their placings in the first heat after finishing first and second across or the line – for rule infringements – they had to fight all the way to reach the top two positions. In the end, Bethwaite, sailing Terror, won top spot by less than one point from Bertrand, sailing his new Abbott boat, Odds-n-Ends.

The closest result of the regatta was in the 470s which was also the largest fleet. Going into the final heat any one of five competitors could have won, but the experienced Sydney sailmaker Gary Gietz and his crew Greg Johns, both of whon played a vital role as part of the support group in Canada, topped off their Australian championship win by winning by .4 of a point from young West Australian, Rod Beurteaux. Beurteaux finished second in the 1978 World Youth Championships in the 420 dinghy.

Another member of the 1976 Olympic team, Western Australian Brian Lewis, faced one of his race championship defeats in the Tornado catamaran class. Lewis, who finished fourth in the 1976 Olympics after losing a mast in a vital race, clinched the series by point and one place in the final heat. The man who almost beat him was Queenslander Keith Hunter who bought and se up a Tornado built by Lewis. He sails as crew and tactician with Denis Kelly steering.

In the Flying Dutchman class, that demanding, high-performance centreboarder, 38 years old Carl Ryves made a remarkable comeback to comfortably take out the double of the Australian championship and the Olympic Regatta. Ryves, who now has James Cook as crew, represented Australia in the Flying Dutchman class at the Mexico Olympics in 1968.

Skipper of the runner-up in the FDs, Andy Allsep, another veteran sailor also got the nod in the Pre-Olympic team for Europe.

Victorian Keith Patterson was the only helmsman who was in a position to pack up his boat after six heats, scoring a comfortable victory in the Finns. Patterson is a newcomer to the Olympic scene but the second Finn skipper in the team, Geoff Davidson, the Australian national champion from Sydney was the support Finn skipper in Canada.

Manager of the Pre-Olympic yachting team is former world 505 champion and two-time president of the Australian Yachting Federation, John Parrington, of Adelaide. The Olympic coach is John Cuneo from Brisbane who won the gold medal in the Dragon class at the 1972 Olympics at Kiel, Germany. He is a widely experienced sailor in many classes, from Flying Dutchman to 12-metres. Tim Alexander, the meteorological adviser, was crew for Mark Bethwaite in the FDs at the 1972 and 1976 Olympics and in 1978 won the Pacific Laser championship. □

Above. *Keith Hunter and Dennis Kelly. Tornado, Soling and Star are the three classes where the Australians have the best chances at the Olympic Games in 1980.*

Following pages. *The Sydney bridge is the back-ground for this Australian 18-footer.*

What can be next in windsurfing ?

by Alastair Black and Gilles Pernet

A million ? Even more ? Just how many people have experienced surf board sailing along the coasts of Europe ? From Kiel to Gibraltar, taking in all the inland waters on the way, you might well have been able to count even more than that last summer.

Introduced to Europe just five years ago, the sailing surfboard has seen an extraordinarily rapid expansion - unique in the field of leisure activities. Paradoxically, this happy invention from Califonia, has not been the centre of such a spectacular growth in its country of origin. Invented by Hoyle Schweitzer and Jim Drake at the end of the sixties, the Windsurfer failed to take off for some time, and even four years after its invention nobody could have predicted the extraordinary explosion of interest. In fact, for Schweitzer and his friends a sailing surfboard was something of a stopgap. Madly enthusiastic surfers, they couldn't bear to stay ashore on those days when the sea was too flat for real surfing. Even though it caught on elsewhere, board sailing in the United States was to remain the joy of a select few at any rate, until 1979.

In contrast to the United States, the Windsurfer was not protected by a patent registration in France, and it was the commercial enterprise of the various manufacturers which played a big part in the unusually rapid growth of sailing surfboards there. It seems likely that the first European Windsurfer imported was to Germany. In France, Charles Daher, a boat chandler from Marseilles, was the pioneer. It happened that a German on holiday on the Cote d'Azur was disinclined to hump his plaything all the way back to Germany : Daher bought it.

" To start with, we didn't really know how to sail it ' says Nano Dubout, one of the very best board sailors in France. We put in several weeks of practice before we even began to make any progress. At one time we actually thought we were short of some parts which might make it easier to sail the diabolical machine.

At that moment we really believed that board sailing would be limited to very sheltered waters, such as inside a port, and that it would only be done in very light winds. Everyone seemed to find our constant capsizes very amusing ". But the board sailing techniques suddenly improved. And so did the commercial exploitation of the idea. Though there wasn't a single one on show at the Paris Boat Show in 1973, by 1979 the January exhibition at La Defense saw no less than 60 different manufacturers peddling their wares. In France, Patrick Carn, with Charles Daher, was one of the first to break new ground and launch the Windsurfer. In less than five years the whole scene has changed enormously.

By the end of 1978, there were about 40 000 sailing boards made in France. And even though the figures for this past summer are not yet collated, it seems likely that the total number of boards has doubled during 1979 alone. Nowa-days everybody seems to be into making sailing boards. Undoubtedly the most impressive example is Dufour of France. This boat yard, which normally specialises in cruising yachts, launched a new board on the market with a first year production of 12 000 units. It should be mentioned that Dufour has been bought by Marcel Bich, the man behind the various French challengers for the America's Cup, and the industrialist who made his name through the Bic ballpoint pens and throwaway razors. However, sales figures of boards do not correspond to the number of people who go board sailing. In fact, it's quite possible that any one board would be used by all the members of the family. And then you have to remember all the schools for board sailing on every beach around the coats.

A rule was introduced in 1978 to allow owners of different makes of board to compete together on equal terms. This rule, called the A or Open rule, limits the overall length of a board to 3,9 metres, with a maximum beam of 600 centimetres and a minimum weight of 18 kilos beneath a maximum sail area of 6,3 square metres. This Open rule was quickly adopted throughout Europe. To even out the chances for everyone, classes for featherweight, light, medium, light heavyweight and heavyweight – plus a series for women – were also introduced. At world level, the Americans, and particularly the Hawaiians, are the masters, especially in heavy weather. Matt Schweitzer, Mike Waltze and Ken Winner are among the best of the bunch, but Robby Naish is still the idol. Unbeaten champion of the world for three years running, this blond youngster of just 16 simply wiped the floor with everyone else at the first world championship organised in the Bahamas. He was just as far ahead of the pack the next year in Sardinia and still beating them all at Mexico in 1978. Just when the European board sailors reckoned that they had caught up with the crack Hawaiian stars, they discovered at Cancun, in Yucatan, that they still had an awful lot to learn.

In the old world, a board sailing event remains close to the traditions of conventional sailing regattas. But for the Americans, the board sailer is still a marvellous plaything with plenty of undiscovered potential. Robby Naish goes out in weather conditions which would put off even the bravest surfers. And the sailing board has led to the evolution of new disciplines and tests such as leaps off rollers, long distance races, free-style sailing and even football matches on boards.

Those who went to the recent events in Hawaii came back with a tremble in their voices every time they spoke about what they had seen. In March 1979, the Pan An Windsurfer World Cup took place on the island of Oahu, in Hawaii, to provide competitive conditions for those young spirits of the sport who are filled with the joy of their new craft.

In the week before the Cup, the regular north-west trade winds blew perfectly. The early arrivals had plenty of opportunities for pratice – especially leaping off waves and surfing under sail around famous Diamond Head.The breakers there form up to just the right height – about five or six feet – and the wind blows steadily enough to hurtle the boards across or off the top of the waves.

But those very same trade winds changed into light breezes from the south-west. The whole series was reduced to nothing, with the exception of one day, when Robby Naish won both the races. The minimum 15 knots of wind required didn't appear for the rest of the week. The 75 contestants just didn't have a chance to show their talents in the conditions. Just the same, during the days preceding the races, it was possible to capture on film the new vogue for leaping a surfboard off the waves. With the latest Windsurfer Rocket and Naish Mistral boards, specially designed for competition and wave jumping, we were witnessing the beginnings of a new era. These boards have a mast step and a dagger board as well as twin ailerons. They are also equipped with straps over the sailor's feet so that he can stick to the board and control it. As a result, he remains in touch with his craft, no matter what happens – over the top of the waves as well as in the surf. But look out if you fancy having a go – this is not a sport for beginners. If you happen to have the right sort of board and breaking rollers in which to practice, go gently. The feet need to be rapidly withdrawn from the straps – and you need very quick reflexes – if ever you are overturned by the waves or if your board is thrust up into the air out of control by the fierce winds.

There isn't – yet – a handbook showing how to make flights into the air and leaps off waves in ten easy lessons. It's the result of infinite practice wedded to natural talent. Ask Robby Naish, the undisputed master of the art of board sailing, how he does his fantastic leaps without apparent effort. He'll tell you that he just does this or that and it happens – that's because for him the sailing board is a natural sport and he doesn't even have to think about it.

Just look at these pictures of the masters of the art, most of them Hawaiians. They will give you a good idea of the latest techniques of board sailing. But more than that, they will convey the enormous sense of fun which permeates the whole sport.

What are the sailing ideas of this new generations of board sailors ? To give you some idea, they have started calling conventional sailing boards " cruisers " ; the little boards (about ten feet long) for fun in the rollers, are called " Go-karts ", and the boards for leaping waves are called " rockets ". Have a good time, with your dreams of matching them ! □

Outboard Races

The European Season

by Ray Bulman

24 heures de Rouen

April 30th – May 1st 1979, France.

The European season always opens in Rouen in France on April 30/May 1 with the famous 24 Hours Marathon. The event is limited to outboard powered craft under 850cc and, because they are thought to have less performance and reliability, inboard engines of 2,000cc are also eligible. It was this latter factor which proved the exception to the rule in 1978.

The 1978 Rouen 24 Hours confirmed two issues ; one, that a well prepared inboard engine can hold its own in an outboard powered fleet ; and the other that immaculate preparation of craft and crew – more common at motor race fixtures – is the answer to eventual success, regardless of problems suffered in the course of an event. No driver is more professional than Italian Renato Molinari. Not only are his craft and engines impeccably prepared, his attitude to the sport is totally professional. In this respect any team led by Molinari is in a class of its own and makes all the others look the rank amateurs which they generally are.

These factors were in evidence in Rouen when a team consisting of Angelo Vassena, Augusto Panzeri and Ettore Cagnani led by Molinari himself, achieved outstanding success. Despite being hampered with mechanical problems for the first six hours when they

slipped back almost 28 laps behind the leader, their perseverance in resolving their mechanical failures – where many would have conceded defeat – and determination to prove their engine and hull, saw them through. They drove a Molinari catamaran in Class R3 (Racing Inboard 1,500 – 2,000cc), and what was a completely new venture for the Molinari stable, used an Abarth tuned fuel-injected Fiat inboard engine instead of the outboard normally associated with this prime Italian team.

Their victory was decisive. They crossed the finishing line 42 laps ahead of Frenchmen Jean-Pierre Masurier and Bernard Balkou who took second place in a Mercury-powered OE Class (Racing Outboard 700-850cc) French built Cormorant.

Inboard engines have not seen success for

some years in Rouen, and although its capacity was over twice the largest outboard in the line-up, this Fiat-powered outfit had a performance far ahead of any outboard competitor. The Italians not only annihilated the outboard competition, they achieved their victory against tremendous odds.

The winners completed 536 circuits of the Ile Lacrox which forms the centre piece of the River Seine course. They averaged 49.84mph (80.40kph) for the 24 Hours and when one considers that Molinari and his team lost several hours while their engine problems were being cleared up, this average was achieved in well under the programmed duration and included the fatigue of driving through the hours of darkness. The next craft to finish, a Mercury powered OE Class Gardin driven by Frenchmen Jacky Mohamedi and Albert Izard finished 52 laps behind the winners, representing an incredible 130 kilometres lead for Molinari over this third placing.

The Italians led the 43 boat fleet from the start and were actually 12 seconds ahead of their nearest rival at the end of their first 2 min. 20 sec. lap. Within thirty minutes however their engine was to suffer overheating problems causing the first of many pit stops over the following six hours. It was at this point that an Argentinian team, which had performed so well in Rouen twelve months earlier, went ahead.

The performance of this Mercury powered OE Class craft, known as an SSB, and built locally in Argentina, was also outstanding. Driven by brothers German and Fernando Barbo who shared the driving with Carlos Garcia Montes, it soon built up a ten lap lead over the second boat – a position it held for seven hours. It was an unscheduled pit stop to change a propeller which lost them ground. This was the moment that Frenchmen Jacky Mohamedi and Albert Izard were waiting for. They took complete advantage of the Argentinians pit stop and moved to the head of the fleet.

Just before midnight – some eight hours after the start – the Fiat mechanics from Italy eventually solved the fault on Molinari's engine. It appeared to be associated with a freshwater cooling system and with this rectified, the Italians made a determined effort to catch up.

They lay eighth overall, 28 laps behind Mohamedi and Izard. Even though the Argentinians were back in the race and frantically trying to maintain a safe distance ahead of the Italian threat, they were dogged with further trouble. Their craft capsized when a crane malfunctioned as it lifted the boat out of the water for a second pit stop. This cost them 45 minutes and relegated the crew to a position where they had no hope of improvement.

Mohamedi and Izard were given a further three hours of supremacy before Molinari and his team began snapping at their stern. The final

blow for these Frenchmen came when the steering on the boat failed, opening up the way for Molinari. He took the lead in the early hours of May 1st and never looked back.

There was little other competitors could muster against such a formidable performance. Rain settled in in the early daylight, but the Italian craft with its mechanical problems now solved, was playing with the fleet. By 10 am – six hours before the finish – they were over 30 laps ahead of the nearest challenger while the gallant Argentinian crew had fallen to ninth, some 78 laps astern. Not being content with this lead, Renato Molinari, taking his turn behind the wheel, set a new lap record for the course of 74mph (118.8kph) totally disheartening the remaining drivers.

All categories receive class awards but nothing could draw the attention of the huge number of spectators from the overall leader. The honour of driving the craft across the finishing line at 4 p.m. went to Renato Molinari himself, after one of the best demonstrations of top class powerboating seen for many years. □

Pages 186-187. The winners-to-be push on through the night.
Left-hand page, top. In the lead for seven hours, the Argentine racers Barbot and Montès were forced to stop to change a propeller.
Below. An overheating 2-litre Fiat engine slowed Molinari down for 28 laps at the start of the race.
Opposite, top to bottom. Jean-Pierre Masurier was second with Bernard Balkou in the Cormorant/Mercury.
Mohamedi and Izard, third overall in their Gardin/Mercury, side by side with Favede-Romangas in their Barracuda/Johnson.
There was a camera aboard !
Under. A popular success.

A dual to the death

The last two years have seen a steady rise in the support for serious championships. Such championships particularly appeal to the works team managers, a constant points battle throughout the season holding a far greater attraction for the media. Serious championships of this type can result in a great deal of publicity and thus the privately entered driver keen to gain notoriety for his sponsor, also joins the competition. The calender of the Union Internationale Motonautique (UIM) still shows one day sprint championships but such competitions are slowly dying out.

The idea of a world series championship on the lines of motor racing was suggested to the UIM as long ago as 1973 but instead of being received with enthusiasm the proposal was passed over and in its place an experimental series – later known as the European Endurance Championship – was introduced. Unfortunately by then the UIM was out of touch with the commercial side of the sport.

The European Endurance Championships had heats of mixed duration but none less than 3 hours. They could be split into two 1 1/2 hour heats over à two-day meeting, but unfortunately, most of the spectator public are unable to follow such long competitions. So, in 1977 (almost following the type of breakaway seen in motor racing and motor cycling) a professional public relations company stepped in.

This organization acted for Mercury Marine in Europe. They also handled several other accounts including Canon – the Japanese business machine company. Canon also make mini-computers and had produced the printed result sheets for several important powerboat fixtures. Canon soon became attracted to the sport, which they considered an untapped source of potential publicity.

Canon's publicity agents suggested they support a six heat championship. Management accepted and, in 1978, the Canon Trophy, as it became known, had its first full season. It was an immediate success. Although the European Endurance Championship still exists, it now gains little support. The Canon Series has completely taken over in status, and while the UIM recognises its existence, it is a first class example of how commercial thinking can benefit an exciting but expensive sport.

Mercury Marine decided to give the Canon Trophy their total backing in 1979. It would obviously gain maximum publicity and the very fact that Mercury was involved, forced the Outboard Marine Coporation (OMC) – who manufacture Evinrude and Johnson outboards – to support the series against their commercial competitors. The brand of engine which won the Canon Trophy was certain of an increased slice of the market.

Although UIM-approved races were chosen as heats in the Canon Series, the public relations company still held tight control over which six events would count for points.

Many lessons were learned in 1978. Some organisors insisted on races being 3 hours or more in length which was unacceptble to the Canon Series idea. Others with few spectators were also dropped. Exceptional events of long duration, but still attracting large spectator audiences and good media coverage – such as the Paris 6 Hour – were included.

The six heats in the 1979 Canon Series were : the British Embassy Grand Prix, the Casale Monferrato in Italy, Drammen in Norway, the Dutch Grand Prix in Amsterdam, the French Paris 6 Hour and the Grand Prix of Barcelona in Spain. Scoring was simple. It is based on the principles used in motor racing. Points are awarded down to sixth place with the winner taking nine. Whoever finishes the season with the greatest score, either from wins or high placings, takes the Canon Trophy and becomes unofficial European Champion.

The Canon Series is the only one of its type in the world and hence attracts all Formula I drivers including the top Americans.

The series is applicable to overall finishers. Therefore, as Formula I craft are the fastest, it il obvious that only these drivers will gain points when several categories compete alongside each other, as in Paris. This means that the championship organisors do not need to stipulate the type of craft taking part. For instance, if the factory teams decide to use engines of only two litres in Formula I and these craft finish at the head of the fleet, then it is these drivers who collect the points. On the other hand, should their boats compete in the OZ Unlimited category (2,000 cc-infin.), then these would obviously win overall again attracting points. But nothing exists for the Formula II craft, which usually finish further down the field.

OE (700-850 cc) and Sports Boat SE (700-850 cc) tend to be overshadowed in the Canon Series. Instead, these drivers still support the old traditional UIM one day sprint championships. The exception in Formula I in 1979 was the World Unlimited Sprint Championships for Class OZ.

The World OE Sprint Championships took place in Evian in France, while the OZ category was held two months later at Milan in Italy. This type of competition involves 4 x 10 lap heats and although it is probably the most exciting form of powerboat racing for the spectator, the competition is almost over before it begins and any competitor who suffers mechanical problems in the early stages has no chance of making up lost ground.

Embassy Grand Prix, Bristol

The Canon Series was once again by far the most popular Championship in 1979 and began with the British Embassy Grand Prix at Bristol in July – probably the world's foremost circuit event.

Although only Formula I OZ craft are eligible for the Canon Trophy, this did not deter a record entry of 119 craft from nine countries in this classic event. While these attracted a great deal of attention, the eyes of the top drivers were focused on the new Mercury engines which made their debut at Bristol.

Two Formula I boats were fitted with these monsters. One was driven by the previous 1978 winner, Billy Seebold of the United States, the other by fellow countryman and Mercury teammate Earl Bentz. He was not only competing at Bristol for the first time, but also set a new Bristol lap record with an incredible speed of 98.24 mph (158.10 kph) during practice. His performance confirmed two important factors : that high speeds are possible on this circuit – a fact doubted when Bristol was first inspected as a circuit in 1972 – and that the power produced by these new Mercury engines is enormous.

Earl Bentz in his Seebold catamaran led the first race from start to finish with his teammate, Billy Seebold, in an identical outfit second. There were just no other boats on the water to match their performance and they looked certain to gain maximum Canon points. The only close battle occurred further down the fleet between Birger Halsaa from Norway, in another Seebold but using a Mercury T3 racing outboard, and Britain's Tom Percival in a similar combination under the same Long John team colours as the overall leaders. But Percival moved into third place on the 14 th lap so making it Long John one, two and three.

One driver who seldom sees success at Bristol is Dutch Champion Cees Van der Velden. He was dogged with bad luck yet again in 1979. His Johnson-powered craft hit a bank at the end of the second lap and he spent the rest of the two-day meeting as a spectator.

The second Formula I race followed the pattern of the first, except that Bentz fell back in the eighth lap to let Seebold take the flag. The real excitement was again further down the field

when Italian ace, Renato Molinari in his Evinrude-powered Molinari – a name usually up at the front of big international meetings – lost his third slot to Britain's Bob Spalding in the Carlsberg-sponsored Johnson powered Velden.

Tom Percival was also not so lucky this time. His engine gave trouble from the start and he slowly slipped back to finish seventh overall. The final qualifying heat in the Canon Series at Bristol took place without Seebold or Bentz in the line-up. Earl Bentz had damaged his engine as he entered the pits after the second race. As he and Seebold had already qualified for the line-up in the Duke of York Trophy, there was little point in taking unnecessary risks.

The Duke of York Trophy was the finale of the two-day meeting and only those in Classes ON (1,500-2 cc) and OZ (2,000 cc-infin.) who set high placings in the three qualifying heats were eligible to join the line-up. Points in the Canon Series were therefore not easy to achieve at Bristol. It meant that drivers had to qualify for the points-attracting Duke of York Trophy by achieving high standards in the early events.

Bentz led the 13 qualifiers for the first lap and then, as predicted, Billy Seebold with the prototype Mercury went ahead where he stayed for the remaining 24 laps with his American teammate second.

Tom Percival held third slot for the first four laps before being passed by Renato Molinari, but the Italian's efforts were short-lived. The 12th lap saw him in the pits, where he withdrew completely from the competition. The only Outboard Marine Corporation (OMC) fight left came from Britain's Alf Bullen in his new Evinrude powered Molinari catamaran, but try as he might, he could not take Percival's third slot. Bullen actually fell back three laps before the finish to be overtaken by ex-World Champion Roger Jenkins in his Gordon's Gin Seebold – one of Britain's top six drivers. Even Jenkins found the Embassy weekend just too much of a challenge to make an impact.

For the second year in succession, Billy Seebold took the coveted Duke of York Trophy, thought to be worth £ 20,000 (41,000 US Dollars) and nine vital points in the Canon Series. With the type of craft at his disposal and an engine which was obviously the most powerful outboard in the world, Billy Seebold would be a tough driver to topple from his leading position in the remaining heats.

Casale Monferrato

The second qualifying race in the Canon Series was held at Casale Monferrato at the end of July. It consisted of 2 x 45 minute heats: spread over a two day meeting.

Page 190. *Roger Jenkins gave up his Cougar boats this year and started at Bristol with a brand new Seebold. Second in the Canon Trophy the season before, the British driver stayed in the frame (he was second at Amsterdam) but is still looking for his first outright victory.*
Page 191 above. *Peter Inward, seen here at the wheel of his Hodges-Mercury, is one of the few amateur European drivers in the OZ class.*
Below. *Bob Spalding, winner of the Canon Trophy in 1977 and 1978 with Mercury-powered boats, changed this year to the Johnson camp.*
Page 192. *Bill Seebold carries off the Embassy Grand Prix at Bristol. He was one of the leading contenders for the Canon Trophy.*
Opposite, top. *On the difficult Bristol course, the monohulled boats of the Open Class provide a mavellous high speed spectacle for 25 000 spectators.*
Opposite. *During one of the three Class OE races at Bristol – which were dominated by the English driver John Hill – Peter Derby lost control of his boat. Happily, he emerged unhurt.*

There were eight OZ craft in the first heat which was led from the start by Italian Renato Molinari competing on his home course. This time Mercury did not use their prototype engines which cost them the meeting. It was a decision they corrected for the season's following events.

For the first twenty minutes of the first heat, Dutchman Cees Van der Velden was the only driver capable of challenging Renato Molinari but he eventually retired into the pits with engine failure, leaving second place to his OMC teammate, Britain's Bob Spalding (Velden/Johnson).

The OMC outfits had the more powerful engines and a margin of one lap lead over the third place of Bill Seebold – who had driven so brilliantly at Bristol four weeks earlier– confirmed this fact.

The second race had almost the same outcome. Renato Molinari again led from the start with Cees Van der Velden hot on his heels and Bob Spalding third. The Mercury challenge relied entirely on Bill Seebold and Tom Percival; who failed to finish the first race because of mechanical problems.

The pace again proved too high for Cees Van der Velden and his boat was withdrawn with engine trouble which left Bob Spalding chasing after the Italian with little hope of victory. Tom Percival – now with his earlier mechanical trouble solved – had moved into third place as Bill Seebold slipped back to fourth. But ten minutes before the end, Spalding began losing power which allowed Tom Percival to pass into the third place.

This meeting was a complete disaster for Mercury Marine, and for the following heat in the Canon Series their team manager, Gary Garbrecht, made sure his drivers used the new Mercury racing engine.

Bill Seebold gained four Canon points for his efforts and these, coupled with the 9 he already held for winning the Duke of York Trophy, maintained his leading place. Renato Molinari collected 9 points but he had a zero score for

Bristol. He did not enter the following two events in Norway and Amsterdam and virtually gave up the challenge even though he lay third at this stage.

Drammen

The Norwegian event at Drammen on September 2nd resulted in another resounding victory for American Bill Seebold.

Driving his Long John OZ catamaran, he had no intention of repeating his performance at the Italian race and therefore used the new Mecury engine with its undisclosed power output. But the overall result was in doubt right up to the last of the four 20 minute heats. Seebold had to better the performance of his teammate Tom Percival, and Dutchman Cees Van der Velden behind the wheel of a Johnson powered craft of his own design. This he managed with spectacular ease, leaving second place for Tom Percival with fellow British driver Roger Jenkins, in the Mercury powered Gordon's Gin craft, pushing Spalding back into fourth place.

Cees Van der Velden made a spectacular start in the first race and drove his boat into a healthy lead with OMC teammate Bob Spalding second. Seebold crossed the starting line in last place but quickly moved through the field and on lap two was in third place chasing Spalding and passing him seven laps later. Once ahead of Spalding, Seebold continued to close on the leader gaining five seconds each lap, but the Dutchman managed to stay in front to finish just ahead of the American.

Conditions deteriorated for the second heat on the first day. Again Van der Velden headed the start this time with Seebold on his tail. Two laps later however Bill Seebold moved into the lead and in another two laps was almost 100 metres ahead when his throttle cable suddenly snapped. Tom Percival, who at that time was third, began chasing Velden and for the last two circuits these two were side by side until,

with only a few seconds of the race left to run, Percival crept by to take the chequered flag.

The third heat was held the following day. Conditions were misty but this did not deter the crowds : estimated in excess of 30,000. It was Bill Seebold's turn to lead from start to finish with Tom Percival in second place. Cees Van der Velden lying second pulled out at the halfway stage with engine trouble. Although he rejoined the race on the last lap, he had lost too much distance and his chances of victory were now slipping away. Bob Spalding finished third and Roger Jenkins fourth.

The fourth and final heat was held with very bad visibility and was again convincingly won by Billy Seebold. He was followed for the first four laps by Bob Spalding until Tom Percival – Seebold's teammate who was also using one of the new Mercury engines – crept by. Roger Jenkins later moved into that place relegating Bob Spalding to fourth.

Bill Seebold finished with 22 points to his credit while Bob Spalding and the hopes of the Outboard Marine Corporation (OMC), were second with 15 points.

Amsterdam

The Dutch Grand Prix in Amsterdam was held on September 15/16. It was Cees Van der Velden's home venue and, regardless of any tough competition in past years, he has always performed with distinction in this particular event. The Formula I racing again consisted of four heats : two held on each day.

As predicted, the race became Van der Velden's show. Driving his Johnson powered Velden catamaran, he finished first in three of the four 30 minute heats to take the major prize on points aggregate. Huge crowds were delighted to see him topple the competition offered by the Mercury Long John team when the Canon points leader Bill Seebold, began suffering mechanical problems after he won the first heat.

Mercury hopes rested with Seebold and Tom Percival. Percival, however, had a dramatic crash in the first heat and was lucky to escape with his life. This meant he was out of the competition for the rest of the meeting, and for the first time, the new Mercury engines began to show the effects of fatigue.

Britain's Roger Jenkins in the Gordon's Gin Seebold cat was also using a new Mercury but was no match for the Dutchman, and he finished the weekend in second slot. Bill Seebold was well down in the final placings but still managed to collect two points for fifth, and with his earlier high score of 22, maintained his leading position in the series.

What looked like a certainty for Seebold early in the season now depended on the outcome at Paris in October plus the result of the final race in Spain later that month.

Seebold was in a commanding position but with the falling reliability of the prototype Mercury, the driving ability of Cees Van der Velden could easily turn the tables.

The German Grand Prix in Berlin was not included in the 1979 series mainly because the organisors insisted on 2 x11/2 hour heats. This was not acceptable due to lack of excitement and spectator interest. It had been found in 1978 that a race of 11/2 hours was too long for the noninvolved enthusiast on the shore and the Berlin event was replaced in 1979 by the Spanish Grand Prix, whose organisors were willing to modify their heats in accordance with the Canon objectives.

World OE Championship

25 Formula II OE catamarans (700-850c) entered the World OE Sprint Championships at Evian at the end of July.

Evian on Lake Leman (Geneva) was the setting but its size was very vulnerable to changing surface conditions. Strong winds meant that the race was more akin to an offshore meeting than a competition for small high-speed lightweights. Conditions were not helped in the run-up to the first heat when several rescue boats drove across the circuit, creating an enormous wash. Two drivers, Britain's Andy Bullen – son of Formula I driver Alf Bullen and Frenchman Didier Jousemme did not even reach the start line. They submarined in the gigantic wash which resultad in Andy Bullen being taken to hospital with a badly cut hand.

Italian Renato Molinari was competing in these championships as was Britain's John Hill – one of Europe's top Formula II drivers. Molinari had a greater top speed but Hill found more acceleration. Both were driving craft powered by OMC engines but the first heat was to be Molinari's race.

John Hill was running neck and neck with the Italian when a plug lead came off his engine relegating him to the back of the fleet. The second heat was again dominated by Renato Molinari. Conditions were no better. Several rescue craft and other organisors would accept no protests, but when a deputation of officials from Germany, Italy and Sweden intervened, the protest was adjourned until after the racing had finished.

The start of the third heat was postponed ten minutes to allow the ferry to pass. This time John Hill managed to get ahead of Renato Molinari, finishing first overall, but the final heat was without Renato Molinari who had already won two heats and taken a second in the third race. Hence he had sufficient points to take the title.

It is obvious that in 1980 the International Authority will have to closely vet organisors' ability to hold World Championships of this stature. Commercial craft and the ignorance of

official course marshals as to the requirements of top sophisticated racing boats can prove fatal to those out to achieve titles.

World OZ Championship

Billy Seebold repeated his 1978 success when he won the World Unlimited Outboard (Class OZ-2,000 cc-infin.) Sprint Championships on Idroscalo Lake in Milan on September 23. Driving his Long John catamaran, which he designed and built himself, he finished the 4 x 10 lap 20 kilometre (12.42 mile) heats with a 200 point lead over the pre-race favourite, Renato Molinari of Italy.

An unwritten agreement was made some years ago between the two major outboard manufacturers : Mercury Marine and Outboard Marine

Preceding pages. *American Bill Seebold, Formula I (OZ) World Champion, drives a Seebold Long John, powered by a Mercury. 3.4 litre T4.*
Page 196. *Cees Van der Velden, encouraged by his home crowd, achieved his first win of the season in the Canon Trophy at Amsterdam port.*
Above. *Frenchman François Salabert from the Bénéteau team, world vice-champion in Formula II (OE) at Evian, gives a driving demonstration in his Velden hull, equipped with a Johnson RS.*
Below. *At the Formula I (OZ) World Championship, Italian Renato Molinari, unbeatable in a hull of his own design, equipped with two 3 litre V6 Evinrude motor.*

Corporation (OMC), who manufacture Evinrude and Johnson, that neither side would compete with twin-engined craft. However the new Mercury racing engine which was outstanding in the Canon Series was, at this stage of the season, virtually unbeatable. OMC found they had nothing to match it in level competition. It was therefore obvious if they were to gain any marketing pulicity in Milan, they would require a power unit with greater output.

The International Unlimited Rules are completely free from restrictions of any kind, which means that a competitor can enter a craft fitted with more than one motor. this was exactly the ploy adopted by OMC at Milan.

Italian Renato Molinari arrived with a huge catamaran fitted with a pair of Evinrude racing outboards. Protests were made and two of the eight drivers in the line-up even threatened to stay in the pits, but after much discussion all decided to take part, if only for the sake of the sponsors and the huge crowd of spectators who were sitting on the edge of their seats waiting for battle to commence.

Young American driver Earl Bentz, in another Long John Merury powered Seebold catamaran, shot into the lead in the first 10 lap heat only to be disqualified for jumping the gun, but within three laps Molinari was in front. Bill Seebold moved up to third only to discover at the end of 10 laps he had won overall. It appeared that Renato Molinari had struck a course marker costing him a 1 lap penalty.

This heat therefore finished with Seebold first, Cees Van der Velden of Holland second in his Johnson powered Velden and Britain's Roger Jenkins fourth in the Gordon's Gin Mercury powered Seebold. The unlucky driver who was to sit out the remaining heats was Britain's Bob Spalding. His Carlsberg sponsored Velden had to retire when his Johnson engine smashed a cylinder block beyond repair. The remaining three heats took place the following days.

Seebold leapt into the lead on the second heat chased by Molinari, but the large Italian boat was baulked by the American's Mercury teammates allowing Seebold to take the winner's flag by a small margin.

The third heat threw the competition wide open when Mercury drivers Roger Jenkins, Earl Bentz and Bill Seebold, in their eagerness to leave Molinari behind, jumped the starting gun and were disqualified. Renato Molinari just cruised home to an easy victory with Cees Van der Velden in second place. this result left the outcome of the Championship hanging on the final race.

Bill Seebold was determined to retain his title and creamed into the lead. Renato Molinari was again held back by the other Mercury team drivers and it was not until the third lap that he managed to move into second position – a place he should have gained easily with the huge power advantage of his twin engines. By then, however, the American was almost half a lap in

Preceding pages. At 11.05, 60 boats leap into the infernal merry-go-round of the Paris 6 Hours. For the first time unlimited cylinder OZs took part.
Above. Norwegian Halsaa fast as usual, dirves an extra-short Seebold, powered by a Mercury Black Max.
Below. Dutchmen Pelster-Zimmermann sixth at Paris, are among the best amateur teams, in a Velden hull powered by an Evinrude ccc.
Following pages, top. Dutchman Van der Velden and American Posey from the Bénéteau team take the lead the first hour, and keep it to the finish. Velden with a fresh victory at the Spanish Grand Prix on October 28, wins the Canon Trophy.
Below. The Italian-American pair Molinari-Woods, helped by McConnell, are sure of second place ; Molinari hull, 3 l. V6 Evinrude motor.

front, and with such short events, that was a distance that could not be made good.

Bill Seebold therefore won the title – a first class effort against what seemed initially impossible odds. It also proved that in the right hands, no other outboard existed in the 79 season even when used in twin form, to match the Mercury on power output.

Paris Six Hours Grand Prix

October 7th, Paris, France

The Paris 6 Hours was to be a trial reliability.

The three prototype Mercurys in the line-up had never raced for more three hours and the feeling in the pits on the eve of the event favoured the smaller models and craft fitted with the three litre Evinrude and Johnson outboards.

Paris always attracts a top class fleet and the 79 event with its 13 OZs was no exception. Sixty craft joined the line-up including

10 ON, 7 inboards and several 30 OE and among the international stars were ten drivers from the United States.

Awarding Canon points was not quite as straightforward as in the earlier heats. The duration of the Paris race is such that most craft need two drivers. Canon points are only allocated to overall placings and therefore it was decided to award these to one pre-selected driver who had been behind the wheel for at least 40 per cent of the race.

The first lap gave an immediate indication of the battle to follow. Speeds were extremely high. Bill Seebold in his Long John Mercury went to the front and showed his paces as the new World champion of OZ. As the other members of the leading bunch approached the pit turn, fellow American Jimbo McConnel in an Evinrude powered Molinari lost a sponson at over 100 mph (166 kph) and spun off the course in a cloud of spray.

Although the pace was high it was not the reliability of the engines which was to be a problem for Mercury. Driftwood and other

flotsam began taking its toll. Son of the leader, Mike Seebold, entered the pits after three laps with a broken keg on his underwater unit.

At the end of the first hour Dutchman Cees Van der Velden, head of the French Beneteau team, held first place overall in a hull of his own manufacture fitted with a Johnson motor. Englishman Bob Spalding, winner of the 1978 Paris 6 Hours lay second in a similar craft with a Mariner motor – a Hodges cat driven by John Nicholson with a Mariner motor was third.

The top Mercury challenge began to falter in the second and third hour. Americans Mike Seebold and Lee Sutter had both barrel rolled leaving Mercury hopes in the Formula I league resting on Bill Seebold in the only Mercury powered Long John craft left in the race. But this was a position well down the fleet in 11th place. If Mercury were to feature at all, then the fight would come from Britain's Peter Inward. Inward was behind the wheel of an OZ Seebold catamaran fitted with a standard T 3 Mercury.

Cees Van der Velden and his partner, Tom Posey from the United States, were invincible. They had taken the lead on the fourth lap and maintained this position for the rest of the event while lesser crews slipped back and retired astern.

By the fourth hour the Mercury challenge was over. Most of their leading craft were on trailers in the pits with crews now reduced to insignificance among the many spectators. Cees van de Velden and Tom Posey were six laps ahead of their nearest rival, ace Italian Renato Molinari and Bill Woods (Evinrude/Molinari).

In the last hour of the race all the competitors had problems.

Peter Inward went from third to fifth place while Britain's Bob Spalding – the 1978 Paris winner – who had held second slot at the third hour was now fourth after suffering ignition trouble leaving third place to Werner, the former OE world champion, with co-driver Brimkert in a catamaran equipped with a Mercury T3 motor.

Although Van der Velden and Tom Posey took overall victory at Paris, the earlier retirement of Bill Seebold and the fourth placing of Bob Spalding left the outcome of the Canon series resting on the final heat at Barcelona. Seebold still held the lead but Bob Spalding was only a matter of three points behind...

In the ON category, limited to 2l.cylinders, victory hovered between the Dutchmen Backer-Klinkhamer in a Cougar-Mercury and the English brothers Wilson in a Hodges-Mercury. The latter pair squeezed in first by a narrow margin. They followed in the footsteps of the Brazilian brothers, the Corbettas, who won in 1978, making this a family affair.

The OE category, with 30 boats entered was a real race within a race. Limited to 850 cm3 and slower than the OZ, the OE catamarans still make a very good showing. The fight was fierce and Vanessa-Colombo, among the leaders at the 3rd hour, had to retire, being the first to suffer. Frenchmen Salabert-Izard, part of the Beneteau stable, in a Veden-Johnson shared the lead with the English pair Hill-Larsson followed by the Swedes Sjöberg-Strôm in 3rd place. □

From top to bottom. *The Hill/Larsson couple gain the victory at the last minute in the OE category in a Burgess hull driven by a Johnson motor.*
The « family » Wilson in a Hodges/Mercury carry off the prize in the ON category.
The winners of the S3, Högberg/Dahlquist, led the race the whole way.

The American Season

Mercury and OMC played hide-and-seek

By John Crouse

Traditionally the first big outboard perfomance craft race of the year in the U.S. is the famed Parker 7-Hour enduro which is staged in the middle of the Arizona desert where the fabled cowboys and Indians once roamed in search of, or to get away from, each other.

Once upon a time it was also the first of many confrontations between the vaunted American factory outboard racing teams... i.e. Mercury and the OMC twins Evinrude and Johnson.

Fortunately for the OPC fans at Parker, and unfortunately for them almost everywhere else in the States, save at the last big race of the year at Lake Havasu in November, the factory teams have been making more of an effort to duck one another than to challenge each other here in recent seasons.

The reasons seem to be as much, if not more for political causes... real and imagined... as for anything mechanical.

Mercury has long dominated the famed World Mod U championships in St. Louis, Missouri which is run in the backyard of its most productive factory driver, Billy Seebold, the ice-nerved young man whose tunnel hulls have become almost as renowned as their creator.

This year Seebold's son Mike won the Mod U Class II title in the same race in which his dad captured the Mod U Class I world crown and the world Mod 120 title !

The reason why Mercury runs away with everything but the water at St. Louis and hulls powered by the OMC engines do not, is quite simple. OMC's factory teams never show up. In a situation which the top racing executives of both Mercury and OMC admit is silly, Mercury boycotts the annual race at Beloit, Wisconsin billed this year as the U.S. continental OZ class championships... which almost all the racing people and almost none of the spectators know is the same as the APBA's (American Power Boat Association) Mod U class.

Anyway, back to the circuit and Parker on March 4th where teams from all three, Mercury, Evinrude and Johnson, made the scene. Mercury's race people vow that Parker is where OMC likes to pop their new machinery, but this year it was OMC watching for new things under the famed black hoods. Word had it that Mercury would show up with its new giant 207 cubic inch (3.4 liter) six cylinder T-4 engine. Word was wrong ! With hopes of discovering

what the enemy was doing in its race shops both teams found little mechanical and mostly matters mortal at Parker... which still proved a more fruitful search than in most of the other U.S. OPC races in 1978.

On hand at Parker for Mercury was its ace of aces Billy Seebold, who would prove more than a thorn to the OMC legion throughout the season, its great charger Reggie Fountain, Earl Bentz who would drive with Seebold, and Mike Seebold and his co-driver Curt Todd. OMC's troops were loaded with talent too. The near legendary Jimbo McConnell and Ken Stevenson were teamed up as were the Flying Dutchman Cees Van der Velden and Barry Woods and Mr. Steady, Johnnie Sanders, and his co-pilot, England's Alf Bullen and the incomparable Italian Renato Molinari and his U.S. co-driver Tom Posey.

Below. the Parker Enduro Seven Hour Race : in the magnificent setting of the Arizona desert, the boats and crews line up, waiting the start, while the mechanics get their feet wet to make the last minute adjustments.

Another familiar face showed up to test a prototype aluminum block Mercury inboard engine, which reportedly pulled a giant 465 horses from its 256 cubic inches with the help of turbocharging. He was the veteran Bob Hering. Unfortunately the mill broke early in the race as the factory outboards set a pace that is still all but unbelievable.

To say that the Men of Mercury were a bit hungry after almost three years of coming out of this fray sans victory, is an understatement.

The race, once called the Parker 9-hour Enduro, was shortened to seven hours to show the outside masses that boat racers are also conscious of fuel economy.

Mercury's Seebold Sr./Bentz team was clocked for 62 laps over the slightly under 12 mile course at an average 108 miles per hour in an historic perfomance for U.S. boat racing. As Bob Brown, editor of Powerboat magazine put it so succinctly, "Never before in the history of U.S. endurance racing has a boat been driven so fast, so far, for so long a period of time". Random radar speed guns around the course revealed that the black and blue painted Seebold-Bentz boat was whizzing down the chutes at 115-120mph !

If you think that is impressive hear this. For 42 of the 62 laps they were running second behind the Molinari-Posey duo in an Evinrude V-6 183 cubic inch (3 liter) powered boat. For four hours the crack OMC duo led after grabbing the front position from the start.

Then the lead boat begin to come apart. Two blown gear cases and a ruined prop spelled its doom as Seebold and Bentz pressed on relentlessly to win by a reasonably comfortable four laps over Seebold's son Mike and Todd. Thus the fans looked eagerly to a summer-long circuit full of more hotly contested confrontations. They would wait in vain as the two teams would almost magically motor to such places as Lake Charles, Louisana ; Beloit, Wisconsin ; Lake Alfred, Florida ; Valleyfield, Quebec, Canada ; St. Louis, Missouri ; Eufala, Alabama ; Memphis, Tennessee and a dozen or so other way-out places and never officially tangle again.

Which does not mean that there were not exciting things happening anyway. As the circuit progressed not only was it evident that the latest breed of tunnels seemed to be trimmed out much better than before, but mid-way through the summer at least one manufacturer, Mercury, would unwrap a phenomenal, huge new engine... and at the same time let the public take its first gander at a new braking system for boats.

Parker was Billy Seebold's third straight win after victories at the 1978 Lake Havasu race and in Miami, Florida's Race of Champions in February. Before we join the black Max people at our next stop, we must add that Seebold the Younger and Todd caught Molinari on the last lap to take second at Parker. Borth the Seebolds were driving dad's boats, of course.

Since the OMC drivers weren't there, Lake Charles, Louisiana's race May 6th wouldn't ordinarily draw much ink except for the fact that it was the first event ever for the newly-formed Professional Powerboat Association. Mercury's Earl Bentz came from behind to win all three of the 15 minute heats in his 18.5' Seebold hull. Hering, the man who has driven for both Mercury and OMC over the years, while surviving some terrible crashes, took second in a boat made by himself and powered by one of the new Mercury Mariner V-6 engines.

Next battle of note was the controversial Beloit, Wisconsin, Race on May 26-27 where OMC's legions, like Mercury's do at St. Louis, do their thing in mime... sans the enemy actors. Despite being an OMC "backyard race" the absence of the big guns from Oshkosh, headquarters for the Mercury racing team, did not dampen the proceedings that much as the famed Jimbo McConnell put on a show for the local fans in his 17.5' Molinari, Evinrude V-6 powered hull, winning the U.S. Continental Championships for OZ class which is the same thing as the U.S. Mod U. Teammate Ken Stevenson took second in a near identical Evinrude propelled rig.

On June 9-10 Stevenson would get his bit of glory at the U.S. OPC Marathon Nationals on Florida's Lake Alfred.. While Mercury's Seebold the Elder was in Bristol, Eng, successfully debuting the new 400 horsepower Mercury 207 C.I. (3.4 liter) engine to win the coveted Duke of York Trophy in the Embassy Grand Prix, OMC's team members and some of its top independents, would sweep the boards at Lake Alfred. Stevenson would win the Mod U class setting a new world record of 102 mph for one hour using an Evinrude V-6 300 hp engine. The previous mark of 105 set last year in a Texas race by Fred Hauenstein in a Johnson powered boat, was disallowed because of some race technicalities. It's doubtful that this one will wind up in the books either, since Molinari and Posey who led the first four hours at Parker had to be topping 108-109 mph.

Preceding pages : *The fabulous machines on the American circuit.*
Top, left. *Earl Bentz won the race staged on Lake Charles in Louisiana at the controls of an 18.5 Seebold boat with a Mercury V-6 engine, having dominated the three heats of 15 miles each.*
Below. *In sharp contrast to the fine lines of the out-board boats, the powerful inboard boats look very heavy. This is the mount of the American Walker, U.S.A. champion in 1978 - another craft powered by Mercruiser.*

A month later on July 7-8, the North American Championships... it's getting near impossible to tell what kind of championship you're looking at anymore... were held at Valleyfield, in Quebec, Canada, where Stevenson once more did himself proud even though he switched to Johnson power.

Once more, as had happened at Beloit and Lake Alfred, the OMC boys had only one another to contend with, as the Mercury aces were noticeable by their absence. Stevenson and McConnell locked horns at Valleyfield to see who would wind up with the Mod U title of North American Champion. Stevenson won. McConnell, who has got so many trophies at home he could get ample solar energy by just setting them all out in his front yard when the sun's out, got some solace a week later in a Chippewa Falls, Wisc. backyard race when he set what is expected to be a new 1 2/3 mile sprint record of 102.56 mph in a Molinari-Evinrude package.

Now it was Mercury's turn to shine without any OMC factory challenges as the OPC limelight in the States swung south to St. Louis for the Mod U and Mod 120 world championships. It would be all Seebolds on the tight little course.

St.Louis was an attention-getter no matter how you looked at it. Not only would the American public get their first real look at the new big Merc 207 cube (3.4 liter) powerplant and the controversial boat brakes on the Mercury factory team boats, they would see a show put on by the father son Seebold team that would truly dazzle.

Correctly figuring that OMC's soldiers would not show, race officials at St. Louis added another dimension. With only Billy Seebold, Earl Bentz and Reggie Fountain entered in Mod U div. I with their fuel injected Mercury T-4 engines, they included the Mod II boats, which used the older carbureted Mercury V-6s. In the first heat Pop Seebold won by a huge margin as son Mike won the Mod U II division. Bill would capture all three heats in like manner as Fountain, who was injured in a crash in a later race, was second. The show put on by the new Mercury engines was enough to satisfy the estimated 30,000 spectators.

There were other happenings of note at St. Louis. The observer could see that in order to accommodate the new engines, Mercury had Seebold build some bigger, wider hulls. The combination had the team drivers turning laps a full five seconds quicker than the carbureted older V-6 powered hulls could. Seebold reportedly turned some 115 mph laps which is absolutely phenomenal.

The Mercury team boats also had brakes... a pair of small feet that lowered hydraulically off the transoms... allowing them to go into turns much faster than previously possible. Not all of their drivers dug this feature. Bentz reportedly complained of a sore stomach from slamming into his steering wheel because of the abrupt changes of speed. But the device does seem to have great merit, especially when one considers its possibilities when fitted out with an altitude detector that could automatically bring a boat's nose down before it could blow over backwards.

Later in the day Mike Seebold would add the world Mod 120 championship which would give the family three titles for the session.

OMC race director Jack Leek was not overly impressed with Mercury taking the world Mod U championship at St. Louis saying.'..the real Mod U of OZ championship would be held at Milan, Italy.' a month later. He had to be somewhat impressed then, when Seebold won that one too !

A week after St. Louis, some of the OMC team drivers showed up for the U.S. National Sprint championships at Eufala, Alabama on Aug. 25-26. Mercury's racing chief Gary Garbrecht says his company's policy is to keep its hot dogs away from such events in order not to "...compete against the customer". Of course, the two teams have been sending their best men into such events for years under the guise of.independents.' but it is true that none of Mercury's leading men were at Eufala while most of OMC's were.

Ironically enough a true independent, Jim Hunt from Florida, did win the main event Mod U race in a V-6 Johnson powered 18' Broughton hull. McConnell won the Mod 120 national title in an Evinrude/Molinari rig and Terry Leather-by the Mod 50 race with a Johnson engine.

Above. *Jimbo McConnell repeats the success he enjoyed last year at Beloit in the OZ class - Mod U in the USA - with his Molinari 17.5 hull powered by Evinrude V-6 3-litre engines.*

The opposing factory team drivers did meet in some force on Sept. 8-9 in Memphis, Tenn. to support another of the new Professional Powerboat Association's races. Bentz won with one of the 207 c.i. (3.4 liter) mills clamped on the back of his 18.5' Seebold racer, and Seebold was second with a simliar package. The outing cost Mercury one of its top drivers for the forthcoming Paris race when Fountain suffered kidney damage when his boat flipped. OMC's Stevenson and McConnell were both at Memphis.

The final and perhaps most important confrontation of the year so far as the meeting of the giants is concerned, is at Lake Havasu, Arizona on Nov. 23-24 where the factory teams tangle for the second time in 1979.

Seebold won the 1978 race which saw all sorts of disastrous things take place. He is back this year in one of the new hot team boats, as are his Black Max cohorts. □

Preceding pages : at the Parker Enduro, the inboard were formidable opponents for the fastest outboard.
From top to bottom. It was a transitional season for Bob Hering, who has left OMC for Mariner and is now building his own hulls. With the V-6 Magnum Mariner he finished second at Lake Charles.
Deserved satisfaction for Bill Seebold, number one driver for Mercury. He was champion of the world in the OZ speed championships at Milan and an outstanding winner at the Parker Enduro, at St. Louis, at Bristol and at Brammen in Norway.
After a disappointing season in 1978, Earl Bentz, of the official Mercury team, at last saw his efforts rewarded with several victories, including the Parker Enduro Seven Hours, in association with Bill Seebold, and the race at Memphis, Tennessee...
Sniping for honours in the OZ class (Mod U in the USA), the British driver Jacky Wilson raced this season once more with the powerful 3-litre Cosworth Formula One motor racing engine. But his results were not very convincing, despite meticulous preparation work.

Offshore Races

The American Season

*Lady Cook and cats
the big news in States*

by John Crouse

Many things happened on the North and South American offshore powerboat racing circuits but two stood out above the rest.

When the spray had settled from the seven U.S. and three South American races a 56-year-old lady racer and the big English-built and designed tunnel hulls got the major share of the publicity.

For the second year in succession Betty Cook, the 1977 world champion and defending American titlist, won three races at Miami, Detroit and Oakland, Calif. She made boat racing history all the way, winning her second straight U.S. open class crown.

The world offshore season traditionally starts off in Argentina in January and this year was true to form, although the first race wasn't routine as a class II boat, Pira Pita, a 28' Pira made in Buenos Aires, won with 1978 world champion Juan Taylor, son-in-law of the late Dick Krieger, at the wheel. Co-favorites Billy Martin's 39' Cigarette Bounty Hunter and Michael Doxford's 35' Cigarette Limit Up both broke, leaving the field open to Taylor in the 189 mile race.

The first race was run on January 13th. A week later a second Rio de La Plata contest was held over the same course. This time Martin got his act together, easily topping the 43 mile per hour pace clocked by Taylor in the first race, winning at an average speed of 61.3 mph in the Mercruiser powered Bounty Hunter.

It was Doxford's turn the following week, January 27th, at the Punta del Este race in Uruguay. Running all by his lonesome in the open class I, all the Englishman had to do was finish to gain victory. His pace averaged out at a slow 54.2 mph. Based on the number of starters in the three races, Martin wound up with his second straight South American continental championship although four class II open boats completed the three races with more points overall. Regardless, Martin, Doxford and Tim Powell, who drove the other Doxford boat to a second behind Martin in the second Buenos Aires event, all qualified for the world championship showdown scheduled for Venice, Italy, October 20th.

Whatever glee Martin may have felt about slipping by with his second South American title didn't last long for the winner of eight 1978 races when he got to America. In the first race of the U.S. circuit, he tore a large chonk out of Bounty Hunter in a test run the day before the race. Patching it up, he could do no better than seventh in the Bushmills Grand Prix race off Newport Beach. Calif., on March 17th, despite the encouragement of movie star John Wayne who waved the fleet on from his home, only a few yards from the race docks. It was one of the famed actor's last public appearances before his death from cancer.

While Martin was floundering about in the Pacific a young rookie, Charlie McCarthy, who had dreamed of being a big time ocean racer for years, saw it come true as he won his first open class race in a prototype hull designed and built by Frenchman Jean-Claude Simon. The two would later get into a dispute as to what to call the 38' hull, but McCarthy, of Irish descent, was ecstatic to say the least. The race sponsors, Bushmills Irish Whisky, were not depressed either, especially since McCarthy won the 205 mile race on St. Patrick's Day! His Top Banana's average speed was 72 mph.

Almost a month later, on May 12th, and 3400 miles away the second race on the U.S. circuit was held... again backed by a spirits firm... the Bacardi (rum) Trophy event. With two of the big English cats tied to the docks at Miami's Four Ambassadors Hotel, former American national champion Joel Halpern's 35' Cougar Cat Beep Beep and Betty Cook's brand new 38' Cougar Cat Kaama, the press and fans anticipated an historic sea war. Unfortunately, Mother Nature did not co-operate and heavy weather prompted both drivers to leave the boats ashore. Cook opted for her deep vee Scarab Kaama thus setting the seeds for a controversy that would finally erupt at the last race of the season at Oakland, Calif. where the practice of bringing two boats to each race was openly criticized by a group of less endowed drivers led by Howard Quam.

Driving with the deliberation and intelligence that has become the trademark of the Kaama team of Cook, throttleman John Connor and navigator Bill Vogel, Jr., Kaama won the 194 mile race at an average pace of 67.3 mph. A third place by the upstart McCarthy maintained a tie with Cook for the lead in national championship points for the young, wealthy trucking company owner but Cook had given notice that she was already back in the groove with only two races run.

Last year's inaugural Guy Lombardo Classic off Freeport, Long Island, New York, the final race on the 1978 U.S. circuit, was moved up to June 2nd this year and picked up a new sponsor... Halter Marine, the purchaser of Don Aronow's Cigarette Racing Team firm.

In a brilliant display of a deep vee hull tangling with one of the new cats, Cook led the 179.3 mile race in her new tunnel Kaama as Quam and throttleman Keith Hazell gave furious and heroic chase in the 38' Kevlar Bertram Flap-Jack, considered to be the fastest of its design in the world today. Cook seemed to have the race wired, showing speeds that were simply beyond the reach of the vee bottoms when it happened. With only 16 miles left, one of the engines on Kaama elected to take a holiday. Quam flew by to register the first open class win in his career, setting a respectable 77.6 mph pace.

But win or no Kaama's performance shook the offshore establishment. By the end of the next race, the Manufacturer's Bank/Spirit of

Detroit bash at the Motor City, she and her wooden sea horse from England, had severely jarred the advocates of the vee hulls.

On hand in Detroit were three of the monsters... Kaama, Beep Beep and Rocky Aoki's Benihana, well known in Europe as the former Yellowdrama of Ken Cassir, holder of the existing straight away record for offshore boats of 92.2 mph.

Benihana would blow before it could get to the starting line on race day, June 29th, but Beep Beep and Kaama would lock into a duel so close that Cook would later swear that she could see the screws on Beep Beep before the Halpern tunnel holed out and nearly sunk. Cook went on to win and break her own U.S. race record of 82.5 mph set at Cedar Point, Ohio last year ('78) with an 83.9 mph pace. Now there was no doubt in anybody's mind that the cats were the breed of the future for offshore racers.

But that story was just beginning.

Next came the Benihana Grand Prix off Pt. Pleasant, N.J. on July 18th... the biggest offshore race in the world. Race officials reported almost 60 entrants in the combined open and production fleet. Fifty four would start. It should have made any sponsor happy... especially the publicity-oriented Oriental Aoki whose Japanese steak house chain backed the event. Sales of Benihana souvenirs were heavy enough to make the local shops edgy. Crowds flocked around Aoki everywhere he went, but still the little man frowned.

Aside from his record run from Key West, Fla. to Cuba earlier in his tunnel hull his fortune cookies had all been crumbling for Aoki who had failed to finish his last dozen races.

So distressed was he, that Aoki told a New York Times reporter in an interview prior to the race, that he was quitting the sport if he failed to finish. Aside from finishing a race Rocky hadn't won since his victory at San Diego on February 12th, 1977. To say he was due was an understatement.

Rocky couldn't have picked a worse day to make his vow. The waters off Pt. Pleasant were foggy and drizzly, a condition that grew worse by the minute. It got so bad that once underway the first three boats... unable to see the beaks of their boats, opted to run for the shoreline to get their bearings.

Benihana's throttleman Errol Lanier, with a bit of terror still showing, would later recall how he ducked in the cockpit to adjust his headgear, when he casually glanced up to see how Aoki was doing. Aoki was heading straight for shore at 70 mph! While the likes of Cook, Aoki and Quam were taking the scenic tour along shore, Michelob Light driver Joey Ippolito chose to blast through the murk at high speed. It appeared at first that the tactic would win the race as Michelob Light moved up from fourth to first place with only 25 miles left in the 178 mile race and a comfortable 7 mile lead... then the beer backed boat lost its suds with an engine gone.

As whatever spectators were insane enough to brave the driving rain and fog from boats, and the les' miserable press corps who had lit-tle choice, watched in amazement, Benihana popped out of the weather near the finish, first. It was immediately decided that poor Rocky had missed a check point. But poor Rocky was about to collect $13,000 of his own money which he would later haul off to a local charity.

Forty-two seconds behind Benihana came Quam's Flap-Jack. Later at dock-side the miracle would magnify as Lanier revealed that Behihana's battery had broken loose early in the race and was bouncing around the sensitive boat's guts, a compass had dropped through the dash wiping out wiring, an alternator belt slipped off and around a fuel injector, the trim tabs ceased functioning, and the hull had split in two places!

Despite all this Benihana had averaged 69 mph. It was the fourth coup for the celebrated hull. Its previous owner, Cassir, had won three with it before selling it to Aoki.

On August 25th the U.S. offshore fleet lined up for the 189 mile John Wayne Memorial race off Long Beach, Calif. With conditions ideal for the cats, Cook and the once hapless Aoki were listed as co-favorites. This time things went as advertised at sea. Cook held the lead for the first part of the race before an engine went. Jacoby grabbed a bit of glory later as his Ajac Hawk flashed past Aoki but Aoki's throttleman Lanier had ample power left to take the Cigarette anytime he wished.

On the final leg Lanier wished and blew by Ajac Hawk which finally died in the water with a blown engine, with 20 miles to go in the race. Once more Aoki would idle up to the finish boat to get the checkered flag. After 12 straight DNFs he had won two races in a row in his battered cat!

Ippolito was second and Quam third. With

Cook down, the 225 points for third was enough to give Quam the lead for the U.S. championship with one race, the Benihana Grand Prix West, left on the circuit.

But that one race proved almost too fateful to describe in words.

Before they could fire the starting flare, disaster would strike. With the threat of both fog which is almost omnipresent off San Francisco, and memories of '78's brutal conditions, race sponsor Aoki decided he might need a backup deep vee hull for race day and leased a 38' Cobra hull named "Mollewood" from owner Gerald Dehenau. The day before the race Aoki, Dehenau and Lanier took the boat out for a test run.

A mile outside of the famed Golden Gate Bridge the 38' hull dove its nose into a sea, a routine incident that should not have been any real problem. It became one as ten feet of the boat's bow broke off hurtling its crew into the controls and then out into the water. Fortunately, Lanier, a fireman from Ft. Lauderdale, Fla., was trained for such emergencies... and was the least injured.

Quickly gathering his wits, Lanier spotted Aoki lying unconscious, face down in the water nearby and Dehenau not far away, conscious but obviously hurt badly. Lanier swam over to his boss and pulled him back to the badly damaged boat which, by some stroke of good fortune, remained afloat. Hauling Aoki over the outdrives, Lanier applied mouth to mouth resuscitation. Aoki came to life, muttered he was okay, then repeatedly lapsed into unconsciousness. As luck would have it a U.S. Coast Guard vessel was stationed near the accident and was soon on the scene. The three were rushed to the famed U.S. Letterman Army Medical Center in San Francisco where Aoki hovered near death for two days from near fatal injuries. They took his spleen and gall bladder out, sewed up a lacerated liver, performed open heart by-pass surgery, and mended a broken right leg, both arms and a cracked wrist. Last word from the incredible little man was he was coming to Venice for the world championships... but he didn't make it.

After extensive surgery they feel they were able to save Dehenau's right arm. Lanier's most serious hurt was a cut leg suffered when he hit his leg on one of the props as he worked on Aoki.

The next day with the gloom of the mishap on their minds, the racers headed out into San Francisco Bay for more gloom... this time in the form of patches of fog which hid all sorts of monsters... among them the huge U.S. aircraft carrier "Coral Sea"...

As the boats roared past the start and finish line and ran up and back along the coast line, it appeared that Quam would be the new American champion. His Flap-Jack and Ippolito's Michelob Light were locked into a fiercesome duel, with Quam a boat nose ahead. Cook seemed out of it in her deep vee Scarab Kaama... then, as Aoki had done at Pt. Pleasant, she came out of the murky horizon all by herself. Again nobody believed it, despite her reputation for being almost always correct. By now the race committee had instructed its check boats to flag the open boats down after three full laps.

They got to Cook who ran three laps totalling 148 miles, but blew it with the rest of the fleet, Quam and Ippolito included, signalling them to stop after only two laps. Through no fault of Cook's who went on to win, the others never got a chance to take a shot at Kaama in the last 48 miles !

Both she and Aoki had proven without a shadow of a doubt that the catamarans or tunnels, however you wish to label them, are the way of the future for the sport. So convincing have been the Americans' performances with the big double-beaked hull that the line-up for the October World championships in Venise listed as many as five of them. Included were Cook in a 38' Cougar Cat named Kaama, possibly Quam in Aoki's Benihana, perhaps Doxford in either an English owned Cougar Cat or in Halpern's Beep Beep which will race as a Limit Up, and Niccolai in a new Molinari Dry Martini. Last but most important, the defending world champ Francesco Cosentino, in a prototype Don Aronow –Hal Halter hull built by the celebarted outboard tunnel ace Billy Seebold for Cigarette.

No matter how you view it, the year 1979 was something else offshore. □

Left-hand page. *Howard Quam's Bertram 38, built in Kevlar 49 and powered by twin 625 h.p. Mercruisers, is currently considered the fastest V-hulled boat in the field. It won the Guy Lombardo/Halter Classic at an average speed of 124.8 kilometres an hour.*
Above. *The American Jo Ippolito finished third in the Open Class of the American Championships. He drives a Scarab 38 called Michelob-Light, one of the few boats powered by Kiekhaeffer Aeromarine engines.*
Below, left. *Billy Martin took the South American championship title for the second year running. His boat is a 39 foot Cigarette, Bounty Hunter.*
Below. *Newcomers to the Open Class, Howard Quam (left) and his co-driver Keith Hazell (right) finished a brilliant second in the American championships.*
Following pages : *Tim Powell drove Michael Doxford's fast 35' Cigarette Limit Up in the World Championship.*

The European Season

Italians Niccolai De Angelis
account for an eight races

by Ray Bulman

The eight races which counted for points in the 1979 European Offshore Championship were virtually dominated from start to finish by Italian Guido Niccolai. Driving his 38 ft. (11.5m) Don Shead designed Class I racer, built in aluminium by Picchiotti in Italy, he finished the season with a huge points lead over his nearest rival, Britain's Derek Pobjoy.

While this success gave Niccolai the European Championship. the more coveted prize was a place in the World Championship at Venice in October. The international powerboating authority, Union Internationale Motonautique (UIM) stipulates that only Class I and II drivers who finish first, second or third in each of the six continental championships can compete for the world crown. It was a system which received a great deal of criticism in 1979 and it looks almost certain that the Championship will revert to a series of grand prix races in 1981. Meanwhile the old system will continue for another season. The next World Offshore final is due to take place in Australia in 1980.

The 1979 European series began on England's south coast in June at Poole.

The Poole international Races

There is little doubt Britain currently provides

the toughest competition in Europe and Poole was no exeption. Later events in Spain and Italy attracted a handful of competitors but this first event, organised by the United Kingdom Offshore Association, saw 15 Class I and II craft on the start line.

With two exceptions, all offshore craft competing in Europe in 1979 had seen at least one season's racing.

Dry Martini 2 was built in 1979 and the two Italian craft racing under the Alitalia banner were also at least a year old ; the second Alitalia Due, a Mercruiser powered Cigarette 36 (10.9m, was even older and first used by Italian Vincenzo Balestrieri under the name of Black Tornado in 1972. The main British challenger was also far from new. She was the 38ft. (11.5m) Don Shead designed racer built in aluminium by Enfield Marine in 1971. All were still capable of giving a good account of themselves. It was one of these Italian built Picchiotti's in which Italian Francesco Cosentino had won the 1978 World Championship in South America the previous December. The two new boats were Dry Martini 3, a Jean Claude Simon Coyote-Picchiotti, moulded in fibre glass, and the brand new Cougar catamaran Toleman Group which was still being constructed for newcomers to offshore. Nick Cripps and Ted Toleman, when the Poole event took place.

The weather conditions at Poole were ideal. Guido Niccolai immediately showed the superiority of Dry Martini 2. She held second place in the early stages of the 161 mile (257.6 kilometre) course between the Needles on the Isle of Wight and the town of Swanage to the west. Alitalia Tre driven by fellow Italian Giulio de Angelis - an identical craft to Dry Martini 2 - led the fleet with Britain's Derek Pobjoy in Uno Mint Jewellery third. Another Italian craft, the older Cigarette 36 (10.9m) Alitalia Due driven by Tommaso de Simone was up in fourth place but was forced to retire within two miles with a split manifold.

The first lap was completed with Dry Martini 2 still holding second place but shortly after Alitalia Tre blew an engine and fell back. Dry Martini 2 immediately took the lead with Derek Pobjoy in Uno-Mint Jewellery about 1 mile (1.6 kilometre) astern.

These positions were maintained until the finish with Niccolai crossing the line to take a well earned 400 points and Pobjoy finishing second with 300. Third place was taken by another veteran. this time the wooden Apache driven by David Hagan giving him 400 points in the European Class II series.

San Feleu de Guixols

The next race in the European Championship took place at San Feleu de Guixols in Spain on June 25. It was here that the Toleman Group catamaran made its debut, but if the newcomer looked a potential winner on arrival, then the poor weather was to be its downfall.

Five Class I boats joined the line-up but the severe conditions were to decimate this fleet. Nick Gripps in Toleman Group ran no further than 1 mile (1.6 kilometre). They were overwhelmed by rough seas and wisely retired. Italians Giulio de Angelis in Alitalia Tre (sistership to Dry Martini 2) and Tommaso de Somone in the 36ft. (10.9m) Cigarette Alitalia Due both retired well before the half way mark leaving Guido Niccolai on his own. Derek Pobjoy in Uno-Mint Jewellery covered the course slowly to finish second overall.

Viareggio - Bastia - Viareggio

The third heat was held between the Italian towns of Viareggio and Bastia on July 22. This time Guido Niccolai used Dry Martini 3 : a new boat designed for Jean-Claude Simon and moulded in fibreglass by Coyote-Picchiotti. This race was also far from calm and the Toleman Group catamaran fell back yet again. It was also the one race in Europe where Niccolai failed to score. His new grp craft was no match for the rough seas. Her hull delaminated forcing him to slow. Guilio de Angelis went on to score his first victory in Alitalia Tre with Derek Pobjoy in Uno-Mint Jewellery taking second place for Great Britain.

Naples

The fourth heat at Naples on July 29 was flat calm.

The same handful of competitors took part and, not wishing to be outshone by using the weaker hull, Guido Niccolai once again drove the aluminium Dry Martini 2, and won easily.

The weather was ideal for the Toleman Group catamaran but unfortunately, as if cursed with a Jonah, the boat ran out of fuel two miles from the finish and was forced to retire. Alitalia Tre driven by Giulio de Angelis – sistership to Dry Martini 2 – took second place two minutes behind the winner with Uno-Mint Jewellery third.

The state of the Championship after four races meant that Niccolai of Italy led with 1,500 points, Derek Pobjoy of Britain lay second with 994 points while Giulio de Angelis held third with 700 points. Four races remained with the next taking place on August 12 in Oregrund in Sweden.

Oregrund

This event was almost a walk-over for Guido Niccolai. Only the Italians took part which meant that Dry Martini 2, Alitalia Tre, (Giulio de Angelis) and Alitalia Due (Tommaso de Simone) were the sole Class I competitors.

Dry Martini 2 completed the course in 2hrs. 43 mins. and was the only finisher, the Italian entries having to withdraw with mechanical problems. Guido Niccolai now had the Championship within his grasp.

The Needles Trophy

Competition in this race mainly consisted of the four craft which had taken part in the earlier events, but in this case the fleet was supplemented by several Class II contenders including Italian Alberto Smania who had been competing in the earlier heats in his single-engined monohull. His close class rival was British driver David Hagan in Apache – a diesel-powered contender originally built by Souter of Cowes to a Don Shead design in 1969.

The Needles Trophy was again won by Italian Guido Niccolai but tough competition came from the American 39ft. (11.8m) Cigarette Bounty Hunter and Uno-Mint Jewellery. Dry Martini 2 took the lead immediately and

Left-hand page. The Italian driver Niccolai deservedly won the European title by carrying off most of the honours. He drives Martini 2, a 38-footer in aluminium, built by the Picchiotti yard and driven by twin 625 h.p. Mercruisiers. He also drives Martini 3, a Coyote 38 built in polyester by the same yard to the design of Frenchman Jean-Claude Simon Opposite. In his first season in Class 1, the British driver Dereck Pobjoy ended up second in the European Championships, thanks to five seconds and a third. His boat Uno Mint Jewellery is eight years old and powered by twin 625 h.p. Aeromarine engines. It si the same 38 foot Enfield Marine aluminium craft which was previously known as Enfield Avenger, Unowot and Uno Ambassy.

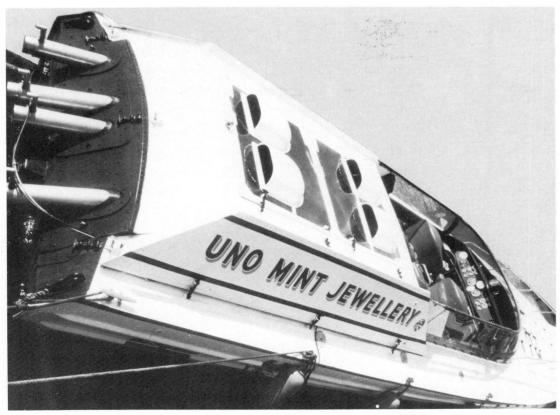

opened up a large gap over the rest of the fleet. Derek Pobjoy lay third in Uno-Mint Jewellery until Francesco Cosentino in Alitalia Tre fell back with mechanical problems. This promoted Uno-Mint Jewellery into second place. Bounty Hunter driven by Michel Meynard held third for the first 75 mile circuit but his starboard engine seized on the final lap and ne was forced to retire.

Dry Martini 2 crossed the line at an average speed of 67.73 knots to collect 400 points and the chequered flag 10 minutes ahead of Uno-Mint Jewellery.

Cowes-Torquay-Cowes

The Cowes/Torquay/Cowes class is without

doubt the premier offshore race in Europe. Held on August 25, it was also the seventh in the European points series and the fact that it clashed with an American fixture in Long Beach California, meant that the group of Americans, who nearly always attend this event, could not take part. The battle for points therefore remained with a small band already competing on the European circuit.

Dry Martini 2 driven by Guido Niccolai led once again at the gun closely chased by Uno-Mint Jewellery. This time, however, they were to be challenged by a brand new 37ft. (11.2m) Cigarette which had arrived from its builders on the even of the race and driven by Britain's Mike Doxford and Tim Powell. Called Limit Up, she was to closely challenge Niccolai well before the half-way stage of this 220 mile offshore marathon.

Dry Martini 2 and Uno-Mint Jewellery ran neck and neck to Portland Bill where competitors enter the notorious Lyme Bay. Niccolai held the lead with Derek Pobjoy in second place until Uno-Mint Jewellery picked up a plastic bag in her cooling system which resulted in an over-heated engine. This put paid to Pobjoy's chances. Although he finished the course he had to limp home at a fraction of his earlier speed.

Dry Martini 2 was the next to suffer problems when she lost the blade off one propeller. The boat came to a standstill 10 miles east of the Brixham half-way mark and the crew hastily fitted a replacement. Meanwhile Mike Doxford in Limit Up moved ahead and began his return crossing of Lyme Bay.

There is little doubt that the newer Limit Up had the edge over the Italian. Doxford widened his lead by almost two miles (3 kilometres) but no sooner had he repassed Portland Bill on the homeward run than he split the block of his starboard engine and ground to a halt. Niccolai moved past into an unchallenged leading position and although Limit Up eventually managed to proceed ahead, it was at a snail's pace.

Guido Niccolai was now European Champion with Derek Pobjoy in second place. Neither had to rely on the results of the Sardinia race to

qualify for the World Championship of Venice. But the third position went to Giulio de Angelis atten a victory in the Costa Smeralda race off Sardinia, sept. 16.

The Putney-Calais Class III race

Class III racing is the offshore section which gains greatest support in Europe. It began as a cheaper alternative to the large Class I and II in 1962, with a return event between Putney on the River Thames in London and Calais in France for small outboard powered runabouts.

Such a race was a mammoth undertaking for these small craft. At 225 miles, it was the longest event in Europe and as the minimum hull length was 14ft. (4.2m) it can be seen that the trial of skill and endurance of those taking part soon captured the imagination of runabout owners. From this particular race Class III was born. Today the majority of boats average between 20 to 23ft. (7.0m) overall and are powered with engines of 250 cu.ins. (4.1 litres).

The 18th event in the series took place on July 1, 1979 and because long races of this type are no longer popular with many competitors, only 18 craft crossed the starting line at Tower Bridge in London.

It was a race of contrasts. Calm water on the down run of the Thames to the port of Ramsgate where competitors stop for refuelling. The trip across to France this time was moderate but only five completed the return leg to Ramsgate; the rest retiring.

The winner is calculated on the elapsed time and the first place was taken by husband and wife team Peter and Jan Armstrong competing in the event for the first time.

Driving their 23ft. (77m) Class IIID (4 litres) Phantom monohull Aphrodisiac powered by a single 235hp Johnson outboard, they averaged 41 knots for the course to win by less than four minutes from Englishman Terry Evans in his IIIC (2 litres) Stapley designed and built catamaran Concord.

Third place was taken by another monohull also in the IIIC category. It was the Mercury-powered Marshan Moody Blue driven by Bruce Mash who lost second place by a mere 77 seconds.

The outstanding performance of the 1979 race was without douth the effort of twin brothers Graham and Michael Toleman. Only 17 years old, they were the youngest ever to enter and drove the smallest craft, a little IIIB (1,500cc) Phantom Fayanagin. They took over 3 hours on their return crossing between Ramsgate and France but unfortunately these efforts were in vain, for their engine seized completely, forcing their retirement less than half a mile from the winning line in London. □

Preceding pages
Betty Cook used a 38-foot Scarab for bad weather racing and also a formidable 38-foot Cougar powered by twin 625 horse power Mercruisers. Offshore Europe captions.
Opposite. *The Italian Giulio de Angelis, third in the European Championships, is qualified for the world championships, thanks to his victory in Sardinia. This year he was driving Alitalia 3, sister ship of Dry Martini 2 – a Picchiotti 38 in aluminium, powered by two 625 h.p. Mercruisers.*
Offshore USA.

Results

Cowes Week, Isle of Wight, Great Britain

Admiral's Cup

Final position	Nation	Yacht	Designer	Rating	Skipper	Points
1	Australia	Police-Car	Ed. Dubois	32	P. Cantwell	
		Impetuous	R. Holland	31.5	G. Lambert	1.088
		Ragamuffin	D. Peterson	35.5	S. Fisher	
2	U.S.A.	Imp	R. Holland	30.9	D. Allen	
		Aries	R. Holland	36.3	M. Swerdlow	1.013
		Williwaw	D. Peterson	35.8	D. Connor	
3	Italy	Yena	D. Peterson	33.4	D. Durgan	
		Vanina	S. Kaufman	35	V. Mandelli	944
		Rrose-Selavy	D. Peterson	33.1	R. Bonadeo	
3 ex.	Hong Kong	La-Pantera III	D. Peterson	32.4	C. Ostenfeld	
		Uin-Na-Mara	Ed. Dubois	35.5	H.H. Ross	944
		Vanguard	Ed. Dubois	35.6	T. Yourieff	
5	Argentina	Acadia	Frers	39.6	G. Frers Jr.	861
		Sur II	Frers	34.4	E. Mandelbaum	

The Fastnet

Final Position	Yacht	Skipper	Nation	Designer	
1	Tenacious	T. Turner	U.S.A.	Stephens	93 h 44'18"
2	Eclipse	J. Rogers	Great Britain	D. Peterson	97 h 5'27"
3	Jubile VI	R. Santieux	France	D. Peterson	97 h 40'15"
4	Revolution	J.-L. Fabry	France	Finot	97 h 42'53"
5	Impetuous	G. Lambert	Australia	R. Holland	97 h 53'33"
6	Police Car	P. Cantwell	Australia	Ed. Dubois	97 h 56'26"
7	Imp	D. Allen	Holland	R. Holland	97 h 57' 9"
8	Condor	B. Bell	Bermudes	Sharp	97 h 57'24"
9	Kialoa	J. Kilroy	U.S.A.	Stephens	98 h 3'40"
10	Red Rock IV	E. Mandelbaum	Argentina	Frers	98 h 35' 5"

Transat en double, France

Final position	Yacht	Team	Nation	Elapsed time
1	V.S.D	Eugène Riguidel - Gilles Gahinet	France	34 j. 6 h 31'
2	Paul Ricard	Eric Tabarly - Marc Pajot	France	34 j. 6 h 36' 42"
3	Télé 7 Jours	Michael Birch - Jean-Marie Vidal	Canada/France	34 j. 13 h 53' 33"
4	Kriter V	Michel Malinovsky - Pierre Lenormand	France	34 j. 19 h 57'
5	Fernande	Jean-Claude Parisis - Olivier de Rosny	France	35 j. 8 h 15'
6	Serenissima	Marc Vallin - Bruno Bacilieri	France/Italy	37 j. 5 h 52'
7	Pen Duick III	Patrick Tabarly - Philippe Poupon	France	37 j. 6 h 01'
8	Kriter VI	Olivier de Kersauson - Gérard Dijkstra	France/Netherland	37 j. 6 h 35'
9	Avi 3000	Patrice et Jean-Michel Carpentier	France	40 j. 9 h 10' 50"
10	Biotherm	Florence Arthaud - Catherine Hermann	France	41 j. 12 h 25'

Southern Ocean Racing Conference, U.S.A.

	Final position	Yacht	Skipper	Designers	Points
Class A	1	Tenacious	T. Turner	S & S	1992
	2	Kialoa	J. Kilroy	S & S	1972
Class B	1	Williwaw	S. Sinett	Peterson	1969
	2	Acadia	B. Keenan	Frers	1967,5
Class C	1	Midnight Sun	J. Pehrsson	Holland	1990
	2	Secret Affair	T. Greenawalt	Holland	1957
Class D	1	Infinity	J. Thomson	Holland	1982,5
	2	Imp	D. Allen	Holland	1978
Class E	1	Celebration	Geneve Synd.	Cook	1991
	2	Firewater	R. Barton	Cook	1985
Class F	1	Robin	E. Hood		1996
	2	Illusion	R. Taylor	Hawkanson	1981,5

Transpacific Race, U.S.A.

	Final position	Yacht	Owner	Design.	Corrected time
Fleet	1	Arriba	D. Choate	King 48	11.14.42.51
	2	Miyakodori III	O. Hiroshi	S & S 54	11.18.44.54
	3	Secret Love	B. Herman	Swan 44	11.19.00.16
	4	High Roler	W. F. Power	Peterson 44	11.22.05.29
	5	Zamazaan	N. H. Price	Farr 53	11.22.16.05
Class A	1	Jader	S. R. Carson	S & S 80	12.00.25.44
	2	Drifter	H. C. Moloscho	Moloscho 70	12.02.25.08
	3	Natoma	D. B. Dalzial	Rhodes 58	12.08.10.26
Class B	1	Arriba	D. Choate	King 48	11.14.42.51
	2	Miyakodori III	O. Hiroshi	S & S 54	11.18.44.54
	3	High Roler	W. F. Power	Peterson 44	11.22.05.29
Class C	1	Secret Love	B. Herman	Swan 44	11.19.00.16
	2	Wings	J. N. Wangenheim	Peterson 42	11.23.50.08
	3	Mondo	G. Eisenberg	Santa Cruz 33	12.01.45.08
Class D	1	Brown Sugar	U. H. Werner	Peterson 38	11.22.24.24
	2	Bingo	B. Gardner	CF 37	12.00.33.57
	3	Chutzpah	S. Cowan	Lee 36	12.02.16.49

12 Metre J.I. World championship Brighton, Great Britain

Final Position	Yacht	Skipper	Nation	Points
1	Lionheart	J. Oakeley	Great Britain	2
2	Sverige	P. Petterson	Sweden	8
3	Gretel II	G. Ingate	Australia	9
4	Constellation	G. Gurney	Great Britain	12
5	Windrose	T. Romke de Vries	Holland	16
6	Columbia	J. Caulcutt	Great Britain	18

6 Metre J.I World Cup Seattle, U.S.A.

Final position	Boat	Nation	Skipper	Designer	Points
1	Irene	Sweden	P. Petterson	P. Petterson	8,5
2	St. Francis VII	U.S.A.	T. Blackaller	G. Mull	14-3/4
3	Warhorse	U.S.A.	B. Wertheimer	B. Wertheimer	14-3/4
4	US 100	U.S.A.	G. Philbrick	G. Mull	21-3/4
5	Ranger	U.S.A.	T. Turner	G. Mull	27

Ton cups

Mini Ton Cup Estartit, Spain

Final position	Yacht	Team	Nation	Designer	Points
1	Wahoo	Maletto-Nava-Musetti	Italy	Fontana	278,63
2	Honey Moon	Kolius-Baldridge-Gastas	U.S.A.	Holland	271,25
3	Garfio VI	Hernandez-Cuenca-Jacquemin	Spain	Holland	235,00
4	Seveso II	Falciola-Albano-Stella	Italy	Santarelli	227,00
5	Coque-Ton	Balcells-Galofre-Anglada	Spain	Holland	220,50

Quarter Ton Cup San Remo, Italy

Final position	Boat	Nation	Skipper	Points
1	Bullit	France	Fauroux	325,50
2	Sun of a Gun	Denmark	Elvström	318,50
3	Lisa	Italy	Albarelli	297,50
4	Los Angeles	Switzerland	Guglielmetti	295,50
5	Mister Magoo	France	Langlois	290,00

1/2 Ton Cup Scheveningen, Holland

Final position	Yacht	Nation	Skipper	Designer	Points
1	Waverider	New Zealand	Bouzaid	Davidson	210
2	Roller Coaster	Great Britain	Hoyle	Humphreys	215
3	Swuzzlebubble	New Zealand	Gibbs	Farr	214,3
4	Jina	France	Moureau	Joubert	213,2
5	Kat's Lamstraal	Holland	Hellmans		219,5

3/4 Ton Cup Hundested, Denmark

Final position	Yacht	Nation	Skipper	Designer	Points
1	Regnbogen	Sweden	Norlin	Norlin	238
2	Northstar	Germany	Hoffman Berndt	Chance jt	173
3	Partaj	Sweden	K. & et L. Ekblom	Jones	168
4	32 AN	Sweden	I. Boding		168
5	Gunsmoke	Great Britain	Harrisson		159
6	Vitres	Sweden	U. Wikman		154

One Ton Cup Newport, U.S.A.

Final position	Yacht	Nation	Skipper	Designer	Points
1	Pendragon	U.S.A.	J. Mac Laurin	Davidson	49,25
2	Indulgence	Great Britain	G. Walker	Holland	47
3	Archangle	South Africa	T. Kuttel	Lavranos	41,375
4	Oystercatcher	Great Britain	R. Matthews	Jones	35
5	Firewater	U.S.A.	R. Barton	Cook	34,5

Two Ton Cup Poole, Great Britain

Final position	Yacht	Nation	Skipper	Designer	Points
1	Gitana VII	France	Baron E. de Rothschild	Frers	105,25
2	Sur	Argentina	D. Peralta Ramos	Frers	103,5
3	Winsome Gold	Great Britain	D. May	Dubois	94
4	Police Car	Australia	P. Cantwell	Dubois	98
5	Dugenou 1	France	M. Belingard & Y. Pajot	Joubert	88

Small Class-Boats

Finn

	Final position	Nation	Helmsman
Hyères	1	Sweden	G. Liljergren
	2	Holland	M. Neeleman
	3	Great-Britain	C. Law
Weymouth	1	Great-Britain	C. Law
	2	Great-Britain	N. Starling
	3	Belgium	L. Van Keirsbilck
Kiel	1	U.S.A.	J. Bertrand
	2	Sweden	K. Carlsson
	3	Canada	L. Lemieux
Tallinn	1	U.S.A.	J. Bertrand
	2	U.S.A.	C. Lewis
	3	Spain	J. Doreste
Cork	1	U.S.A.	Van Cleve-Annapolis
	2	Canada	Woodbury-Brockville
	3	U.S.A.	Hahn-Edgewater
World championship	1	U.S.A.	C. Lewis
	2	U.S.A.	J. Bertrand
	3	Holland	M. Neeleman

470

	Final position	Nation	Team
Hyères	1	Canada	Matthews-Cross
	2	France	Richer-Claude
	3	Germany	Hunger-Diesing
Weymouth	1	France	Delage-Wattine
	2	Israël	Brockman-Friedlander
	3	France	Russo-Narbonne
Kiel	1	France	Fountaine-Fountaine
	2	Switzerland	Kistler-Dreyer
	3	France	Peponnet-Peponnet
Tallinn	1	New-Zealand	Paterson-Mac Kay
	2	U.S.A.	Ullman-Linsky
	3	G.D.R.	Borowski-Svensson
Cork	1	Canada	Mattews-Cross
	2	U.S.A.	Benjamin-Fowler
	3	Canada	Roufs-Robitaille
Europe championship	1	Israël	Brockman-Friedlander
	2	Germany	Hunger-Korte
	3	Poland	Wrobel-Stocki
World championship	1	Japan	Kai-Komiya
	2	France	Delage-Wattine
	3	France	Richer-Claude

Flying Dutchman

	Final Position	Nation	Team
Hyères	1	Germany	Batzill-Batzill
	2	Holland	Vollebreght-Vollebreght
	3	Italy	Savelli-Gazzei
Weymouth	1	Great Britain	Blake-Houchin
	2	Great Britain	Loveday-Dann
	3	Spain	Abascal-Noguer
Kiel	1	U.S.A.	Diaz-Reynolds
	2	France	Bouët-Poirey
	3	Germany	Batzill-Batzill
Tallinn	1	Holland	Vollebreght-Vollebreght
	2	G.D.R.	Steingross-Schramme
	3	U.S.S.R.	Gusenko-Gruzdev
Cork	1	Canada	McLaughlin-Bastet
	2	U.S.A.	Taylor-Penfield
	3	Canada	Tawaststjierna-Mawson
World Championship	1	France	Bouët-Poirey
	2	Spain	Abascal-Noguer
	3	Holland	Vollebreght-Vollebreght

Star

	Final position	Nation	Team
Hyères	1	U.S.S.R.	Mankin-Muzitschenko
	2	Italy	Scala-Testa
	3	Spain	Gorostegui-Gorostegui
Weymouth	1	Spain	Gorostegui-Gorostegui
	2	Great Britain	Howlett-Boyce
	3	Great Britain	Mac Donald-Smith
Kiel	1	Canada	Louie-Lawson
	2	Italy	Gorla-Peraboni
	3	Switzerland	Wyss-Soss
Tallinn	1	U.S.A.	Buchan-Knight
	2	Italy	Gorla-Peraboni
	3	U.S.S.R.	Mankin-Muzitschenko
Europe championship	1	U.S.S.R.	Mankin-Muzitschenko
	2	Italy	Scala-Testa
	3	Italy	Gorla-Peraboni
World championship	1	U.S.A.	Melges-Josenhans
	2	U.S.A.	Wright-Cozzens
	3	U.S.A.	Buchan-Knight

Tornado

	Final position	Nation	Team
Hyères	1	Germany	Neuhann-Plenk
	2	Germany	Splengler-Heinimann
	3	Germany	Ettl-Vosslamber
Weymouth	1	U.S.A.	Smyth-Hill
	2	Great Britain	Reg White-Olle
	3	Great Britain	Rob White-Johnson
Kiel	1	New-Zealand	De Thier-Moffat
	2	U.S.S.R.	Potapov-Zibin
	3	Germany	Splengler-Heinimann
Tallinn	1	U.S.S.R.	Potapov-Zibin
	2	Germany	Splengler-Schmann
	3	Great Britain	White-Olle
Cork	1	U.S.A.	Bossett-Kent
	2	Canada	Woods
	3	Canada	Osborn-Jackson
Europe championship	1	U.S.S.R.	Kliver-Fogelev
	2	Denmark	Due-Kjoergerd
	3	Germany	Neuhann-Plenk
World championship	1	Great Britain	White-Olle
	2	Denmark	Due-Kjoergerd
	3	Germany	Neuhann-Plenk

Soling

	Final Position	Nation	Helmsman
Hyères	1	Switzerland	Corminbœuf
	2	Great Britain	Crebbin
	3	U.S.S.R.	Budnikov
Weymouth	1	France	Haegeli
	2	Denmark	Bandlowski
	3	Great Britain	Crebbin
Kiel	1	U.S.A.	Haines
	2	Australia	Bertrand
	3	U.S.A.	Melges
Tallinn	1	Germany	Kuhweide
	2	Australia	Bethwaite
	3	G.D.R.	Richter
Cork	1	Canada	Hall
	2	U.S.A.	Allen
	3	U.S.A.	Haines
Europe Championship	1	Brazil	Souza Ramos
	2	Holland	Bakker
	3	Sweden	Gruenewaldt
World Championship	1	U.S.A.	Haines
	2	Denmark	Jensen
	3	Sweden	Wennerstrom

World Cup 1979 – Trophée l'Equipe

	Final position	Helmsman	Nation	Points
Finn	1	J. Bertrand	U.S.A	28
	2	Law	Great Britain	19
470	1	Courarie/Richer	France	23
	2	Brokman	Israël	18
Flying Dutchman	1	Vollebreght	Holland	31
	2	Bouet	France	28
Star	1	Gorla	Italy	25
	2	Gorostegui	Spain	24
Soling	1	Haegeli	France	21
	2	Haines	U.S.A.	18
Tornado	1	Red White	Great Britain	25
	2	Potapov	U.S.S.R.	20

24 Heures de Rouen, France

Final position	Drivers	Nation	Boat/Engine	Class	Laps	Distance (km)	Average time (Km/h)
1	Molinari-Vassena-Panzeri-Cagnani	Italy	Molinari/Fiat Abarth	R3	536	1929,60	80,40
2	Masurier-Balkou	France	Cormorant/Mercury	OE	495	1782,00	74,25
3	Mohamedi-Izard	France	Gardin/Mercury	OE	484	1742,40	72,60
4	Visser-Torenvliet-De Vreng	Holland	Burgess/Johnson	SE	471	1695,60	70,65
5	Barthelemy-Touron	France	Burgess/Evinrude	OE	468	1684,80	70,20
6	Riondet-Deguisne	France	Cormorant/Renault	S3	463	1666,80	69,45
7	Hedge-Rowe-Knights	Great Britain	Johnson	OE	459	1652,40	68,85
8	Covill-Covill-Rodrigues	Great Britain	Blu-Fin/Johnson	SE	458	1648,80	68,70
9	Barbot-Garcia Montes	Argentina	Mercury	OE	447	1609,20	67,05

Embassy Grand Prix Bristol, Great Britain

	Overall position	Driver	Nation	Boat/Engine	Average speed Mph
Formula I Class OZ more 2000 cc	1	R. Spalding	Great Britain	Velden/Johnson	140.50
	2	B. Seebold	U.S.A.	Seebold/Mercury	137.16
Formula I Class ON 1500 - 2000 cc	1	T. Williams	Great Britain	Velden/Mercury	126.98
	2	A. Lawson	Great Britain	Hodges/Mercury	126.77
Formula II Class OE 700 - 850 cc	1	J. Hill	Great Britain	Burgess/Johnson	113.59
	2	R. Torrance	Great Britain	Burgess/Johnson	111.33
Formula III Class SE sport 700 - 850 cc	1	P. Faithful	Great Britain	Barracuda/Johnson	100.45
	2	J. Giggins	Great Britain	Clerici/Mercury	99.49
Formula III Class SD sport 500 - 700 cc	1	D. Hutchings	Great Britain	Molgaard/Volvo	79.75
	2	P. Ainge	Great Britain	Burgess/Evinrude	79.60
Formula IV World Championship Class NF	1	R. Hedge	Great Britain	Burgess/Mercury	82.57
	2	J. Woods	Ireland	Burgess/Mercury	82.10
Formula IV World Championship Class NE	1	J. Jones	Great Britain	Concorde/Suzuki	78.33
	2	P. Wilde	Great Britain	Bristol/Suzuki	77.88

World Formula II OE Championship, Evian, France

Overall position	Nation	Driver	Boat/Engine	Points
1	Italy	R. Molinari	Molinari/Evinrude	1 200
2	France	C. Salabert	Velden/Johnson	1 125
3	Germany	H. Hubel	Velden/Evinrude	788
4	Great Britain	J. Hill	Burgess/Mercury	625

Casale Monferrato Grand Prix, Italy

	Overall position	Nation	Driver	Boat/Engine	Canon points
Class OZ - 2000 cc	1	Italy	R. Molinari	Molinari/Evinrude	9
	2	Great Britain	R. Spalding	Velden/Johnson	6
	3	U.S.A.	B. Seebold	Seebold/Mercury	4
	4	Great Britain	R. Jenkins	Seebold/Mercury	3
	5	Great Britain	T. Percival	Seebold/Mercury	2

Drammen Grand Prix, Norway

	Overall position	Nation	Driver	Boat/Engine	Canon points
Class OZ - 2000 cc	1	U.S.A.	B. Seebold	Seebold/Mercury	9
	2	Great Britain	T. Percival	Seebold/Mercury	6
	3	Holland	C. Van der Velden	Velden/Johnson	4
	4	Great Britain	R. Spalding	Velden/Johnson	3
	5	Great Britain	R. Jenkins	Seebold/Mercury	2

World Formula I OZ Championship, Milano, Italy

Overall position	Nation	Driver	Boat/Engine	Points
1	U.S.A.	B. Seebold	Seebold/Mercury	1 200
2	Italy	R. Molinari	Molinari/Evinrude	1 000
3	Holland	C. Van der Velden	Velden/Johnson	825
4	Great Britain	R. Jenkins	Seebold/Mercury	521
5	Great Britain	T. Percival	Seebold/Mercury	423

Amsterdam Grand Prix, Holland

	Overall position	Driver	Nation	Boat/Engine	Canon points
Class OZ - 2000 cc	1	C. Van der Velden	Holland	Velden/Johnson	9
	2	R. Jenkins	Great Britain	Seebold/Mercury	6
	3	R. Spalding	Great Britain	Velden/Johnson	4
	4	B. Halsaa	Norway	Seebold/Mercury	3
	5	H. Pelster	Holland	Brugess/Evinrude	2

Paris Six Hours

	Final position	Drivers	Nation	Boat/Engine	Laps
Class OZ	1	Van Velden/Posey	Holland	Velden/Johnson	185
	2	Molinari/McConnell	Italy	Molinari/Evinrude	184
	3	Werner/Brinkert	Germany	Seebold/Mercury	180
	4	Spalding/Stevenson	Great Britain	Velden/Johnson	178
	5	Inward/Williams	Great Britain	Seebold/Mercury	166
Class OE	1	Hill/Larsson	Great Britain	Burgess/Johnson	147
	2	Salabert/Izard	France	Velden/Evinrude	143
	3	Sjöberg/Ström	Sweden	X/Evinrude	134
	4	Barthelemy/Bisbal	France	Gardin/Evinrude	122
	5	Favede/Romangas	France	Barracuda/Evinrude	121
Class ON	1	Wilson/Wilson	Great Britain	Hodges/Mercury	157
	2	Backer/Klinkhamer	Holland	Cougard/Mercury	157
	3	Florianci/Babich	Yougoslavia	Molinari/Mercury	147

American Outboard

Lake Havasu, Arizona

	Overall position	Driver	Engine
Class Mod 50	1	T. Leatherby	Johnson
	2	J. Slack Jr.	Johnson
	3	D. Beaulier	Johnson
Class Mod UJ	1	T. May	Evinrude
	2	L. Holden	Evinrude
	3	R. Milford	Johnson
Class S J	1	B. Barrett	Mercury
	2	K. Mayhue	Mercury
	3	R. Geilenfeldt	Mercury

Parker 9 Hours, Arizona

Overall position	Driver	Boat/Engine
1	Seebold/Bentz	Seebold/Mercury
2	Seebold Jr./Todd	Seebold/Mercury
3	Molinari/Posey	Molinari/Evinrude
4	Sutter/Percival	Seebold/Mercury
5	McConnell/Stevenson	Molinari/Evinrude

World championship, Beloit, Winsconsin

	Overall position	Driver	Boat/Engine
Class SE	1	Chris Bush	Mercury/Seebold
	2	Bob Hamilton	Johnson/Gann
	3	Paul Heathman	Evinrude/Hauptner
Mod 50	1	Terry Leatherby	Johnson/Broughton
	2	Gene Thibodaux	Evinrude/Seebold
	3	Bill Kelly	Johnson/Hering
Class OZ	1	Jimbo McConnell	Evinrude/Molinari
	2	Ken Stevenson	Johnson/Molinari
	3	Johnnie Sanders	Johnson/Molinari

OPC Marathon, Lake Alfred, Florida

	Overall position	Driver	Boat/Engine
D. Production	1	M. Osborn	Johnson/Osborn
E. Production	2	S. Hancock	Johnson/Allison
G. Production	1	W. Strickland	Mercury/Critchfield
J. Production	1	D. Kelly	Mercury/Hydrostream
Sport D	1	B. Ross	Johnson/Bunky
Sport G	1	M. Hauptner	Mercury/Hauptner
Mod UJ	1	R. Gore	Mariner/Al Martin
Mod 120	1	K. Olson	Mercury/Seebold
Mod U	1	K. Stevenson	Johnson/Molinari

Race	Date	Country	Name	Driver	Nation	Boat/Engine	Miles/h
Rio de La Plata	13 jan.	Argentina	Pira Pita	J. Taylor	Argen.	Pira/Mercruiser	43
Rio de La Plata	20 jan.	Argentina	Bounty Hunter	B. Martin	U.S.A.	Cigarette/Mercruiser	61.3
Port Phillip	26 jan.	Australia	Courage	J. Dicieri	Austr.	Magnum/Mercruiser	NA
Punta Del Este	27 jan.	Uruguay	Limit Up	M. Doxford	G.-B.	Cigarette/Mercruiser	54.2
King of Straight	10 apr.	Australia	Slingshot	T. Low	Austr.	Cigarette/Mercruiser	67.7
Bushmills Grand Prix	17 mar.	U.S.A.	Top Banana	C. McCarthy	U.S.A.	Prototype/McNamara	72
Val. Paul Carr Mem.	25 mar.	Australia	Haines Hunter	K. Wyld	Austr.	Hunter/Mercury OBs	37
Bacardi Trophy Race	12 may	U.S.A.	Kaama	B. Cook	U.S.A.	Scarab/Mercruiser	67.3
Poole Bay Int.	2 june	Great-Britain	Dry Martini	G. Niccolai	Ital.	Picchiotti/Mercruiser	NA
Lombardo/Halter Cl.	2 june	U.S.A.	Flap-Jack	H. Quam	U.S.A.	Bertram/Mercruiser	77.6
Palmdale Int.	10 june	Australia	Whippy's Eagle	B. Stevens	Austr.	Cigarette/Mercruiser	57.6
San Feliu Guixols	17 june	Spain	Dry Martini	G. Niccolai	Ital.	Picchiotti/Mercruiser	NA
MFG's BNK/Spirit Det.	29 june	U.S.A.	Kaama	B. Cook	U.S.A.	Cougar/Mercruiser	83.9
Mercury Trophy	8 july	Australia	Whippy's Eagle	B. Stevens	Austr.	Cigarette/Mercruiser	NA
Benihana Grand Prix	18 july	U.S.A.	Benihana	R. Aoki	U.S.A.	Cougar/Mercruiser	69.2
Viareggio/Bastia	22 july	Italy	Alitalia Tre	G. de Angelis	Ital.	Picchiotti/Mercruiser	NA
Atami Cup	28 july	Japan	Benihana	R. Aoki	U.S.A.	Bertram/Mercruiser	70
Naples Trophy	29 july	Italy	Dry Martini	G. Niccolai	Ital.	Picchiotti/Mercruiser	NA
BP Ocean Classic	5 aug.	Australia	Courage	T. Low	Austr.	Magnum/Mercruiser	NA
Gettingloppet	12 aug.	Sweden	Dry Martini	G. Niccolai	Ital.	Picchiotti/Mercruiser	60.5
Poole Bay Trophy	18 aug.	Great-Britain	Dry Martini	G. Niccolai	Ital.	Picchiotti/Mercruiser	NA
John Wayne Memorial	25 aug.	U.S.A.	Benihana	R. Aoki	U.S.A.	Cougar/Mercruiser	78.6
Cowes Torquay	25 aug.	Great-Britain	Dry Martini	G. Niccolai	Ital.	Picchiotti/Mercruiser	NA
Morton Bay Classic	26 aug.	Australia	Whippy's Eagle	B. Stevens	Austr.	Cigarette/Mercruiser	NA
Benihana Grand Prix	15 sept.	U.S.A.	Kaama	B. Cook	U.S.A.	Scarab/Mercruiser	73.8
Costa Esmeralda	16 sept.	Italy	Alitalia Duo	G. de Angelis	Ital.	Picchiotti/Mercruiser	NA
World Championship	20 oct.	Italy	1 Kaama	B. Cook	U.S.A.	Cougar/Mercruiser	73.97
			2 Dry Martini	G. Niccolai	Ital.	Picchiotti/Mercruiser	69.61
			3 Limit up	M. Downie	G.-B.	Cigarette/Mercruiser	69.60

Poole Bay International, Great Britain

	Class position	Overall position	Name	Driver	Nation	Boat/Engine	Points
Class II	1	3	Apache	D. Hagan	Great Britain	Souter/Ford Sabre	225
	2	4	Pobjoy Mint	R. Allen	Great Britain	Allday/Ford Sabre	169
	3	5	Romans Sabre	J. Craxford	Great Britain	Cougar/Ford Sabre	127

Cowes-Torquay-Cowes, Great Britain

	Overall position	Class position	Name	Driver	Nation	Boat/Engine	Points
Class II	1	3	Apache	D. Hagan	Great Britain	Souter/Ford Sabre	225
	2	4	Romans Sabre	J. Craxford	Great Britain	Cougar/Ford Sabre	169
	3	6	British Buzzard	R. Allen	Great Britain	Enfield/Ford Sabre	95

Putney-Calais-Putney

	Overall position	Class position	Name	Driver	Nation	Boat/Engine	Points
Class IIID	1	1	Aphrodisic	P. Amstrong	Great Britain	Phantom/Johnson	30
Class IIIC	2	1	Concord	T. Evans	Great Britain	Stapley/Mercury	24
	3	2	Moody Blue	B. Nash	Great Britain	Marshan/Mercury	16
	4	3	Blu Blud	B. Drinkwater	Great Britain	Blu Fin/Mercury	10

Needles Trophy, Great Britain

	Overall position	Class position	Name	Driver	Nation	Boat/Engine	Points
Class I	1	1	Dry Martini 2	G. Niccolai	Italy	Picchiotti/Mercruiser	400
		2	Uno-Mint Jewellery	D. Pobjoy	Great Britain	Enfield/Kiekhaefer	300
Class II	1	3	Apache	D. Hagan	Great Britain	Souter/Ford Sabre	225
	2	4	Jus Gus	P. Sinclair	Great Britain	Phantom/Mercury	169
	3	5	Romans Sabre	J. Craxford	Great Britain	Cougar/Ford Sabre	127